CONTEMPORARY CINEMATOGRAPHERS ON THEIR *ART*

Illustration credits

Page 132: Courtesy of Jody Wodrich.

Page 133: Courtesy of Jody Wodrich.

Page 147: Courtesy of Donald A. Morgan.

Pages 156-157: Courtesy of Donald A. Morgan.

Page 215: Courtesy of Clairmont Camera, Inc.

CONTEMPORARY CINEMATOGRAPHERS ON THEIR *ART*

Pauline B. Rogers

Focal Press
Boston   Oxford   Johannesburg   Melbourne
New Delhi   Singapore

Library of Congress Cataloging-in-Publication Data
Rogers, Pauline B. (Pauline Bonnie)
    Contemporary cinematographers on their art / Pauline B. Rogers.
       p.   cm.
    Includes bibliographical references.
    ISBN 0-240-80309-4 (pbk. : alk. paper)
    1. Cinematography.   2. Cinematographers—Interviews.   I. Title.
TR850.R63   1998
778.5'3—dc21   97-40152
                                                   CIP

British Library Cataloguing-in-Publication Data
A catalogue record for this book is available from the British Library.

Table of Contents

Foreword

As a child, I escaped a world that was out of my control by creating pictures in my head. I would write the words and direct the actions of real life scenarios or put myself into current television or movie dramas, making events come out as I willed. Most of the time, the pictures were in black and white. However, there was the occasional vivid Technicolor story. There was never a thought of who created the colors and the pictures. Even when I began working on television and feature film sets, the cameras and lights were only those "things" that got in my sightline as I tried to concentrate on the words I needed to hear. The cables were merely obstacles that helped me trip over my own feet.

It wasn't until ten years ago, when I began to write about how pictures were made, that I had any sense of the importance of the cinematographer. Even after doing close to 400 interviews and visiting several hundred sets, I am still amazed at what the Director of Photography does. I'll never forget the incredibly beautiful lighting I saw on Stephen Goldblatt's Batman Forever set, or the complex, yet simple, overhead rigs Dean Cundey had designed to fly Robin Williams as well as cameras and lighting over a basketball set, for one of the funniest sequences in Flubber. I still can't believe Tom Ackerman could silk so much foliage inside the Hughes hangar and make it really look like George of the Jungle was really in the Jungle! And a few days ago, while I was playing tag with the television remote control I landed on not one, but two of Emmanuel Lubezki's projects. The texture of Like Water for Chocolate still intrigues me and I found yet another incredible visual in A Little Princess.

Fortunately, many of these interviewees have become life-long friends. Occasionally, I will stress those friendships by asking some very dumb questions. Payback time comes when I visit their sets. I've been talked into riding a buckboard onto a remote location, only to find out that it is a breakaway – the hard way. To understand the reality of a gimbaled set, I've been cajoled into taking a ride, assured that it will rock only 15 percent – Sure! To see how rigs work below the water in tanks, I've been invited to look over the edge, and landed inside!

It's okay, because the childishness is all part of the making of a motion picture or television show. I admire every one of these people who ply their art, and it is an art, often under tremendous pressure, in highly volatile political situations, and sometimes in extremely tense moments, yet still retain a wonderful sense of humor.

Although I understand only a little of how they do what they do, I know they are often highly underrated individuals. Although technically classified as "below the line," they are responsible for one of the most important parts of a project – the picture. I agree with the Vittorio Storaro's concept – lighting is another actor in the drama. And the cinematographer is responsible for that actor's performance.

I hate to see this all important quotient of a project discounted – or even ignored. I've received hundreds of press kits, yet rarely is the Director of Photography mentioned, let alone his background and credits. When I see one-sheets or newspaper and television ads, or even trailers, everyone's name seems to flash on the screen or be printed on the paper – but the cinematographer.

I've heard horror stories about the break down of contract negotiations, when an agent asks for a reasonable salary for pre-production and post production involvement. It is only right that these talented people be involved in the whole process – not just the days on the set. If Tom Ackerman hadn't camp in the art department's offices when Jumanji was being prepared, there surely would have been even more difficulties in putting this intriguing picture together. If Don Burgess or Dean Cundey weren't allowed to participate in the post process of Forrest Gump or Contact, and Jurassic Park or Casper, carefully created visuals could have gone amok. Often times, to protect the integrity of what they have worked so hard to create, cinematographers will literally donate their time, to follow through effects, post production, timing, and whatever else is necessary to keep a single vision throughout the project. And that isn't right. However, that is the way it often happens as budgets get more and more out of control on the "above the line" side of the picture.

Fortunately, directors and actors are beginning to go to bat for their cinematographers. And, as pictures become more and more intricate, studios are beginning to see the light. (No pun intended). However, instead of making the job easier, these pressures to perform on ever shortening schedules takes a toll on the cinematographer and crew. It becomes a trade off, "we'll give you the equipment, the CGI, but you better not fall behind, or else."

In approaching the design of this book, I have tried to select significant cinematographers who are working in all fields of lighting, camera, and CGI. Each chapter isn't just about what technique these people used on a particular project, it is as much the sum total of how they got to each film they discuss. Who they were before they began "in the business" has contributed to how they function within this world unlike any other. As Donald M. Morgan says, he "failed miserably" at several things before he became a cinematographer. An unprecedented four A.S.C. Awards, numerous Emmy Awards, and other nominations have shown that he found more than a home behind the lens. Jo Mayer thought she would be an economist until she spent her "spare time" lighting productions at Smith College, then in her off time while working on Capitol Hill. An introduction to John Houseman made her career take a sharp turn.

　　To include the paths and lessons that brought each of these cinematographers to where they are today meant I was able to cover fewer people than originally intended. Fortunately, or unfortunately, many of the original list of interviewees became so involved in current productions that it became impossible to complete their chapters to satisfy us both. Although I have learned much about how John Seale A.S.C. created a few of the images in The English Patient, we haven't been able to cover this or his other projects completely due to his involvement in City of Angels. Jack Green A.S.C. and I started to discuss the 20 plus films he has done with Clint Eastwood, as well as his involvement in Twister and the two Speed pictures. However, fine tuning his first directorial debut (Traveler) took precedence. Over the years I've worked with and watched John C. Flinn III A.S.C. do amazing things on television projects such as Jake and the Fatman and Babylon 5. However, Babylon's grueling television schedule and back to back Babylon two hour movies have precluded our conversations on his work, going back to Gunsmoke and Hawaii 5-0.

It is my hope that these cinematographers, along with other highly talented Directors of Photography such as Laszlo Kovacs A.S.C., Vilmos Zsigmond A.S.C., John Schwartzman A.S.C., Phil Meheux, Dante Spinotti A.S.C., Robert Richardson A.S.C., Michael Ballhaus A.S.C., Daryn Okada A.S.C., Ken Ralston, and many others will be at the top of the list for a part two should the readership demand a follow up to Contemporary Cinematographers on Their Art.

Until then, I salute every one of these men and women who fight the political battles, the ever surprising invasion of Mother Nature into their well planned exterior shots, and the often exasperating nuances needed to perfect their stunning interiors. I hope to continue to visit sets, ask dumb questions, and even be the butt of tension-breaking practical jokes, as long as the industry and the talented people behind the images will allow me. Maybe, some day, I will really understand the difference between HMI and Tungsten lighting and be able to see why they send a grip running for a double in place of a single.

When you are trying to fight a computer, with very little knowledge of that tool, patience, knowledge, and tolerance of friends and associates is vital. Of course, this book could not have been accomplished without the help of the cinematographers involved. I could not have made my deadlines with out Hollie Meyer's help in transcribing hours and hours of interview tape. Thanks to Chandler Warren, The DiLeo family, Maria Carpenter, Dixie and Michael Robillard, and Doug Barnard, several computers managed to turn out camera-ready art that actually looked like the original concept of the project. Also, special thanks to Marc Messenger (for the over/under rig art) and Frank Kaye at Panavision.

"You have to have a colossal stockpile of faith in yourself to do this job. There's no personnel office where you consult a neatly printed job description. And, ultimately, when you crack open your meter case at six in the morning, feeling like you aren't exactly God's gift to cinematography, you are left with only one resource – yourself."

Tom Ackerman A.S.C. and his family moved to Montecito, a quiet and elegant suburb of Santa Barbara, California, in 1995. However, until recently, he still had to pause when he gave visitors directions to the new house. Ackerman is one of the busiest cinematographers in the business, known for his calm and controlled approach to the challenging task of shooting comedy.

"Maybe it is because of what I like to call a 'normal' childhood," he says, as he settles into the office in his classic Monterey Colonial home. "I grew up in Iowa, far from where movies were made." Ackerman's father had been a newsreel "stringer" during the 1930s, later becoming a projectionist. Ackerman grew up at his father's theater, hanging out in the projection booth or in the manager's tiny office with a bay window that allowed a view of the screen.

"It was sort of a mid-western *Cinema Paradiso*," he recalls. "My view of the world was essentially the movies. It was classic black-and-white, pure Hollywood." Ackerman was hooked. He began to scour movie fan magazines for behind-the-scenes photographs. The tweed-jacketed crew members and exotic array of shooting gear caught his attention.

"The activity was usually centered around the camera," he says. "With the director often hunkered down right next to the matte box, it was obviously the core experience.

"When I went to the University of Iowa, I became a Theater major and took every broadcasting and film production course available. But, despite some great teachers, I never really saw any connection to working in the industry. It was a more academic approach."

Ackerman's introduction to the "industry" came during the summer break following his freshman year, as a mail messenger at NBC's Rockefeller Center headquarters. "I got pretty good at finishing my mail runs under schedule, which gave me time to hang out in the master control room," he says. "I saw the first Telstar satellite feed live from Europe. I also got a kick out of watching the guys wrangle the studio cameras down on the stages where they were taping soap operas. They were unbelievable, the way they wrapped around those pedestal dollies, making all their own moves, pulling their own focus."

Ackerman returned to the University of Iowa excited about the possibilities in broadcasting. By that time, the war in Vietnam was well underway. Enrolled in Air Force ROTC, he was intrigued to hear that career opportunities existed for Motion Picture Officers. "When I went on active duty as a 2nd Lieutenant with the 1365th Photo Squadron in Orlando, Florida, I was actually very gung-ho. Of course, my enthusiasm waned a bit when I did my tour in Southeast Asia. The motto of the 600th Photo Squadron was 'We Kill 'Em With Fillum.' I think that was overstating the case, since we posed, in my opinion, next to zero threat to our opponents.

"We had production abilities that could have been used to make documentary films about the air war. We had eager-beaver film school grads commanding detachments all over Southeast Asia. We had cameras, labs, unlimited film stock, and free access to what was going on. But no. WE got to bolt gun cameras to F4a and give briefings not on the great photography but on our gun camera failure rate."

While in the Air Force, Ackerman began what would become a life-long friendship with documentary filmmaker Peter Vogt. After his discharge, Vogt became Production Manager for Oscar-winning documentarian Charles Guggenheim, also an Iowa grad. With Vogt's help, Ackerman wrangled an interview with the Washington based Guggenheim, and eventually a job.

"Charles Guggenheim had a tremendous influence on me," Ackerman says. "He was a great lover of photography.

But he also wanted an idea behind the image. I did a lot of editing at that time and he taught me how to be ruthless, especially with my own footage. He was a purist in that he used voice-over very sparsely. He wanted the pictures and the live dialogue to convey the story. The narration he did write tended to be poetic rather than nuts-and-bolts descriptive."

It was a concept that would be echoed years later when Ackerman was working as camera operator with Vittorio Storaro on Francis Ford Coppola's *One from the Heart*. Storaro also advocated cinematography as a thoughtful process, rather than the slapdash form it sometimes had assumed in Hollywood.

"Vittorio insists that the photography authorship isn't an 'add on' element," Ackerman explains. "So, on the set, it is not just 'pop this' or 'roundy-round and slam in for a tight one.' If you can't support the shot with an idea then maybe it shouldn't be a shot. If the lighting has no design philosophy behind it, just a random process of whatever seems nice on the day, then how can it express the values of a story being carefully told. Now, it is hard to be this principled when you are setting a five-camera stunt and the sun is going down. But it helps set the tone for a more informed approach to the work."

In 1973, Ackerman moved to Los Angeles to form a production company with another ex-Air Force friend, Mike Robe. The partners did well, but in 1979, Robe sold his first spec script and Ackerman finally received a much-coveted card in IATSE Local 659. The decision was made to downscale Robe/Ackerman and get on with what they had originally come to town to do.

"I got in the Union as a Director of Photography, but the DP thing didn't mean much, coming out of the world of small non-union production. It was obvious – there were some great photographers out there to learn from. And I was ready to pay my dues," he says.

Ackerman dropped back to operator, working as a day player and on many B-camera assignments. Eventually, he graduated to A-camera, working on projects like *The Gangster Chronicles* mini-series and several television movies. One of his last operating assignments was *One from the Heart*; "It was a nice way to go out," he reflects.

"Coppola was onto the Electronic Cinema thing way ahead of the time when most other people in town felt comfortable with it," Ackerman reflects. "The die-hards didn't even want a video tap on the camera. It was thought to be a sort of 'intrusion' into what had been the province of the operator. And a director was supposed to be able to trust what happened in the frame until dailies. I think the last few years have shown that Francis was exactly right in his predictions. There has been a revolution in the way video has changed film shooting and finishing."

After *One from the Heart*, Ackerman resumed working as a DP, doing commercials, music videos, and the occasional low-budget feature. "The hours were brutal on the music videos," he remembers with a slight wince. "My own record was a 27-hour day. I saw dailies I hardly remembered shooting. The most fun I had shooting was with Marty Callner. The first time I met him he told me 'Lighting is God.'

"One of the clips we did was for Stevie Nicks, where I designed what came to be called the 'mirror matrix,' an array of 48 two-inch mirror squares mounted on a monofilament grid. The monofilament was stretched taut, like a drum skin. When the stage was smoked up and the Xenon was directed onto the mirrors it bounced back as a cluster of brilliant shafts of backlight. We tapped rhythm on the monofilament grid and choreographed them to Stevie. Computerized light cues were a rarity then, so we had to find crew guys who understood music." Several weeks after the video was released, there was a parody of it on David Letterman, Ackerman's technique and all. He had arrived.

When pushed to reveal the name of his first feature, as Director of Photography, Ackerman is vague at first. "It was a good experience but not one to write home about," he says. "A cheesy horror film for Cannon called *New Year's Evil*. It was an 18-day schedule for about four hundred thousand dollars.

"We were using one of the last Cinemobile production vans in which all camera, lighting, and grip equipment was compartmentalized on a single vehicle. It had an on-board generator and the crew, in theory, could work very efficiently. The company's equipment and rolling stock had a low reputation for reliability.

"We had one Brute arc. It was my only 'big gun' for night exteriors, along with a couple of Maxi-brutes and four big-eye 10ks. The negative was ASA 100 and without Zeiss super-speeds, which were T1.3, we couldn't have done much night work. Still, there are some parts of the film I can look at and see that the craft was pretty good. At least, not embarrassing.

"In fact, it is amazing what you can accomplish with very little. In *New Year's Evil*, there was an elevator shaft scene in which the killer, played by Kip Niven, terrorizes the passengers in the lift. It was all shot on a practical location downtown – no mock ups, no blue screen, no process work. For some of the coverage, we mounted an Arri llc on the roof of the elevator. I was doing my own operating and could hear the counterweights whizzing past my head as we moved up and down the shaft. We're talking about three inches of clearance!

"I think we had one night to do the entire sequence, which on our schedule was a bit of a luxury. A big contrast to the elevator scene at the construction site in *Baby's Day Out*, where we used a set that filled the National Grand Armory in Chicago and had 16,000 amps of light, lots of prep, lots of days, and lots of visual effects.

"Obviously, it's better to have the big tools in your kit," Ackerman says, pragmatically. "But there was a strange sense of freedom on the really low budget projects. You couldn't have much equipment, so this required a simpler approach. No distractions. When I do a picture now, we usually have all the bells and whistles. It can give rise to a certain anxiety level. If you've got a Super Technocrane on the set, you're going to be trying really hard to find a way to use it. There's no doubt in my mind that we make certain shots just to exploit the equipment."

Ackerman's first job as a Union cinematographer was in 1983, on Tim Burton's *Frankenweenie*. "Tim wanted to emulate the look of the great J. Arthur Rank horror films of the 1940s and 1950s," he explains. "He wanted to convey that extremely graphic, almost wood block simplicity of those black-and-white B-movie images. I was also influenced by Gabriel Figueroa's brilliant work and Stanley Cortez A.S.C.'s photographics on *Night of the Hunter* for Charles Laughton. Tim also wanted to edge it with the surreal, almost Da-da-ist feeling of the German classic, *The Cabinet of Dr. Caligari*.

"In *Night of the Hunter*, there was another parallel to *Frankenweenie*," Ackerman continues. "Cortez was working on some very elemental sets. The film was being done inexpensively and the scene in which the children escape Robert Mitchum by floating away in a pram was shot on stage with little more than water to float the boat, clumps of reeds and cattails, and a painted backdrop featuring a silvery moonlit sky. It was mostly the light that made the illusion.

"Tim always wanted to boil down the shot to the basic elements. It was a half-hour film and every minute had to be strong. He kept urging us to 'keep it simple.' This was an aesthetic choice, not something to keep us on schedule.

"What made the project really unique were the elements created by Tim and his close ally Rick Henrichs," Ackerman explains. "They designed all the gravestones with a surreal quality, whimsical and ominous at the same time. They took the light beautifully."

When *Frankenweenie* was finished, the story of a boy resurrecting his dead dog was deemed too unsettling for a G-rating. It was never shown theatrically, only belatedly seen on the laserdisk release of *Nightmare Before Christmas*. However, the powerful talent that created it had not gone unnoticed.

"A cinematographer's opportunities accelerate tremendously if he works with a director whose career takes off,"

Ackerman says. "But, when Tim asked for me on *Pee Wee*, I didn't have big screen credits to convince Warner.

"You have to have a colossal stockpile of faith in yourself to do this job," he continues. "There's no personnel office where you consult a neatly printed job description. And, ultimately, when you crack open your meter case at six in the morning, feeling like you aren't exactly God's gift to cinematography, you are left with only one resource – yourself."

Soon *Girls Just Want to Have Fun* and *Back to School* catapulted Ackerman onto the A-list of comedy shooters. "There used to be a misconception about how comedy should be lit," Ackerman asserts. "'Broadly and flatly.' My approach has always been to light in a way that intrigues the eye. Why should a comedy be shot differently?

"There are certain disciplines I observe. One has nothing to do with the look but relates to composition. At some point in a comedy, and this is especially true in John Hughes' work, there is a need for the camera to set up a joke, to include some elements in the frame and exclude others, to express a certain point of view that helps draw the audience in. Often it is a series of cuts that add up to the joke, each one of which rests on the others. You can look at Buster Keaton's movies to see how brilliantly this can be done.

"But, the need for precision doesn't need to conflict with beautiful imagery," he continues. "When I did *Dennis the Menace* for Nick Castle, in 1992, John Hughes had conceived a movie with several levels of interpretation. On one hand, the brief was to paint a loving portrait of small-town summer in the eyes of a little kid. On the other, we were to carefully assemble specific comedy beats that showed the torture exacted by Dennis upon Mr. Wilson (Walter Matthau). Added to this challenge was the need to shoot many of the idyllic summer scenes on a soundstage. Restricted night work hours with children plus the onset of a harsh Chicago winter made it impractical to stay on the Evanston neighborhood streets beyond mid-October.

"The night situations were no more difficult than usual. We always have to impose a look and find practical sources to generate light. I'm not very fond of movie 'moonlight' if it is the only thing happening, or for grossly artificial sources that look glued-on instead of organic to the scene.

"In the Wilson neighborhood, the idea was to create a safe, cozy feeling at night and make it look like the kind of place where kids can go out after dinner and play kick-the-can. I decided to use the warm light from windows, porch lights, and street lamps to key various elements in the scene. Half blue moonlight would etch out the basic shapes and we would paint in pools and nice little nooks of warm light from there.

"In some cases, we could splash things around pretty liberally – a 5k skypan with its wide throw could be placed flat on the ground. It gave a beautiful glow in the distant background. It would be way too crude for use up close, but looked great in the distance.

"The stage day exteriors were another story. To recreate daylight artificially is a major undertaking. There are many elements involved. It isn't just getting a strong source which, thankfully, is easier now that we have 20k incandescent lamps. You also have to achieve the ambiance – the glow of the open sky, the multitude of ways light is reflected. The color contrast between cool sky light and warm sunlight has to be seen.

"Of course, you don't want to overdo it," he adds. "In a real exterior situation, we usually use a lot of 'negative fill,' if the natural light is too flat. And, if reflective surfaces are involved, especially vehicles, you have to make sure the open sky source is seamlessly perfect. This is pretty obvious, when it is a car commercial, using the big Fisher Light. But, when you translate that onto a large set like the Wilson backyard in *Dennis the Menace* or the construction site on *Baby's Day Out*, you are talking about thousands of square feet of gridcloth. Out of necessity, the grid is usually rigged in separate frames or Super coops. So, the rigging reflects like crazy on the sheet metal if you are shooting cars. We usually try to break up the equipment reflections with tree branches or structural elements."

Before Ackerman got to perfect these elements of shooting comedy and recreate the exasperating Dennis, he teamed with the now famous Tim Burton for what has become a cult comedy *Beetlejuice*, a movie that broke all the molds.

"Reading *Beetlejuice* was a bit of a jolt," Ackerman recalls. "Here's a dead guy, a molding lounge lizard, who takes the protagonists on a kinky trip through the after-life. Anyone who has seen the movie knows that level of surreality. But with only the screenplay in hand, the uncharted design aspects were a little unsettling. The look of the film had to work, had to illustrate the bizarre and absurdist qualities that were so much a part of the story.

"I spent a lot of time with Tim during prep, exploring the visual logic of what we were going to do. We couldn't just use surreality as a crutch," he explains. "The use of color evolved from these discussions – yellow and green pervasive in the after-life, white 'color-corrected' light dominating the 'real world.' In some cases, such as the scene in which Beetlejuice is conjured up during a seance, the after-life colors follow him into Charles and Lydia's farmhouse. And, as the action becomes almost carnival-like, with the B-man literally ejecting house guests through the ceiling, I pushed things into a more theatrical mode by using follow spots and shadow 'reveals.'

"The approach to the visual effects also evolved during prep. As had been the case with *Frankenweenie*, Burton urged a simple approach. Although blue-screen was used in the sand worm attack and for when Alec Baldwin and Geena Davis' characters shrink into the model village, several key composites were achieved in-camera.

"When Geena's character had to dissolve away from Beetlejuice's grasp in the seance, we did it as a mirror shot. She's supposed to be sitting next to him, which required that the set geometry be duplicated in a 'black zone' situated 45 degrees off axis of the fully-illuminated set. It's not a very big deal to use a mirror to make a ghost-like superimposure in-camera. But, in this case, she had to appear solid, then become transparent, then vanish. In order for her to be opaque, we had to subtract all light from her position on the main set, her key on the black set was up 100 percent. Then, as she dissolved away, we took her key light down to zero and cross faded the isolated background light on the main set up to 100 percent.

"*Beetlejuice* is a strong film," Ackerman continues, "not as a result of the bells and whistles but because Tim had a vision of it and invited the rest of us onto the ride. Incidentally, as strong as Tim's concepts were, he wasn't very specific about the photography. He would issue some elliptic clues, but was definitely not into macro-management. But Tim had such a profound belief in what he wanted to achieve, that I guess I was inspired to the right conclusions. Visceral is a word that's used maybe too often. However, it really applied here. Tim is very good at getting your gut up to speed."

Tom Ackerman is one of the lucky ones. He builds strong relationships with his producers and directors. They keep asking him to re-team on challenging projects. Eight months after finishing *Dennis the Menace*, he returned to Chicago to shoot *Baby's Day Out* with Hughes Entertainment. Patrick Read Johnson was at the helm. "I don't know of any other director patient enough to work with seven-month-old babies," Ackerman remembers. "Patrick was so gentle and considerate and he was rewarded by getting great stuff. Having never been much of a two camera guy, I soon got into that mode, since it was necessary when working with the babies. Two camera coverage can be dueling matte boxes with lighting and angles terribly compromised, or it can be a tremendous asset.

"John Hughes wrote the mother of all climax scenes in which the child is elevated up to the 45-story level of a skyscraper under construction. Joe Mantagna and his cronies are in pursuit. For obvious reasons, and not just the safety aspects of working with infants, production designer Doug Kraner placed the action on stage, or rather in the Chicago National Guard Armory. The five-story-high structure required 16,000 amps of power and at one point threatened to exhaust the supply of electricians and grips available in the Chicago local.

"The set was complemented by a 500-foot-long by 60-foot-high painted backing in what has to be one of the great achievements in scenic painting. Production Designer Tom Valentine created a generic city, composited in Photoshop from several plates taken at the proper altitude in the Loop. The whole enormous piece was designed to have a nodal point at the 45-story level. There were also several free standing cut out buildings. They were deployed for added depth and could be dressed to camera. From within the set, the sense of height was totally convincing.

"After Tom got the composition organized, I worked with him on 'lighting' the painting, based on how I intended to light the construction set. We did extensive pre-lighting tests on a quarter scale model during prep. This helped us determine the 'sun' position. Since the backing covered 270 degrees, the directionality of our sun had to shift from side light to back light to side light again.

"One other factor we had to address was to get the scenic artists back in Los Angeles to abandon their traditional contrast range, which tended to be flat, without much punch at either end of the scale. I insisted on whites that would pop and rich blacks for a more photo-realistic quality. Where normally you only get a veiled sense of the backing through a dirty window in the set, here in some shots, the backing WAS the set. In committing to a painted drop on this scale we were extremely vulnerable.

"Achieving a credible exterior look was much the same challenge in *George of the Jungle*, as it had been in *Baby's Day Out*. With a major exception. In *Baby*, we had vast open spaces, with only the open girders of the skeletal building to blend one 20k into another. Since I'm fussy about strong, single source shadow when we're reproducing sunlight, this got to be a headache. On *George of the Jungle*, there was a thick tropical forest. The foliage hid a lot. The background greens could be directly backlit from a variety of angles and because of the confusion of leaves and branches, any multiple shadows were completely swallowed up. Also, the greens were forgiving of uneven densities that point the way to a phony source of sunlight. Foliage, basically, eats up the intensity. In fact, we usually overexposed the greens to enhance their color saturation and give a more realistic spin to parts of the image. It's these out of control anomalies that help us believe we're shooting outside."

Forgiving as the backgrounds were, the foreground lighting scheme proved rigorous and inflexible. Ackerman evolved a style of dappled light, similar to his backyard simulations in *Dennis the Menace*, but on a much grander scale. Once he committed to the leafy shadows, key grip Ted Rhodes and his crew found themselves in a symbiotic relationship with the greens department.

"As agreeable as they were, I'm sure they got to dread the sound of my asking for just one more leaf cluster," Ackerman laughs. "We would position a 20k and then block in the shadows. For some of the wider shots, we had to fly entire branches or leaf bordered grids. Getting it to look natural was a matter of trial and error, but we got to a fairly well-organized approach. Sam Weisman, our director, was very fond of the look – protecting the actors' faces with diffused open shade, while dappling their bodies and the rest of the set with sizzling hot sunlight."

Visitors to the cavernous hangars that once housed the construction of Howard Hughes' "Spruce Goose" were struck by the enormous amount of diffusion material rigged over the *George of the Jungle* sets. "Each 20 by 20 foot section covered a bank of coops and I could furl or unfurl them as needed," Ackerman explains. "Making an open style source was the final component in the equation. This not only gave me a beautifully soft ambiance to moderate the sunlight, it also reflected in the foliage. The best highlights, the stuff that really makes the jungle look great, came from the grid.

"In a way, the fake jungle was the best challenge we could have had. When you looked at it in the morning with the work lights on, it was appalling. Nothing but mush. In fact, one of the concerns during prep was whether we could sustain 60 percent of the show on this set without being seriously dull and repetitive. But in the early tests, I found it to be responsive. You got out what you put in. Nothing looked like anything unless you gave it the right light."

Between shooting *Baby's Day Out* and *George of the Jungle*, Tom Ackerman took on another Robin Williams classic comedic project. *Jumanji* combined physical comedy and often monstrous special effects. Based on the Chris Van Allsburg children's book, this was a comic adventure with decidedly dark tones. Although the film went on to gross 240 million, it's opening was marred by controversy.

"Several reviewers took umbrage with it because they thought it was too scary," he recalls, "that we were luring kids in, disguised as a 'children's movie,' then popping out of the closet and scaring them gratuitously. In fact, Joe Johnston directed the picture with a lot of respect for the unique mood that Van Allsburg creates in his illustrations. It isn't all sweetness and light, but that's the essence of how he tells a story. There is an edge to it. That's what Joe wanted to carry through to our photography.

"*Jumanji* was a wonderful project," he says. "In addition to the pure pleasure of working with Joe, who is as clear and decisive a director as you're ever going to meet, I had a great time with Jim Bissell, our Production Designer. During prep, I asked to have my office located in the art department, that way, when an idea or question came up, everybody engaged in visualizing the movie would be sitting in the same office. For a project with so many sets and locations to knit together, it was a godsend. As Jim worked with the sculptor to create the quarter-scale jungle version of the Parrish house, I could envision the light. It was sort of a low tech virtual reality. Later on, when we were shooting the monsoon sequence, neck deep in floodwater over at B.C. Research, there was a certain sense of been-there-done-that. That's when you know you got the value out of your preparation time.

"When you are preparing a film, you are making a roadmap. The good news is you'll be able to have all the big toys to use as long as you can fit them into a coherent plan. But it requires that you adapt a very disciplined, long view into the schedule. On day one or day 101 you had better know what your vision is. It's not unlike the preparation an actor undertakes. The story arc is shot out of continuity, so he/she has to know how to find the character at any point along the way.

"The bad news is that if you don't plan, nine times out of ten you will be screwed. By the way, this doesn't mean we never improvise! The more buttoned up you are as cinematographer, the more you know your plan, the more you know what the directors' intent is, the more you can throw it all away, if need be, and make a delicious shot nobody dreamed of."

On *Jumanji*, Ackerman used slant focus lenses for the first time. They were ideal for keeping the game board in focus and at a reasonable stop. "Both the 24mm and the 45mm gave me an incredible depth at T4," he says.

"Another new toy was the enhanced Panavision color video taps that came on line in 1995," he adds. "I tested them at very low light levels, down to 16 footcandles, and they still delivered a decent image. Although I never use them as a lighting reference (who would) they are extremely useful in remote camera operations, where it is essential that we have as much information as possible in the time frame to substitute for the human eye. It's nice to see the red outline of a double net that's accidentally been composed, for example, or to be able to say 'Hey, it's that extra in the blue shirt who's clueless about what he's supposed to do in this shot!'"

Ask Ackerman what sequence was almost the straw that broke the camel's back on *Jumanji*, and he will immediately go to the water tank and monsoon.

"I think it was in the very first meeting with Joe Johnston and Larry Franco that I told them the indoor monsoon would be, for me, the most nightmarish. We were going to transplant a major part of the Parrish house set to a huge tank at B.C. Research in Vancouver. Then, somehow, translate one of the most surreal parts of the sequence into a house interior being consumed by a six foot deep blinding rain!

"Conceptually, the first concern I discarded was how to motivate the light. Basically, I decided, 'screw the validity of the source!' We're talking about a monsoon storm inside a New England mansion! Cross-fade to blue rimlight, hit the Lightning Strikes lamps, and have some fun!

"The second concern was safety for the actors and crew. We were literally awash in floodwater, and the electrical circuits had to be protected by means of a GFI (ground fault circuit interrupter). It would close down the power instantly, if a short was detected.

"Ironically, the only injury we had was due to a miscalculation in dropping an 800 gallon 'wall of water,' down the main staircase," he remembers. "Robin Williams and the principal actors were struggling against the rain, and the drop tank was activated. In the movie, you see them looking up: 'Here it comes,' then they are engulfed. At the same instant, our camera operator, Sandy McCallum, was knocked unconscious by a 'rogue wave' that slammed his head against the Platinum's viewfinder. Fortunately, he wasn't injured seriously and was back on set in a week!

"The fact is, there's no exact science to dropping water. Special effects guys are great at what they do, but there are limits to how much R and D the company can afford. If anyone tells you an effects gag or stunt is 100 percent safe, they may be one of the best and the brightest, but they may be wrong.

"But, we had great spirit on that show. Robin was right in there doing a lot of his own stunts, wallowing around neck-deep in some pretty ugly water with the rest of us. Sandy's accident didn't provoke any bad-mouthing or rumor-mongering. It was obviously not due to any negligence or inattention to detail. So, it never got to the 'them versus us' stage." Tom Ackerman stops for a moment, takes a deep breath, and brings himself back from the rigors of shooting *Jumanji*.

"Sometimes, I think we all talk too much. There's so much more verbiage from DPs in print now, compared to our predecessors. It's like everybody's got to justify what they are doing. A layman reading this stuff, whether in trade journals or ads, might wonder what happened to photography that was to be discussed in such oblique terms. We come off sounding like so many self-anointed prophets.

"Unfortunately, we get caught between the need to recite the lists of stuff we use, which is tiresome, and the obligation to somehow explain the artistry. It's like what goes on in the art marketplace. No painter who seriously wants to make the major gallery scene can do without reams of elaborate verbiage. Some of it is so obscure, it is hilarious. I remember a grad student at Iowa who ran around clicking off shots without even looking through the viewfinder. He justified his thesis as 'photographing that which I cannot see.'

"Despite all the pontificating, cinematographers light because they like the way it makes things look. That's their passion. Although the DP's job calls for a whole laundry list of skills, the cornerstone is intuitive and idiosyncratic. It can't be taught. And 98 percent of what is written is pure invention. For example, when I work with a second unit DP, I try to drop a few breadcrumbs, technical details, and so forth. But, ultimately, he has to find the way. He has to synchronize with my technique on the deepest level, not just mechanically. And he has to love his results.

"I'm not suggesting we're just a bunch of idiot-savants, who should never try to talk about the process. Absolutely not. I do think circumspection is in order. Frankly, I think we should use our communication skills to define how we're going to move forward in the CGI world. For all the promise, there are pitfalls that warrant a lot of caution. It's a cliché, but it's true – we've got awesome power to change or enhance photography in post production. Any scripted image can now be put on film. The downside is how many cooks are stirring the broth. Or changing the recipe after the fact. As we speak, there are probably a dozen screening rooms around town where people are running CGI dailies. In some of these rooms, you are going to hear a chorus of voices, not the cinematographer's, making comments. They will discuss in great detail the minutiae of photography, light and shadow, color saturation, contrast, composition. It's a pretty big menu with a lot of tantalizing opportunities for change. These are decisions that until recently were the province of the cinematographer. It's tempting for a director, a producer, an editor, to request a little 'fix' here and there that might seem on it's face innocuous. But in the larger sense, it is an intrusion. And, believe me, it will emerge more visibly as the use of Digital FX widens.

"Directors of Photography are going to have to protect their authority. In my own case, I've never felt remotely 'shut out' or precluded from following my work through the effects process. But there have been times when, due to my involvement on other projects, I haven't been able to mind the store, times when I've had to abdicate to a certain extent because I couldn't be in two places at once.

"This gets into a couple of important areas. First, we can only hope there will be at some point soon a cost effective method of exporting images to all the people who need to see them, in a quality controlled mode. Second, we need to review how the DP performs services in post. Traditionally, we supervise the lab work leading to a final print on a no-fee basis. With the vastly increased time needed to follow through on a visual effects oriented film, this noblesse oblige might have to be amended

"The irony is that CGI, which on one hand, can liberate our imaginations so profoundly, can also rob the cinematographer of his independence. It's like an electronic throwback to the days when studio moguls could tell the cameraman how to light the stars."

Over the years, Ackerman's crews have been observed as models of harmony and efficiency. Time spent with him on set gives some insight to his part in the process. He shows respect, takes time to explain, and seems to genuinely enjoy the process. Although soft spoken, he commands respect in return. During the GMS years, he was affectionately dubbed "The Admiral." He is the collaborator who always welcomes a new idea from others, yet he generally knows exactly what he wants and how to get it.

In speaking with Ackerman about the men and women in whose company he has put out much film through the camera, including a cross-section of producers, drivers, set designers, drivers, set decorators, etc., one perceives a great satisfaction, almost a sense of privilege.

"I worry a little that there is a distance between the crew people and the production staff, and that it is getting wider," he says. "I know it is naive, but it would be nice if we were like a little theatrical troupe, or did movies the way Bergman used to do in Sweden. We'd all pitch in and at the end of the day be friends. Everybody would have read the script and care about the film. Unfortunately, there is a tendency for some crew guys – not all, by any means – to see anything production does as inherently incompetent and evil and anything the crew does as all-knowing and wise. Obviously, the reverse can also be true – production people who view the crew as self-absorbed over-paid slackers.

"Some terribly incendiary things have been said in the press. We all remember Bruce Willis' ranting about how below-the-line crews and the IATSE were responsible for skyrocketing negative costs. Tarantino seems to have the same opinion with all his anti-union diatribes. Their crew counterparts are the guys who are always whining that production is screwed up, that every paycheck error is a conspiracy, and so on.

"People who are lucky enough to work in the entertainment crafts unions are well paid and generally very well treated. Ask our Guild leadership if they've negotiated a good labor contract and you will be informed, correctly, that it's one of the best.

"There are any number of disappointments we all have to deal with. Maybe it's a grip who realizes he'll never write that screenplay, or a producer who knows she's probably not going to get the net point on a blockbuster. The point is we've got to go back on the set, rehearse, light, and shoot. And keep it together as a family with respect. Because you are going to be seeing as much of these people as your own husband or wife and kids."

"I have mixed feelings about this kind of style (the English system). If you have a good operator, it is okay. You can step away from that area and concentrate on the look. If the operator is weak, then you are split between two different jobs, both requiring your full attention."

John S Bartley

John Bartley A.S.C., B.S.C. settles down at the table, cup of tea in hand. As he takes his glasses off, he checks out the room. Is he in Canada or Los Angeles? Since leaving the highly successful series, *The X-Files*, he has been jumping back and forth between countries, like a commuter. He is seriously thinking about making the move to Los Angeles. It isn't that he is unhappy with the state of film and television production in Canada, it is just that he is looking forward to a change. After all, he did make the move from Australia to Canada, even before he began shooting television shows.

A native of New Zealand, he grew up around live, feature films. "There was no television," he recalls. "So, I went to Saturday afternoon matinees and evening shows at the local theater. My brother and I would drop our bags at my mother's ticket booth outside the live theater and go off to the movie house next door. From 11:00 A.M. to 11:00 P.M., we could immerse ourselves in B-westerns from America and England."

His mother's love for stage productions was infectious and Bartley soon began working on local musicals. "At 15, my first paying job was as a second principal dresser on *Hello Dolly*," he recalls with a laugh. "Puberty was interesting, watching all those people in various stages of undress backstage!"

With an uncle who was an electrical contractor, it was only natural for Bartley to start looking toward a career in this field. For five years, he apprenticed with his uncle, doing theater lighting at night and on weekends. "It was a fantastic way to start," he admits. "I learned the basics and limits of the lighting world and practiced theatrical style with the old English Strand lights."

In his early 20s, he moved to Sydney, Australia and became a serious member of the theatrical community. A six month run of *Man of LaMancha*, as a lighting technician, several months of *Boys in the Band*, and the first production of *Hair* after the London opening provided him with quite a resume, at such a young age. When he went as far as he could with stage work, he turned his attention to one of the local television stations.

"I knew little about television lighting but worked with people who soon became well known gaffers. It was the 1970's, the era of free exchange of ideas and the evolution of the stage and variety shows," he explains. "With those experiences under my belt, I thought I was hot. I aimed for work in the American mecca and tried to get a job in New York."

Emigrating to America turned out to be far more difficult than expected, so newly married and concerned about supporting his family, Bartley took a short turn and settled on Toronto, Canada. "It was close to New York," he shrugs. "I thought I could move down eventually."

The high unemployment rate in Canada and lack of resources in television forced Bartley to take a job at a Toronto lighting and grip rental house. "I thought this might be my way into the movie or television world," he concedes. "When the company asked me to run the Vancouver office, I thought it would be three months at the most. Was I ever wrong! Twenty years later, I'm still Vancouver based. But, at least now I am shooting!"

When Bartley finally made it out from behind a desk, he was gaffing hard sell type commercials and then feature projects, working with some very strong cinematographers and directors. One of his all-time favorite projects was with cinematographer Sven Nyqvist B.S.C., A.S.C. "The project was called *Star 80*, starred Eric Roberts and Mariel Hemingway, and was directed by Bob Fosse," he remembers. "Richard Aguilar was the gaffer and I was the Canadian match. I was able to learn a lot from both Sven and Richard. It was very interesting to see two such talented artists working together. The style of this movie focused on the use of many directional soft lights, a Sven Nyqvist style."

Bartley teamed with Nyqvist for another project *The Marie Balter Story.* Directed by Lee Grant, the project starred Marlo Thomas as a woman suffering from schizophrenia. "There is one scene that I remember," says Bartley. "Marie is locked in a closet for punishment. As the door closes on her, the scene went black. Sven dimmed up a light slowly to simulate the audience getting accustomed to the darkness inside the closet."

Bartley went on to do *The Gray Fox*, directed by Phillip Borsos and *The Forbidden Zone*, (a 3-D movie) directed by Lamont Johnson, gaffing for another of his favorite cinematographers – Frank Tidy B.S.C. "*The Gray Fox* was incredible," Bartley recalls. "I received more comments about the look of this show than any other movie on my resume. I learned a lot from Frank, who had shot *The Duelist* for Ridley Scott. Frank lights with little equipment and works quickly. A lot of my lighting style was influenced by Frank – lighting through windows for daytime and using small practical lights as sources. Frank's interiors turned out beautifully and were lit very simply.

"Working with him on the second project was also intriguing," he continues. "We used a Panavision 3-D system, made by a team led by Ernie McNab. This system, two 35mm Panaflex cameras with a half silvered mirror, needed more light than usual. Frank took on the challenge and achieved very high quality 3-D photography. The exteriors were shot in Moab, Utah, and the interiors at the Bridge Studio in Vancouver, B.C."

Bartley was learning about the range of characters in the industry. He was building his own personality and his library of visual experiences on music videos and trailers, as well as a select few movies for television. Oftentimes, production companies seeking funding would ask him to shoot a ten minute "trailer" that was a sample of what the film's story was going to be like. "I did one day on a movie called *The*

Raffle," he recalls. "The film took ten years to make after we did the trailer!

"The budget for that trailer was so tight, we had to shoot on the Panavision stage," he laughs. "We couldn't afford to pay the insurance to take the camera out the front doors!"

It was here that Bartley began to learn the "system" used in Canadian production. It was a style of shooting that leaned toward the English rules. While the cinematographer concentrated on the lighting, the director and operator created the shots. "I have mixed feelings about this kind of style," he admits. "If you have a good operator, it is okay. You can step away from that area and concentrate on the look. If the operator is weak, then you are split between two different jobs, both requiring your full attention."

Bartley also began to learn the pluses and minuses of shooting in the Canadian environment. "In the States you have a lower contrast," he says. "In British Columbia, as well as a lot of rain, there is a lot of clear blue sunshine, sometimes up to four or five stops of contrast. My first feature took place in the summertime. *Beyond the Stars* was a short, four-week shoot starring Sharon Stone, Christian Slater, Martin Sheen, and F. Murray Abraham. One of my problems was to keep Sharon Stone out of the harsh sunlight.

"When I did the Disney film called *Sky High*, not too many years ago, we experienced a lot of rain. We fought to get rid of that saturated green look that always gives away a Pacific Northwest location by using sepia filters on daylight exteriors," he adds.

John Bartley is very philosophical about his first feature film. He had high hopes for *Beyond the Stars*. Although it wasn't filled with attention grabbing visual techniques, it was a platform for his work. Only the film never was released to the theaters. Years later, it was copied to laser disk and for limited cable viewing. "Would a wide release have launched me on a feature career?" he asks, rhetorically. "Probably not. The script was slow. Even though we tried to give the visuals a movement, the story slowed them down. The only shots that really stick in my mind as challenges were scenes done from a boat."

He pauses, dramatically, takes a long sip of his tea and smiles shyly. "I learned one very important thing on these shots," he says seriously. "Try to tie the boat to the wharf! Don't try to do the shots at sea unless you have to!"

With his feature career slightly thwarted, John Bartley made the segue to television. "Stephen Cannell's company was going strong at that time," he says, changing the subject. "There was *Wise Guy, 21 Jump Street*, and the spin off called *Booker*. Although *Booker* was a show the network wanted to let go, I really enjoyed taking it over," he says.

"How did I know they were ready to drop it?" he laughs. "We looked at the *TV Guide*. All it listed is the name of the show. By this time, they weren't even interested in giving the audience a two line description!"

Even with the waning interest in the show, John Bartley was determined to maintain a stylish look on his first television series. "We had lots of equipment, all the toys on *Booker*," he says. "Brooke Kennedy, the producer, helped us maintain a good color palette for set dressing, props, etc. This made the show look good. We lit mostly from practical lights and windows. Light coming through venetian blinds and close-ups using wide angle lenses became the look. Shot with Arriflex BL4 cameras, Zeiss Prime lenses, and on Kodak 5296 and 5247, it was cut on film and transferred to video from a low con print.

"In one particular episode, Booker is hounded by a man and becomes obsessed with catching him. The characters and the story play through as if it was a single day. To give the show a sense of degrading, I got progressively darker as the characters go dirtier and grungier."

Most people who shoot in Canada complain about the quixotic weather, yet John Bartley has always loved to use it in his shows. His first taste of the pressure of schedule and weather conditions came on *Booker*. "I had to shoot in the winter and during the day," he says, shaking his head. "The sun is always in the south in Vancouver. One episode was quite funny. It concerned a house that kept getting stolen and moved from lot to lot. Luckily, every day was sunny and all the locations chosen were on the south side of the streets. This choice of southern exposure was quite by accident, but was very effective as all the scenes were backlit."

When the show finally ended, Bartley and his gaffer Ron Williams moved to do the last season of *Wise Guy*. "Stephen Baur took over for Ken Wahl," he recalls. "I did the three episodes in Vancouver before the show was canceled. I used Arriflex BL4s from Clairmont and tried using Cooke Prime Lenses but had lots of flares, mostly from the practical lights. Like *Booker*, the show was edited on film and transferred to video. The low con print results in a very different look from a transfer taken from negative to video."

Bartley then moved to *Broken Badges*, for ten episodes of another series that was winding down. "We started to call ourselves the terminators," he laughs. "If you hire us, the show will go down the tubes!

"It doesn't bother me to take over a show which is losing its audience," he says. "I didn't walk through the days, but tried to do a quality shoot. The only thing I couldn't do is change the looks. We had to keep the shows consistent, and work with what we had.

"I had shot a pilot produced by Stephen Kronish and directed by John Patterson called *Both Sides of the Street*," he recalls. "While we were waiting for the show to get picked up, I was asked to start a new show called *The Commish*. It became a very popular show. Half of the pilot had been shot by Brenton Spencer using 35mm film. I finished the pilot using 35mm, but the network (ABC) wanted to do the series on 16mm.

"It was quite a challenge. 16mm was used on a lot of Canadian television shows, but not as often in the United States. 16mm film stocks and video transfers were not as good as they are today. Kodak and Fuji have made great improvements in the grain of 16mm stocks and digital tape transfers have made 16mm more acceptable. U.S. audiences are used to seeing 16mm and probably cannot tell the difference now. After a lot of testing and trying different lighting techniques, I think we did okay.

"Post production on the show was done in Los Angeles, while the shooting was done in Vancouver. I did not have much of a say in the final color transfer but, for the most part, the show came off all right. I found I had to light more to compensate for 16mm, particularly at night as video noise and grain were factors to contend with. Again, we were using Arriflex SR cameras and Zeiss Prime lenses."

Years ago, as a gaffer, Bartley did several television movies, one with producer Bob Goodwin. Not long after, Goodwin called to tell him about a very interesting series called *The X-Files.*

"Bob set up a breakfast meeting with Charlie Goldstein from Fox and Chris Carter. We talked about the look of the show. I went home and by four in the afternoon, I wanted that job – badly.

"So, I phoned Bob's wife and left a message. Later, he called and said, in a very sad voice, 'I tried real hard – but they still want to hire you!' Bob's a really funny guy," he says dryly.

When Bartley looked at the pilot, he was surprised that the show got picked up for 12 episodes.

Going in, Bartley knew that getting this kind of series off the ground was going to be a struggle. Fox was not willing to put a lot of money into the show. "We didn't have backings outside the windows or ceiling pieces (which he loves) over the sets – what few we had. However, as the show caught on, we began to get more money to work with."

Gradually, John Bartley began to really push the envelope with this breakthrough series. Word came down – nothing was taboo. If a look fit the outrageous story, he could do it. As the style began to grow, so did Bartley's challenges. "It becomes interesting, trying to top yourself," he laughs. "We had so many 'Oh, my God, what is out there? What are we doing?' type shows, it took longer to single one out."

Each year, when the awards season begins, cinematographers have to dig through their arsenal and almost second guess the people who are doing the voting. What do they look for? How do you choose? "It took a long time to choose a single episode to put up for the awards," he admits. "I would always put up my favorites. I would look at them from a visual point of view and say – 'I like this episode.' As the shows progressed, however, it became a little harder. Easier in the shooting, because we got a bigger second unit. Harder, because I needed to pick the ones that were really focusing on my work."

Bartley's first nomination was an episode called "One Breath." "I put it up because I liked the concept of the show," he explains. John Bartley sits back, thinking. There were so many strange and unusual shows, it is hard for him to focus on one in particular. "And, I think because the exteriors were very unusual for us. The location was on a lake," he says. "It was much more dreamy and far less gritty than most of our episodes. The biggest thing that sticks out in my mind is the sequences with the nurse figure. We got caught with back light on one angle and front with the sun on the other. It was a challenge, yet the awards committee liked it," he smiles.

"I can't remember the second one, at the moment," he laughs. "But I won the Emmy for 'Grotesque,'" he says, smiling. "The show was about this man who kills people and turns them into gargoyles. It was definitely one of my favorite shows!

"The director was Kim Manners – a Stephen Cannell graduate. We both relished the idea that there would be no rules on this episode! Anything would go! Funny, I can't remember the story, past the storyline, however, I do remember this wonderful Russian actor who had won the equivalent of our Academy Award. He brought so much to the episode."

At one point, Gillian Anderson's character goes into Mulder's apartment and sees that he has pictures of gargoyles all over the walls. There is an easel with one picture on it. "That's where the camera ends up," Bartley says. "We began with several 360s around the room, with Gillian turning around and around.

"Difficult to light? I should say so! All we could do is use the practicals. And a hand held light for Gillian's eyes," he adds. "We also had a major chase sequence in an old factory. With a tight schedule, we had to light the location quickly. We just grabbed what we had and filled the area with hidden lights. While we were shooting one direction, the lighting grips were setting up the other. With our time schedules, the idea was always to keep up the momentum."

For everyone on the crew of *The X-Files*, the whole idea is taking things to the absolute limit. "The show called '7-31' was amazing," he recalls. "It was a train sequence, directed by Rob Bowman. It is probably the first show we did with eight days for the main unit and four days for second unit. The first unit did the interiors of the train – a studio train with the aliens on it. We built the railway carriers."

There was a little bit of homage to *E.T.* in this episode and Bartley admits this. "At one point, we had a shot where this little kid peeps through a peephole and sees a little alien," he smiles. "This is the first time we saw the aliens as aliens and we wanted it to stand out.

"To light it, we used a lot of silver paint to get the sheen on the walls and florescent fixtures to extend the sheen. After seeing this episode, I decided to do a lot more with sheens," he adds.

When people are asked which of *The X-Files* episodes stands out in their minds, they inevitably come up with "Gargoyle" and a show called "Soft Light." "That was really ironic, considering there wasn't a soft light in the whole thing – just shadows!" he laughs. "The episode was all about dark matter shadows, which would fall on people. Anyone who got hit turned to dust."

It is obvious, John Bartley had come a long way from shooting product shots and promotional videos when he took on the challenge of *The X-Files*. "You would think I'd learned a thing or two, wouldn't you?" he laughs. "We did an episode called 'Dod Calm' on an abandoned ship, floating in the middle of nowhere.

"I remembered one of the lessons and we did tie it to the wharf, the way I promised myself after doing *Beyond the Stars*! We shot it on an uncommissioned Canadian frigate. It was going to be sent out to be sunk and become one of those diver's reefs.

"Unfortunately, the weather was horrible. It was so damp, the paint wouldn't dry. It got on our clothes, everything. We had to crawl down inside, into a steam room almost. The washroom was three flights up – and we kept hitting our heads on the metal! Charming way to work, isn't it?" he laughs.

John Bartley is the first to admit that meeting an intense schedule on a no-rules show like *The X-Files* can be trying on a cinematographer. There are only so many days when that cinematographer can work solely on adrenaline. "We never knew what we were getting into," he admits. "On 'Calisari' we had to fly a woman against a wall when she is the recipient of her grandson's evil antics. Wire work, well that's okay. But, figuring out how to light a sequence, when the candles on the table (the only light) are blown out is tough. We ended up underexposing the moonlight ambiance, so that the eye would adjust when the candles went out. We used the strangest lighting sources – anything we had on the truck, anything we could get our hands on."

Eventually, John Bartley decided he had pushed his own limits long enough – at least on *The X-Files*. When he decided to move on, it was from more than just a hit show, it was also a lifestyle. While working in Canada, he was an active member of the Canadian Union. As an executive board member, he tried to watch out for the members. "We are set up somewhat like the American unions," he concedes, "but, what we do have going for us is a training system.

"They will carry on very well without me," he says. "Nothing is forever. Right now, I am enjoying the possibilities. I've just finished the pilot for *Fargo*, with Kathy Bates directing. They are going to do the series in Toronto, but I don't want to go up there. I am going to do another series in Los Angeles, called *The Visitor*. Who knows, there just might be an interesting challenge or two that I haven't tried on *The X-Files*."

******

Three A.S.C. Awards and two Emmy Nominations *The X-Files* **– Emmy Award** *The X-Files*

"In filmmaking, we often want to fall back into doing what we know how to do. However, directors like Bob Zemeckis have shown me how to find new ways of telling stories. In filmmaking, you have limitless possibilities. You just have to open your mind and expand your thinking. It's the only way to keep the stories new and interesting for intelligent audiences who respond to the unusual, not the ordinary."

CBurgess

Climb down the narrow side stairs of Don Burgess A.S.C.'s Pacific Palisades home, then enter his long and narrow office set on the rocky mound of a hillside and the first thing you see is an incredible view. A wall of windows looks down a narrow valley between rock-solid landscape to the sparkling calm of the Pacific Ocean. It is a view he never tires of – a view he has seen all his life.

A rare species, especially in the entertainment industry, Don Burgess is a native Californian – born and raised in the upper-class beach community. "I knew the industry existed, of course, but it just wasn't part of my agenda," says Burgess as he settles into one of the office-type chairs that line the long desk facing the beach.

"In high school, I was more of an athlete than a film buff. However, I had a friend who was an avid camera enthusiast. We started taking still photographs together. Then we graduated to Super 8mm ski movies. It just seemed to be a natural progression to go to Art Center College of Design and major in film," he continues.

"While in school, I worked as a loader with a camera operator by the name of Johnny Stephens. Even with professional experience, I couldn't get into the Union, so I started to produce, direct, and shoot public service spots. Eventually, this led to documentaries and second units for action films."

A natural athlete and an admitted daredevil, Burgess hooked up with a second unit director by the name of Max Kleven. Kleven had seen the young camera operator's ski movies and recognized Burgess had no fear. More importantly, the young cameraman understood the mentality of the stunt and action aficionado. "Although most of Max's show *Super Stunts* was shot on videotape, he wanted a slow motion film camera available," Burgess recalls. "That was my first job for him."

He must have been doing something right, because at the age of 20, he was accepted into the stunt world and the world of action photography. Burgess and Kleven did 20 features together, shooting action for *Runaway Train, Batman Returns*, and *Back to the Future II and III*.

"On my first shoot, I had no assistant," Burgess recalls fondly. "I taped a rheostat on the side of my battery belt and shot the stunts. There was only a light camera, the occasional tripod, some incredible scenery, and talented athletes. As long as I could ski with a camera in my hand, I could get work."

One of the important lessons Burgess learned while shooting these action documentaries was how to tell a story in the flash of a ski run. "There is no time for coverage, no time for a second take. In one shot, you have to be able to get that person coming out of the gate, going downhill, and across the finish line. Then there are the crowd and the clock." Those experiences also taught the young camera operator never to be intimidated by the power or speed he sees through the lens.

"It was a great time," he recalls fondly. "We were doing things that had never been done before. Escapism and stunts – popular television programming. We shot stunts like the man who drove his motorcycle out of an airplane and then parachuted to the ground.

"That was tricky long lens photography," he explains. "There is a whole technique to it. You have to find the center point of the shot. Finding something that small in the sky, well, it's a challenge. Some of the men I watched used a real gun-sight to find the 'target.' I didn't have anything like that. I just took my still camera, mounted it on my film camera and created my own parallax."

Burgess traveled around the world, shooting action – from *American Sportsman* to a series shot in New Zealand called *Survival of the Fittest*. "Some of these shoots were amazing," he recalls. "At one point, I was head camera operator of a group of twelve. We were shooting *Survival*. The challenge was where to place the cameras to get all the coverage. Without a director or headsets, it was difficult. The idea was to anticipate where the athletes would go. You place the cameras to capture the moment and hope the operator can get the story.

"Yes, there is a story, an event. Not only do you want to show the person in the lead, but you also have to follow the challengers. It's heart pumping stuff – and I don't just mean the race itself. This wasn't a movie. We couldn't do it over. It hadn't been rehearsed or story-boarded. This was it. We had to know what was going to happen – and how to get it on camera – the first time.

"When we were shooting my second low budget feature, *Nightstalker* in 1987," he continues, "the challenge was to make something interesting out of nothing," he recalls. "We had one film stock – Kodak's 5247 – and we pushed the stop on interiors and nights. I shot with Canon lenses on the MovieCam. This was a relatively new camera that was owned by Pia Zadora. We used a lot of long lenses, smoke, and nets. That's the best, maybe the only, way to make no money look interesting. You discount the background, focus on a long lens, and isolate the subject.

"Of course, my personal favorite is to work with wide lenses," he explains. "They are the story-tellers. You work from minimum focus to infinity and get a lot of story in one shot."

Burgess has just dropped himself into an ongoing controversy within the motion picture industry. Many feature film productions are shot with "protection" in mind. They will eventually go to the small screen, and a lot of people will sacrifice the story, the visual story, to make sure the product can be seen on the television screen. They will be a bit more conservative in the framing, or even go for closer two-shots or more foreground action, anticipating a feature picture being "shrunk" to the video/television screen size.

"I recently went to see *The Rock* and sat ten rows back," says Burgess. "It was impossible to watch the movie that close. Filmmakers should be forced to sit in that row and watch the picture. It's tough to drop back wide and keep the shot interesting, I know. It is also tough to get in very tight and keep it interesting. To do either is a learned art. As filmmakers mature, you will see them drop back and get more comfortable with what they are actually shooting.

"Of course, it isn't just the cinematographer's fault by a long shot," he concedes. "A lot of directors don't stage the actors for the camera. They have to edit shots together to make a scene. I think it is better to try and make it work in one shot and let the camera move to reveal the story."

Early in his career, Don Burgess learned to find a happy medium between the two styles. "When I was shooting *Blind Fury* with Philip Noyce, we had a first day shoot on the Squaw Valley tram," he recalls. "I literally mounted a generator on the roof of the tram car. We put a man up there to adjust the air flow of the carburetor as we gained altitude, put the windows down, and we put a dolly inside. Off we went, shooting from the tram – moving with the vehicle and within the vehicle."

When Burgess shot the youth-on-the-road picture called *Josh and Sam* he was determined to make the shots realistic by showing the visual story through wide lenses and movement. "We had a portable crane with us," he recalls. "We did a whole sequence where the kid has to run into this train. We tried to make it look realistic."

Burgess's eyes sparkle. He leaps from his chair and pulls several photo albums from a nearby shelf. He flips past more ski shots and sailing stills. You can see pictures of him skinny, slight, bearded in one shot, clean shaven and looking 14 in another. Always in the middle of the action – camera close by. He settles on a still of a strange looking train and points to it.

"Because trains, real ones, are unforgiving if someone makes a mistake, we didn't want to put our small stunt person in jeopardy. So, we created a piece of a train with foam wheels in the place of the regular wheels. This way, when we went in tight for the shot of him going underneath the moving wheels, the worst case scenario would be that he would be bumped by foam instead of hard and sharp iron."

He flips the pages, his eyes focused on photograph after photograph. Suddenly, his hand freezes on a shot of a car being towed. "We had a lot of shit attached to that car," he laughs as he looks at the monstrous rig.

"Car work can be boring," he admits. "It is time consuming. And, a lot of times, you put three cameras on the hood so you have a two shot and cross angles. So, in *Josh and Sam*, we decided we weren't going to do that. We were going to do cross angles and overs instead. It worked out really well, it just took a little more time.

"Cross angles and overs work better, because you see the environment going by outside the window and it gives the shot lots of energy. You feel like you are in the car with the actors," he explains. "People are getting too smart. They know what a phony shot is, so you try to make it as real as possible."

Burgess's second unit adventures, as he developed his talents, began to come in handy in the late 1980s and early 1990's. His memory books are filled with spectacular set-ups and interesting rigs. One of his fondest recollections is of working on the second unit for *Batman*. "We did a lot of in-camera effects," he says. "It was both a creative and a financial choice. We had the talent and the abilities, and we wanted to make the shots as real as possible.

"Most of the work was done on the Warner back lot," he recalls. "So, I got to light up the old Hennessey Street. We really took production designer Bo Welch's set over-the-top. We used 60 10ks, 12 arcs, four raybeams, and two brand new 20ks to light the set to a T4, on the old 5295 Kodak film stock. Shooting at T4 gave us great depth of field at night, so you really see all of that wonderful set in the background."

Ask Don Burgess what his favorite *Batman* shot was, and he answers immediately. Actually, he flips the pages of a photo album and points to a spectacularly colored shot of the shiny black Batmobile and several dozen different cars. "That was real, not miniatures," he says proudly.

"It is the shot where the Penguin has control of the Batmobile and it is being driven down the street, knocking car after car out of the way. This Batmobile is made out of plastic," he explains. "If it hit another car, it would break into pieces. The car, driven by a stunt driver, moved down a street about a city block long. The cars, well, they were rigged to a series of cables that ran back through the facades. The cables were attached to air rams that, when rigged, would flip the cars over. We shot with eight Panavision cameras. The wide lens side angles were shot in slow motion to see the action. The long lens front angles were undercranked to speed up the action and foreshorten the distance between the Batmobile and the cars that it appears to be hitting. This is a great example of using lens, camera speed, angles, and editing to create the illusion of something happening that is not," he adds.

The photo below the flipping cars is just as fascinating. It is Batman flying high above Gotham City, of course. "Live action with a stuntman, in this case it was Scott Skool," he explains. "Actually, this looks simple but is rather dangerous for the guy in the suit. When we did this shot, he was actually flying. Well, rigged to a very thin cable, that is. The smaller the cable, the more chance you have of it breaking – that's the danger.

"Shooting this way is also more time consuming, because you have to light it so you don't see the rig. Here we attached a 150-foot cable to a construction crane and created a flight path down the center of the street. Batman was to fly in, hit the ground with a front somersault, and walk to the Batmobile.

"The challenge was to light Batman, who is wearing a black suit at night, and separate him from the dark buildings," he explains. "Nowadays, we wouldn't take the time to hide that cable. We would use a bigger cable, which is safer for the stuntman, and we would take it out of the shot with the computer – in post.

"Here's a great shot," he says, as he flips to another page. "This is where Batman takes all of these guys out with a little boomerang. To make this work, we used the Bowmont lightweight VistaVision camera on a Steadicam, operated by Chris Squires. We shot at 12 frames per second, speeding up the action. Chris ran the path of the boomerang and the stunt people took hits as if the camera was that boomerang. Later, in post, the actual boomerang image was composited into the picture.

"What is the trick to a seamless blend of first and second unit?" he asks, rhetorically. "Sometimes, it comes down to the focal length and lenses you are using. You try to match their lenses. However, when it involves stunt work, often-times you can't do it on an 18mm lens. You have to use a 200mm lens. Then, besides hoping the editor can make it seamless, you try to match the style of the director and camera operator. When you set up a shot, you ask yourself whose point-of-view this is. If the only answer you can come up with is the audience's, then you are in the wrong place."

While *Batman*'s second unit work was invigorating for Don Burgess, his fondest memories are of doing some of the shots in the *Back to the Future* pictures. That is where he got right into the shot and became an athlete once again. "Into it, upside down, around, and whatever we had to do," he laughs.

"My favorite shots are of the hoverboard sequence," he comments. Another photo album comes out and there is Don Burgess, or at least it looks like him from the back. The thin body, the longish hair, upside-down, or at least almost upside-down. "I'm shooting my own feet here," he laughs as he indicates the board and the camera in his hands as it points down.

"When I'm upside down, I have to do a flip with the camera. To do that, I have to be on the arm of the crane, which is then being flipped upside down. The hardest part about this shot – cramming my feet into Michael J. Fox's shoes. They are about this big!" he laughs, as he holds his hands close together.

"These scenes were fun," he adds. "We had to plan carefully. Some, of the shots would be done with visual effects. However, others that you might have thought could be visual effects were actually real – our real, that is.

"In one shot, you see the board sitting by itself, simply hovering. You see two feet come in, drop on the board, and the board takes off with the feet in place. We had two pieces of monofilament attached to little vibrators. As the board sat there, it shook a little. We had magnets in the board and magnets on the shoes. The stuntman was attached to the Titan crane at his hips. As the arm of the crane swung him into position, it set him down on the board. The magnets meeting attached the two securely.

"I had the mirror parallax on the lens and had the lens right on the neck so you can see onto the board. That way, the audience saw there was nothing there. When his feet came in, the board and the Titan crane took off. We then chased them both down the street – with me and the camera mounted on the front of an ATV.

"It was a lot of R and D," he concedes. "We tested many thicknesses of monofilament and found large magnets to attach the hoverboard to the shoes. We tested camera speeds to make the shots work for day exterior with the light at a perfect angle for the shot," he adds. "The challenge with this kind of shot, is to use the correct film stock, filters, shutter speed, and angle to make everything look real and keep the visuals crisp and clean. Mechanical effects are a lesson in patience," he sighs. "You have to wait until it is right, so you see what you want to see and don't see the rigging."

Burgess admits that *Back To The Future* and *Batman* second units allowed him to cut his teeth on blending visual effects and camera work. However, his most fascinating – up until 1996 – work came with the blockbuster feature, *Forrest Gump*. By now, Burgess had already forged a comfortable working relationship with director Bob Zemeckis. This teaming would take both filmmakers where no-one had gone before.

"Bob is meticulous," says Burgess. "Planning was of the utmost importance. On some of the major shots, we literally put stakes in the ground three months ahead of time. This way we could nail down what the shots would be. We picked the cameras, lenses, cranes, and length of the moves based on the voice-over written in the script.

"We had pages of technical notes for every scene in the film. Every filter and film stock was chosen for each decade before we started shooting. This was the most connected I've ever been to the visual style of a picture before shooting. When this happens, everything seems to fall into place."

One of Burgess's favorite sequences is during Forrest's time in Vietnam. "They were spending a lot of time walking through the jungle, looking for a guy named 'Charlie,'" Forrest Gump says in this scene. We spent our time finding and using the sun's window of time and using the sun's window of opportunity," says Burgess. "This was crucial to this shot. Our challenge: A big enough rain drenched area and getting the rain to stop at the proper time. By back lighting the rain effects with arc lights, we were able to pick a spot where the rain stopped and the sun began.

"Our operator, Chris Squires, began by sitting on a dolly wearing the Steadicam. This way, he could make a smooth move following Forrest through a portion of the set. When a GI steps into frame and is shot through the chest, Chris steps off the dolly following Forrest down into a trench. By panning about 180 degrees, we move from quiet to chaos. We used smoke mortars placed in front of the camera move to cover the transitions.

"The more smoke, the more claustrophobic feeling," he explains. "Soon, we had the same set with a totally different atmosphere. We went from a peaceful walk in the rain, to the sun coming out, to all hell breaking loose in the middle of a trench with bodies being blown to bits – all in one shot."

Later in the sequence, Forrest has to carry his friend Bubba out of the jungle, while being chased by a Napalm attack. "Tom Hanks had to run while carrying the actor playing Bubba, who was twice his size," Burgess explains. "We did the shot in two passes with the VistaVision camera. The first pass was Tom running with Bubba attached to two wires for support. The wires were hung off a 100 foot truss that was attached to a 120 foot construction crane. Tom ran at full speed past eight cameras. Seven of the cameras were locked off and the eighth was geared for a tilt past Forrest to the F4A Phantom Jets. The second pass was shooting the Napalm blast, which was huge, close, hot, and safe. By doing this effect in two passes, you eliminate the danger and have your real actor in close-up instead of a wide shot of a stunt double.

"If we had tried to do this kind of shot a few years before, the producers would have had to get expensive planes and hire pilots to fly over the location. The cost of the equipment, bringing in and housing the crew, and maintaining the planes would have been far higher than doing the CGI," he adds. "The computer allowed us direct placement of the effects and even the sun. By changing the timing, we were able to slow down or speed up the plane's flight, reposition hits, and even drop the bombs at exactly the right moment. Not only did we get to control the shots, we also got to protect the cast and crew from errant pyrotechnics."

When anyone talks to Don Burgess about this landmark movie, they bring up three or four of the same scenes. They are fascinated with the technology used to insert Forrest into significant parts of American history. "People always ask me about the Dick Cavett Show sequences," he says.

The set up for this interview involves Cavett asking Forrest questions about Vietnam. "Tell us about China." Cavett says. "People don't have much," Forrest answers. "No material things?" Lennon adds. "They don't believe in God," Forrest adds. "No religion, too," Lennon returns. Cavett caps the moment with his dry comment, "Imagine that." "So, Forrest is now responsible for the song *Imagine*," Burgess smiles. "To do this sequence, we literally took effects to a new level," he adds, getting serious.

"When we shot the sequence with the real Dick Cavett, de-aged by some fantastic make-up techniques, on a set that duplicated his old one, even lit the same way. On this set, he asked questions that could fit into the interview done years before. However, we shot the sequence on film at 30 frames per second instead of 24 frames. This helped when it was converted to video in post. Tom and Dick acted out the scene with a John Lennon impersonator. ILM then took the material we did with Cavett and Hanks and fed it into their computer. They married it with archival footage of an interview with John Lennon and Yoko Ono, taking her out and putting Hanks in her chair."

"At other times, on various other 'conversational' shots, first unit worked carefully to create the correct atmosphere for the effects. Then Ken Ralston and ILM's technicians took over. They used a new technique called 'mouth-morphing.' They watched miles of footage to learn the physical subtleties of the historical characters who were going to interact with Forrest. Then, after breaking down each shot on an animation sheet, they went into computer mode.

"Using a program called Elastic Reality as their jumping off point, they pasted archival footage together with computer manipulated facial expressions. They then married the movements to the soundtrack of words drawn from a variety of interviews. Once that was finished, they had to computer enhance or de-enhance the footage, matching both grain and lighting direction on the archival footage and the shots we did on stage, or in blue screen, or whatever.

"The guys at ILM love these challenges," Burgess adds. "In fact, I heard through the grapevine that there was a major caucus over one of these unique shots. It is the point in the story where Forrest dreams about his grandfather, who fought in the Civil War.

"First unit shot Tom Hanks, dressed in a Civil War uniform as he sat on a horse. We used the Polo grounds at Will Rogers Park and shot with a VistaVision camera. Tom matched his movement to the actual footage to be matted into the original shot in post. ILM used footage from *Birth of a Nation*. Their special challenge was working with the old Kinescope look of the original footage. They started by manipulating what we shot into a sepia tone, then degrading the shot down to fit the grain of this historical picture. In addition to grain, they had to concentrate on the light and dust from the original set – and even had to eliminate frames from the final product to give it the kinescope speed.

"On top of all that, there was this great controversy," Burgess smiles. "It keyed on integrity. While working on the footage, one of the computer whizzes found tire tracks in the shot! They were so exhausted, they thought, maybe, they'd made the mistake. When they finally looked at the archival footage, they realized it was a D.W. Griffith shot that had the tiretracks! Someone hadn't removed the markings of 'modern' equipment from the set!

"Now, the pow-wow. Do they screw with a part of film history, or leave the glitch in the shot? Glad they didn't ask me," he laughs. "I would have been in a battle with myself – part wanting to 'fix' a glitch, the other part not wanting to 'screw' with film history. Fortunately, the historical part won. Now D.W. Griffith's oversight can be seen by a whole new generation of film-goers."

One of Burgess's more complicated marry shots involved Forrest with football coach Bear Bryant. When Bryant sees Forrest's incredible running speed, he arranges for him to go to the University of Alabama on a football scholarship. "One day, Forrest is walking across campus and sees a rather volatile crowd gathering," Burgess explains. "When he asks what is going on, someone tells him that, 'they are letting coons on campus.' 'Oh, we used to have those in our trash cans at home,' Forrest comments. He has no understanding of the black/white issue consuming the South. His attention turns to a young woman, who has dropped her book. He bends to pick it up, inadvertently putting himself in the middle of an old-fashioned showdown.

"We really had to plan this shot carefully," he explains. "We broke it down on storyboards and chose the archival footage of the incident at the University of Alabama and George Wallace's participation with great care. Using the VistaVision camera, we shot Tom Hanks in situations that resembled the campus. This allowed us to play the shot into the archival footage featuring George Wallace. Then, with a seamless look in mind, we had to shoot the scene leading to the meeting on 35mm anamorphic. Oh, we also had to build the image for the television screen shot on 16mm stock. I asked an old friend, who was a news camera operator in the 1960s, to get this footage. He created the whip pans and all the other 'documentary style' shots we needed. I added a little fill, which would help us blend the archival footage with shots of in-studio newsmen, who would talk about the incident as it played across the television screen."

Another *Forrest Gump* shot that seems to fascinate people is a simple scene between Forrest and his war-time buddy on a shrimp boat. "This is where his Lieutenant from the war finally has gotten his life together and joins Forrest in the shrimping business," Burgess recalls. "At one point, he rolls his wheelchair to the edge of the boat and dives into the water with pure joy.

"Easy? Maybe it looks it, but it was a challenge! Since the character played by Gary Sinise had lost his legs during the war, we had to keep them out of the shot. Normally, something like this is rather easy. I learned these techniques while operating for Dean Cundey on the *Back to the Future* films and on *Death Becomes Her.* You lock off the camera and do the shot with the actors and without. Only, on this picture, we were working on water. That meant nothing was stable. No lock off. The reflectiveness of the water was also a factor. So, we worked from a barge with a crane and remote head. That way we could put the camera where we wanted it.

"So, how did we get the shots where he swings his non-legs over the edge of the boat to be so believable? Sure, we could have used old tricks like putting the legs under a sheet or tucking them into the wheelchair. But, Bob Zemeckis never does things that easy way.

"We shot the scene with Gary sitting on the edge of the boat wearing blue stockings – a Chroma key blue," he explains. "A section of the boat was taken out so Gary could swing his legs around as if they weren't there and flop into the water. Then we shot a plate of the boat with the missing piece put back in. Post composited the two shots together, creating the illusion of Gary being an amputee.

"Complicated enough for you?" Burgess laughs. "It got better. Not only did we have to add stumps to Gary's missing legs, we also had to replace parts of Tom Hanks's arm, as the so-called stumps pass by his body. This is where ILM's magic really came in. We had to marry the texture of the first unit picture, a person's arm in this case, with computer animation. Frame by frame, you have to matte back in the background where you take the legs out. Between Gary's performance and ILM's CGI work, the scene is flawless. People were sure we hired an amputee actor for the part."

Burgess's next challenge was taking over on Kurt Russell's disaster film, *Executive Decision.* "It was half-way through production and the whole shoot takes place inside a hijacked 747 airplane on its way to Washington, D.C., loaded with explosives," he says. "Taking over is always difficult until you get up to speed. You are brought in to solve problems fast and get a handle on the look of the film quickly.

"The interiors were being shot on a sound stage with the body of the plane attached to a large gimbal that could rotate it by computer command. We had to make it look like it was diving, flying out of control, and crash landing. Although the computerized motion helped to create the illusion by giving the passengers a sense of movement, the actual sell came from the cameras," he explains. "You had to rotate them on the third axis and shake them. We used remote third axis heads on crane arms and Steadicams to create the effect. Simply rotating the camera over on its side, you can sell the illusion of the plane diving. With the help of the actors simulating their movement, it makes the shot totally believable," he explains.

"One problem was that the windows in a plane are so small it is difficult to see the horizon. When you don't see the horizon, you have no reference and no environmental change. The audience needs a reference. We needed to do things to correct that. On one shot, we put a glass of water into the shot. This way, the audience could see the water move.

"One mistake often happens when the operator doesn't have a visual reference and the camera is mounted to a gimbaled or moving set. It might feel very dramatic when you shoot it, but you get the dailies back and they are boring. The camera is locked down and doesn't move, so no matter how violent the impact may have been or what it felt like, a shot full of energy doesn't appear on the film. You must create the illusion with the camera as well as in the camera. My motto is to shake, rattle, and roll," he laughs.

The challenge of coming in on the middle of a project and making it work against enormous odds helped Don Burgess get ready for his next project – the action and special effects piece called *Contact*. "*Contact* is the story of a young scientist (Jodie Foster) who hears a signal from 26 light years away. In pre-production, we knew we wanted to take the effects a lot farther than we did in *Forrest Gump*," he explains, "so, we came up with the idea of shooting them with Panavision's 65mm Soundsync cameras. They are similar to Panaflex cameras, only much bigger. They even have a full range of lenses. It is a real system. With over 400 effects shots, the system was a blessing.

"The biggest problem when working on a 65mm negative is the time and cost to turn it into an optical reduction," he explains. "This printer takes a 65mm negative and makes a

35mm anamorphic print for dailies, available the next afternoon. *Contact* is a 35mm anamorphic movie, shot on 65mm, 35mm, VistaVision, Super 8mm, and Beta SP. And you thought *Forrest Gump* was a challenge!"

With all the technical mountains to climb on *Contact*, it is hard for Don Burgess to pick a shot that stands out in his mind. "In *Forrest Gump*, my shot was Vietnam. Audiences enjoyed it, but scenes like the feather opening and JFK's shots captured their imaginations. For me, a *Contact* shot that looks so simple on the screen, but was murder to get smoothly was a scene involving the giant satellite dishes in New Mexico. The shot starts in the desert, before sunrise. Ellie Arroway (Jodie Foster) is sitting on the hood of her car at the bottom of a giant Radio Telescope. She has her laptop plugged into the radar dish and is listening for signs of possible life in the universe. She hears a faint sound and calls home base to have them focus all the telescopes on that signal.

"She gets in the car and races across the desert. We boom down off the crane," he explains. "Mark Okane, the Steadicam operator, then steps off the Titan crane as she jumps out of her car and races into the building. She runs through it, with him running at the same pace. She goes down a hallway and through a door. As she makes a right turn, we do an optical blend (a modern version of a hidden edit) from New Mexico to a Hollywood sound stage.

"The second half of the shot was done at Culver Studios where she is racing up the stairs, through the hallway, and into the control room. We finish with a close-up of one of the radio telescopes on a Translight outside the stage window. Of course, the scene has to take place before sunrise! And we had to match exterior locations to interior Translights. The sequence, when finished, was to appear to be one continuous shot!"

Burgess pulls out a huge photo album of images from *Contact*. Even looking at the pictures, the mind is boggled by the complications. You can see the meticulous steps taken to make these images real. The problem is that until they are married together, things don't always make sense. "That's part of the fun," he laughs. "You get to second guess yourself.

"And you get to do insane things," he adds, a twinkle in his eye. "No matter how big a budget you have or how bankable the director is, there is a limit to how far you can push things. We had only so much time in New Mexico. When we ran out, we still had about five shots to do and 20 minutes of the right light to do them in.

"So Bob Zemeckis and the whole team laid out a plan that only people who are totally insane would attempt to do," he laughs. "We literally had a road built where Jodie drives her car past the dishes. We had the car being towed on the Shotmaker and I was on the camera that was mounted in the Libra III remote head on the end of the Shotmaker arm. This way, we could get a clean move into this big close-up of her as she communicates with base on her walkie-talkie.

"At the same time, we needed a wide angle shot from high up on the car peeling out with the double driving. We also needed two more angles of the dishes, actually turning, that we could file for effects. This way Ken Ralston would have them available for other effects shots. All of the shots, by the way, had to be done at Magic Hour, which is really 'tragic hour' that lasts a whole 20 minutes!" he says, still out of breath.

"The only way we could accomplish this was to shoot three separate units at the same time and in the same place!" Meticulous and inventive, and more than just a little daring, Bob Zemeckis came up with a way to get everything – several hours of set-ups – in 20 minutes. Three people would shoot – Zemeckis and Burgess on the insert car with Jodie Foster, Steve Starkey and Bob LaBonge on the Titan crane, and Ken Ralston on the VistaVision camera.

"We were to take off down the road towing Jodie's car. We would do the dialogue and the crane moving in. As soon as we turned the corner and got out of frame, the high angle with the stunt driver on the duplicate car would be ready. She would peel out and go down the road. After she left the frame, we would still be moving, only this time it would be the VistaVision camera shooting the dishes (radio telescopes). Since the dishes had to be turning in all shots, we had to figure out an angle of about a 250 degree loop for when we started turning and when the dishes left the frame.

"As we turned around, everyone literally bailed out of the way and we came back into the shot in almost one consistent motion. It looked like an Indianapolis pit stop! Wash the windows, kick the tires, put make-up on, and back out again for Take Two. We actually got three shots off in 20 minutes! Now, if that isn't a racetrack record!

"In filmmaking, we often want to fall back into doing what we know how to do," he says seriously. "However, directors like Bob Zemeckis have shown me how to find new ways of telling stories. In filmmaking, you have limitless possibilities. You just have to open your mind and expand your thinking. It's the only way to keep the stories new and interesting for intelligent audiences who respond to the unusual, not the ordinary.

"*Contact* is filled with those challenges. Audiences will respond to images that provoke an emotional response etched in their minds. Images that, years later when remembered, bring back those feelings.

"We shot a sequence that plays toward the end of the film," he continues. "Here Ellie has to go in front of a tribunal to convince the world that she really did go on a trip into the universe. We shot the scene in the Melon Building in Washington, D.C. The room is 120 feet by 200 feet with five large windows on each side.

"To me, the scene was about Ellie against the world and how she finally connects with who we are and how important we are as people and a planet," he explains. "Bob Zemeckis staged her sitting at a table isolated from the thousand spectators behind her and the 50-person tribunal in front of her. We also staged television sets on both sides of the room. They would be broadcasting live pictures of Jodie and James Woods trying to make her admit the incident didn't happen. These television pictures allowed us, no matter what way we were shooting, to keep connected with what was going on in the other direction. We could also shoot a wide master of the room and a closeup in the same shot," he pauses to take another breath. This was a physically and mentally exhausting shoot!

"I wanted a strong window source, so we rigged three layers of scaffolding on both sides. On the key side, we used 15 18ks through 250 diffusion. We cut a few openings for some hard light on the architecture. On the fill side, we used 15 12ks through 216 diffusion. Above the lights, we blocked the direct sun. So, no matter what time of day it was, the light inside wouldn't change.

"We also built an 18-inch tower with three 12ks stacked on top of each other. They were covered with 216 to make it one source that matched the quality of light coming through the windows. We could roll around inside the building and get the light just the right angle for the close-ups with this rig.

"Bob Zemeckis and I worked hard at getting just the right focal length lenses and just the right dolly move in on Jodie as she gives her final speech. We both agreed on the concept that we started out with – and finally, in the end, changed it as we shot the scene! There is a feeling you get as you are shooting," he explains. "It's in your gut. It tells you you are doing the right thing or not doing the right thing. You have to trust your instincts and make changes until you get it right."

Burgess's eyes glaze over for a moment. He flips through his photo album of recent memories. He seems to edit several photos together in his head. "We tried so many different things on *Contact*," he says slowly. "There was another 'unique' scene, the one where Ellie Arroway has been selected to take the ride in a transport that the world consortium has built. It will take one person out into the universe, 26 light years away.

"The scene was storyboarded to just over 100 shots, which we worked on for two weeks. Every shot had a different light and mechanical effect to match where she was in the universe. We used background engineers with video projectors to project conceptual visual images of the universe on Jodie's face. We used arc lamps flickering, color faders, and built 20 foot spinning light rigs to give us as many different effects as possible. All light effects had to create not only a feeling of location but also of movement. It had to appear as if she were traveling at light speed. We used a computerized dimmer board to control all the lighting effects. Of course, we had to shoot out of continuity. So we kept detailed notes to be able to recreate the lighting effect on different sets," he smiles, tired but satisfied.

"We shot in 65mm, VistaVision, and 35mm Anamorphic formats at different frame rates and ramps between rates throughout the sequence. The only thing that remained constant was the Kodak 5293 film stock which worked for all the practical sets and blue screen shots. We also used a three axis head so we could rotate the set and camera to create a zero gravity effect. We morphed images of Jodie together at different frame rates to create a feeling of time warping.

"This scene was a true test of everyone's imagination, patience, and endurance. The process from conceptual meeting, to shooting, to final composite was long and arduous but, in the end, hopefully, it was worth the time and effort to have created something the audience has never seen before."

Burgess closes the photo album on *Contact*. It was a long and exhausting shoot. Much more challenging than *Forrest Gump* – partly because of the intensity of the story, partly because of the mixture of technologies. He looks up at several photos on the wall, one is of his two young daughters sitting on the hood of the *Back to the Future* car. "Would you believe she's in college now?" he groans, shaking his head. He's about to say he's feeling old, but he stops himself. Too many people have told him he still looks like he just got out of school himself.

"Got to slow down, a little," he smiles. "*Contact* was a long and challenging shoot. I'll do it again, and again, and again, if I'm asked. But, in-between those monumental effects pictures, I'll take another *Evening Star* or two.

"People often ask me, 'What is a Director of Photography?'" he says, looking out the window to the quiet Pacific. "The job of a DP is a little different on every job because it depends on what the director needs. You have to find some common ground on which to communicate. You have to understand what story he or she is telling and you have to be the visual conduit between the script and the director."

******

British and American Academy, A.S.C. Award Nomination *Forrest Gump* – **ACE Award** *Breaking Point* – **ACE Nomination** *Yellow* – **A.S.C Nomination** *Courtmartial of Jackie Robinson*

"With today's advanced technology we were able to bring 'flash' and 'fantasy' even closer together to tell a story no-one believed did happen, yet reacted as if it could."

Dean Cundey

Dean Cundey A.S.C. stands patiently in the circular driveway of his La Canada, California house on the look out for visitors. There is a quiet braying sound coming from the neighbor's corral, although the horses are nowhere to be seen. Cundey cocks his head and looks down the long driveway. He is used to visitors being just a little late, the house is hidden from view, a quiet retreat from people and problems.

"Come by way of San Francisco?" he asks with a straight face, but the twinkle in his eye is the giveaway. At first glance, the longish dark hair, graying beard, and bushy eyebrows speak of a no-nonsense manner. The twinkle in his eye and the dry voice give away his quiet sense of humor. If he doesn't tease or pick on you, then you have a problem.

"Don't know if I'm going to let you in the house, you're still an IBM person, aren't you?" he asks. A confirmed Macintosh aficionado, Cundey and son Chris have created a new computer system that will revolutionize the melding of special effects and live action footage. It is a system they used to make the straight-to-video *Honey, We Shrunk Ourselves* (his first directorial effort) and was used on his latest Robin Williams project *Flubber, A.K.A. The Absent Minded Professor*, as well as Tom Ackerman's 1998 release, *My Favorite Martian*.

"Watch the boxes," he says, as he winds his way through piles of packed possessions. "We are still trying to remember where everything goes." Cundey and family have just moved back to La Canada from a six month "visit" to San Francisco, where he shot the *Flubber* remake, based out of the Treasure Island Naval Base studio facility.

Cundey settles into a comfortable chair. "It's good to be home again," he sighs. For a man who has shot movies and commercials all over the world, the word "home" has a special meaning. At heart, he is a confirmed family man and nester. Born in Alhambra, California, his background is middle-America and family oriented. His father was a salesman for Dunn and Bradstreet and mother a housewife. Although the senior Cundey's work touched the world of Hollywood, because he had several clients "in the business," the glamour seemed very distant.

"When I was 12 we had a special tour of Disney Studios," he recalls. "I got to talk to Walt Disney for ten minutes. I was fascinated by the architecture of his theme parks. I remember asking him how to get into the world of that kind of design. My mother was delighted that he steered me toward architecture instead of the movie industry," he laughs. "They both thought that would give me a career to 'fall back on,' should I go astray!"

A camera shop located across the street from Cundey's high school captured his eye. Inside, copies of *American Cinematographer* were displayed. After reading the first, he was hooked. He ordered as many back copies as he could get. "In those days, they were cheaper than the newest editions," he laughs. "The ability to create illusion with light fascinated me. I used to think how lucky these members of the A.S.C. were. I never thought I would become one of them."

When Cundey began reading college catalogs, courses like calculus and structural engineering made him think twice about architecture. He switched his attention to theater history and a few light architectural classes at Cal State, Los Angeles, and then the film school at UCLA.

Although he received some grounding from a few teachers who knew the practical side of the business, UCLA film school in the late 1960s did not prepare students for the reality of the business. Cundey realized he had to learn by doing. "It was the height of the flower child era," he recalls, not at all shy about dating himself. "The students were interested in experimenting. Alternative filmmaking and cinema verite were in.

"There was a new awareness of film as an art form," he adds. "*The Graduate* was a perfect example of what could be done. It had smaller, hand-held cameras, quartz lighting units, faster films, the more portable Nagra sound recorders. All contributed to freeing up the creative process. Films could be shot in actual locations under more realistic conditions. For a while, we were seeing more 'personal' films influenced by that style of European filmmaking."

Cundey's first project followed the experimental road. Project One was silent with a music track. He shot a "story" of a young man who wanted to buy a car. To earn the money, he scrounged masonite and old paint and made a piece of abstract art using roller skates, a mop, and other discards. He then cut it into four pieces, selling each at a festival. The proceeds were enough to buy the car. "Who says it had to have a great meaning," he laughs. "Sometimes we over intellectualize things!

"In class, we would sit for endless hours analyzing the deep symbology that is part of a film or a play or book. At the time, I felt impatient. What I really wanted to get to was 'how can I make this really important?' My project was my low key statement to that effect. It was complimented for its visual style."

Cundey and several other students felt restricted. Instead of making a little final project, they banded together and got permission to shoot something more substantial. One would write, another be the production manager, he would shoot and another direct. Their project would be an existential black-and-white Western.

Cundey used his high school machine shop training to build a mount for an anamorphic lens on a 16mm camera, making it possible to shoot the wide format. The crew then coerced the Paramount Ranch manager to let them use the facility. They then prevailed upon Western Costume to lend them period clothes. "It had a pretty authentic look," he smiles, still getting a thrill out of the production. "We even entered it into a few festivals. One of my partners took the film and blew it up to 35mm, and submitted it to the Academy's short film competition. *Cold Sun*, as it was called, became a finalist. It was up against a project called *Amblin*, from a young student at Long Beach State. The filmmaker was an unknown by the name of Steven Spielberg."

The week after graduation, Cundey began Chapter One of his movie career, as a make-up man on a low budget film with several school buddies. The film was produced through Roger Corman's company. The project took a week to shoot. Then, the newly married, out-of-work, Hollywood wannabe went back to his apartment to fret. Before he could work up a sweat, the phone rang. Roger Corman asked him to do make-up on a film called *Gas*. "It was the last film he directed," Cundey says, sadly.

Although he was getting work as a make-up artist, lighting still fascinated Cundey. "I couldn't forget the class I took at UCLA taught by the legendary James Wong Howe," he recalls. "Between *The Heart is a Lonely Hunter* and *The Molly Maguires*, he would teach a practical approach to shooting. We became the grips, electricians, and camera crew. We built a little three-walled set – a window, door, a table, and a few chairs – and he showed us how to light that set for different moods and styles.

"One day it would be a rundown, seedy hotel, the next an elegant room. The set wouldn't change, just the lighting and equipment. We got to use professional tools and we learned the purpose of scrims. We learned where to place the flags to make the shadow sharper or softer.

"When I am lecturing or teaching, I use the same technique. You have to let your students feel the work, get inside the process."

For Cundey, one of Howe's most valuable lessons hinged on inventiveness. When Howe talked about *Tom Sawyer*, he explained how he created the illusion of candles in a cave, where the light source was totally artificial. "Candles with lights inside were revolutionary at the time," Cundey adds. "They added a sense of reality. That's what he was known for. That's what adds to the dramatic needs of the story."

Filmmaking has to move an audience. "In two ways," Cundey adds, that twinkle coming to his eye once again. "It moves the audience into another world, emotionally. And, it has to move them out of their house and into a theater, to spend seven dollars of their hard earned money. It doesn't matter if it is happy or sad or scary, as long as the story moves the audience through an emotional process, it has succeeded." It is a philosophy Cundey learned during Chapter Two of his career from long-time associate John Carpenter.

"Howe had inspired me. I had been experimenting and building my own reel. One day, I just 'happened' to be in the right place at the right time," he smiles, his beard twitching with stifled laughter. "After make-up, I began gaffing low budget pictures. One day, I walked into the producer's office, just as the cameraman I was going to work with quit for a better offer. The producer slammed the phone down and screamed to no one in particular. 'Now what am I going to do?' It just so happened I had my reel in the car!" he laughs aloud. "Talk about timing!"

From 1972 to 1981, Cundey shot over 30 films, many for scare-fare guru John Carpenter. Since the budgets were low, he had to learn to operate the camera as well as create the illusion through light. "It was valuable," he admits. "That's when I learned what a pan does and how to compose a shot for maximum effect."

These low-budget projects were plentiful. Independent non-union filmmakers would design posters with cars and guns and girls and take them around to foreign financiers. They would raise 100 to 150 thousand dollars – then make the picture.

"At times, I would have only about three lights available. Three small lights like 2ks and 600 watt pars. I had to look at the shot and work with what I had. You started with the image and decided what you needed to accomplish with what you had. Most of the time, you found ways to make one light do several jobs."

"I had to find a way to get in on the work," Cundey says. "So I built my own small truck. It was a Dodge van with a totally re-designed interior. It had shelves, compartments, slots – something like the one built for the television show I Spy," he explains. "This allowed cameramen to carry all the equipment needed to any location available. With a leased package of lights and cameras, I had a small production vehicle for rent. I'd circulate pictures – here's a complete package including cameraman and crew."

Cundey and team began to do a string of 14-day 100,000 dollar budget shoots. The director-cameraman collaboration was vital to this kind of project. By helping to design the shot, Cundey was able to save time and money. "You learned to edit in your head," he says. "I would look at a scene and say, 'this is a quick scene, let's play it as a two-shot at the table. We can pan the girl over the bar and we don't need the coverage, because she says only two or three lines. Now, we can spend time on the coverage in this scene....' I began to make on the spot evaluations that would give me time to spend on the more important scenes."

Of course, some of the 'evaluations' make Cundey cringe today. "Not too long ago, I was running *Where the Red Fern Grows*, my second film, for some kids who had never seen it. The picture had a real director – Norman Tokar. When we got to the kitchen scene, I cringed. Boy, did I ever over-light it!

"It's all a learning process," he says, shrugging. "The Carpenter era was another time for experimentation. *Halloween, The Fog, Roller Boogie, Galaxina*, that was a fascinating era. As the industry progresses, there are less and less places to learn. In the 1930s and 1940s directors like William Wyler and DeMille experimented in westerns. In our era, the B-movies that ran in the Drive-Ins.

"Those movies are still being done today, only they cost 50 million dollars to do! It's a shame in a way. People are still renting *Halloween* – and it cost, well, a twentieth of what the 'horror' film costs today. *Escape from New York* is probably the most widely recognized and talked about film we made. We used Panavision's new, at the time, Ultra Speed lenses and the relatively new HMI lights to light up whole city blocks of St. Louis.

"However, *The Thing* was probably the most innovative picture we did during that period." This film is where Cundey met creature-creators Rob Bottin and Stan Winston. It would be the first of many associations with the newly emerging art of special effects make-up. *The Thing* allowed them to use a very experimental technique called morphing. "We used special effects makeup and a rubber creature to morph the transformation. The biggest challenge was to light it so that it wasn't obvious that we were looking at a rubber object.

"When the dog split open, tentacles would come out. The organic material would change. How do you make that believable for an audience? We used very controlled lighting. Rob Bottin was very conscious of the value of accommodating the camera to further the illusion of life out of his creations. I would look for the 'best' areas of a particular rubber creature, light that, and let the weaker parts fall into shadow. Sometimes, the things you don't see are more scary anyway. I then had to design the overall lighting of that particular scene or set to justify the sketchy light of the creature. It became a thought process and technique that I've carried through to my current projects."

Cundey admits he could do a whole semester on the John Carpenter era. The team pioneered slasher films without blood. Most of the emotional reactions from the audience came from within, not reactions to the gore. "We combined images with sound and music," he explains. "We took people on a ride."

Eventually, Cundey graduated to other "rides." One of his favorites was *Psycho II*. "It was interesting, because we were taking a classic film from a classic director, and recreating it," he explains. "How could we create the same feeling with a new audience?

"We had the luxury of a photo book that had been published. It analyzed Hitchcock's original movie on a cut-by-cut basis. It showed us the exact composition of each shot, the lighting, and details about the set that we could study. It became our key to creating as much as we needed to the style and feeling of the original. Also, the producer of the new film, Hilton Green, had been the Assistant Director of the original, so we were constantly entertained by background stories and bits of trivia about the original. We even found some of the original set dressing in the Universal Studios' storage. We became so involved with recreating the feeling of the original, that we decided to have some fun and include Hitchcock in one of his famous cameo appearances. Unfortunately, he was dead," Cundey says, his face suspiciously blank, "so, we had to come up with some alternative way for him to appear. We felt that a photo would have been too blatant. My camera operator, Ray Stella, came up with the idea of a shadow. We cut a silhouette out of Hitchcock's famous caricature from his TV show and used it to throw a shadow of him on a wall. When Tony Perkins turns out the light in his mother's room, the shot lingers just long enough for the knowledgeable or astute viewer to recognize Hitchcock's face on the wall in the center of the frame."

Cundey pauses, listening as his answering machine clicks on. When he hears a familiar voice, he launches himself from his easy chair, jumps over boxes, to grab the phone. "Hold that thought. I have to take this conference call. It's about a commercial I might do in Mexico."

He listens quietly to the excited voice of an Australian producer. The shoot involves some difficult situations to be done in a weather atmosphere. Cundey responds to the sense of panic with the patience that has gotten him through enormously difficult shoots. "That's not a problem, I did something similar in Mexico on *Romancing the Stone*. We can take a look at that location, if you want."

He hangs up the phone, shaking his head. "Sometimes they get excited about the little things," he laughs, settling in once again. "Now, that's a film that pushed me into Chapter Three, and another wonderful relationship and fascinating sets of circumstances," he remarks. "Bob Zemeckis is a fantastic director to work with," he continues. "He loves making movies. He understands what makes an audience-satisfying picture. He uses the camera in incredibly story-telling ways. He was an exercise in wide lenses and incredibly complicated camera moves with remote heads, cranes, and any tool needed to follow the actor, the story.

"The collaboration with Bob and Michael Douglas made doing *Romancing* an interesting experience, even though we were working with an all Mexican crew.

"Flash, I learned when working with Carpenter, is not always the most creative of shots. It's smoke and mirrors. You aren't fooling the audience that this is real, you are entertaining them.

"In *Romancing*, everyone knows the alligator doesn't really bite the man's hand off. However, they really believe Michael and Kathleen slide down a hill in a rain storm. People have called it a lucky coincidence. We were in Mexico during the rainy season, and we happened to find this location. Far from it."

The shot took weeks of experimentation and careful multi-camera placement. At first, the team talked about using a trap door arrangement. "We would put Michael and Kathleen on the trap door. They would have their conversation and then we would drop them out of frame. The stunt doubles would take over and we could cut the sequences together.

"We found a hillside in Mexico that would work. We dug trenches for the water and filled the area with soft dirt so that it would be slippery enough. We even rigged cargo nets to catch the stunt people at specific intervals. To make the slide look more treacherous, we tilted the cameras at an angle to make the hillside look steeper. We also put plants in the frame with a tilt the opposite way, so they seemed to be upright and level with the frame. All we had to do, we thought, was have plants to cover the equipment and water recycling bins."

The scene was shot with Arriflex cameras from a variety of angles. However, when it was cut together, all they had were a series of exciting moments, but no thread. "The audience would recognize the trick," he adds.

The next step was to mount a camera on one of the actors. Then they would make a sled out of wood, pulling it down a speed rail pipe. "It was too fast, and we could see the cable," Cundey remembers. "I was out of ideas," he admits. "Then, I had this flash. Why did they have to go down hill? All we needed was a piece of ground near a hillside! We could create the downhill illusion by digging trenches and putting the plants in crooked!"

Employing an eight-man crew to pull a rig through the muddy water, Cundey created the downhill effect with 'smoke and mirrors.' "We had people with fire hoses and buckets of water drenching the actors as they were pulled along the path."

Cundey and Zemeckis went on to create what has become one of the most often watched series of pictures – *Back to the Future*. "Did we know what we were getting into when we started it?" he asks rhetorically. "One of the greatest rewards in working with Bob Zemeckis is you know you are going on a new adventure. He isn't satisfied with doing the ordinary or obvious. He loves to try new story-telling techniques, equipment, and ideas. And he loves to build a movie, or a scene, in layers. That's why you can watch *Back to the Future* over and over and still discover something new in the story of frame. There are visual jokes throughout the background and story points at the end that only make sense when you see the beginning again.

"From a cinematography standpoint, he always creates a need to stretch and create. Bob loves wide angle lenses, so it is always a great challenge to find somewhere to hide your lights and still create the proper mood. And he loves to move the camera and make the audience a participant. It was on *Back to the Future* that we first used a remote head for the camera on a crane arm. It became a standard tool for us; which I use constantly. It puts the camera on a remotely operated servo motor head on the end of an arm about 80 by 20 feet long. You can take the audience quickly from floor level with the feet of the actor to high overhead, two floors up, and then back down into a hole in the street, or any other strange place the director wants. It's become a new tool that can be every bit as useful as the Steadicam if you are creative enough to know how to use it."

Although the *Back To The Future* pictures were fun to do, Cundey got the biggest kick out of several other innovative projects – *Big Business* and *Roger Rabbit* (which won him an Academy Award nomination). "Technology has a way of building on itself," he explains. "You start something on one project and push it a little farther every succeeding project. We've redesigned cameras, created new techniques from old approaches, and devised new optical effects, as well as motion control equipment, to meet the needs of each new film."

Roger Rabbit required melding two-dimensional animated characters into the time and space of the three-dimensional world. "Audiences had begun to associate camera movement with real life," he explains. "We had to find a way to bring our Toons into and through the real world. We did crude movement tests, then began testing our ability to create shadows and light for animated characters that would be added later.

"If Roger was to go from one part of the room to another, hopping onto a chair, we had to find a way for the camera operator to track that movement. We developed full-size rubber characters to stage the action. The operator could then see movement in real time. He would associate movement with dialogue. We then translated that information for the animators, explaining why the camera was panning or tilting.

"ILM's Bill Tondreau created the 'Tondreau head,' an attachment that allows the operator to follow movement on a video screen, seen through the camera. He could control the camera's movement through a set of wheels. They were tracked electronically and fed into a computer. This allowed operators, animators, and so forth to recall exact movements from the computer memory, duplicating the human action."

It then became a matter of split screen work. Using the motion control camera, Cundey would shoot portions of a sequence while the technicians manipulated puppets in the shot. The optical house was then able to remove the puppets from the frame and replace them with animated characters. The technique, called 'splitting in' characters, dates back to the 1930s. "Only, we could now move the frame," he adds.

Lighting techniques also became more sophisticated. "Mood used to be the key element in lighting a sequence," he explains. "Now we had to use it, but create the illusion that the light was hitting both live characters and animated actors at the same time. The idea was to calculate where the animated character would fit, and what light would hit a 'normal' figure in that scene. We needed to throw the correct shadows in the correct direction, then pass that information on to animation, allowing them to create characters with realistic movements and sources.

"In the simple throw-away sequence where the hand-cuffs holding Roger and Eddie together are sawed off, we combined several lighting elements to create the reality. By having Bob Hoskins hit the overhead light to make it swing, we gave effects cues for light-dark, light-dark patterns. They could then animate shadows against the wall as Roger goes in and out of the light.

"We rigged a special device in the overhead light," he adds. "With an operator above, making sure the swing was consistent, we could assure precise timing from cut to cut. Using the light and dark falling on Hoskins' face, effects could duplicate the same light movement on Roger."

When Jim Abrahams heard about Cundey's work on *Roger*, he called to ask if he could carry it a bit farther on the Bette Midler/Lily Tomlin feature *Big Business*. "The Vista-Vision cameras were now more sophisticated. We had redesigned and built them especially for *Roger Rabbit* to do more than matte or plate work. Although the camera still had to be 'locked down,' we could now do split screen with move-ment," Cundey explains. "Using the computer, we could follow the action in the frame with one image on one side of the split, then duplicate it with the same actor in the other side of the split.

"We even took it a step farther, by having actors cross each other within the frame. The idea was to shoot 'clean' computer controlled shots, of actors moving in half of a frame, then give the optical house the pieces to lay together.

"We choreographed Lily and Bette's movements care-fully. We had Lily's character and her stand in taking up the space where the other Lily would be. Or, we would give Bette the right eyeline, knowing where to look at herself. Then we would make the stand-in disappear in the optical registering the background perfectly."

Cundey pushed the envelope even farther. In the "simple" Ladies' Room sequence, where Bette sees herself in the mirror, he used the locked down shots from *Roger*. By putting the head on a motion control dolly, he could pan and tilt, plus move the camera through sets. These moves duplicated what cameramen do in regular moves."

Then came the next step in the Zemeckis/Cundey teaming, the complicated black comedy *Death Becomes Her*. "We had a great time with this one," he laughs. Another 'throw-away' has become one of the most talked about shots in a movie. "It's the scene where our actress's head turns 360 degrees. This is a more sophisticated version of the 'splitting in' technique," he explains.

"We shot Meryl Streep in the scene on a normal set using ILM's VistaGlide motion control/dolly camera system, which incidentally, we had them build for *Back to the Future II* and *III*," he says. "Another example of how techniques and technology build on themselves. We then concentrated on one particular area of her body, her head, shot against a blue screen. Now, ILM could 'remove' her head from the master shot and replace it with the blue screen version. By using computer generated 'neck' pieces we married the images as they turned."

Death Becomes Her was the last pairing of Cundey with Zemeckis. Cundey had already moved into Chapter Four of his career, and paired up with his old short subject Academy Award nomination rival, Steven Spielberg. "I also started working with one of the most lovable actors in the business, Robin Williams," Cundey says, unconsciously pulling on his graying beard. "I love working with him, but sometimes, he can be a little trying. He's so spontaneous, he never does the same thing twice. Not easy for a camera operator."

In a way, working with Spielberg was similar to working with Zemeckis. "Both use the camera to tell the story," he explains. "Although, Steven is more 'hands on.' Not only will he work with you on placement, he will also help create the camera movement used to tell the story."

Spielberg's biggest problem with this new Robin Williams film, *Hook*, was to find a way to make massive interior stage shots look like they were exterior, and on the high seas. "We looked at movies to determine the way to get the light, and then he would go to the producers to get the money to follow through with our ideas.

"Trying to create a realistic exterior look on an interior stage has to be one of the most difficult things we do," he continues. "When movies began going more and more on location, starting in the 1950s and 1960s, audiences became subconsciously aware of what exteriors on film really look like. An exterior set on a stage doesn't have the 'reality cues' of the real world, like a single source of light from the sun, and the extreme range of contrast from light to shadow. When we light the set in order to get enough light to expose the film, we have to use multiple lighting units. One light just doesn't have the same intensity or spread of the one 93 million miles from us.

"If you look at most movies, especially the early ones, you see multiple shadows cast by the actors on the ground from the many lights overhead. In preparing for *Hook*, I wanted to overcome that stigma. Steven had decided that we wouldn't build the exterior sets outside, because he wanted the look to be somewhere between 'real' and a theatrical or fantasy look. Outside sets would have been just too real, he felt. Steven and I viewed several recent films to see what kind of style seemed most successfully to create an outside look.

"One of the things I had felt was significant was the feeling that real exteriors are not perfect – there is always too much contrast between sunlight and shadow for the film to capture. The sunlit side of an actor is either overexposed or the shadow side is underexposed. We have to add light to see detail. So, I decided to deliberately build in some of these imperfections in the lighting to give the audience subconscious reality cues. As a result, for sequences in Neverland and on Hook's ship, we added hot backlight on the characters as if from real sunlight.

"Another advance the technology gave us was the ability for computer visual effects work to do 'wire removal' – to literally erase from a frame of film or a sequence the wires that suspend a flying actor. In the past, in order to not see the wires holding up a character, you had to use very thin wires and do a great deal of work to keep lights off of them. You also had to remove shine and shadows cast by them. The thin wires and their possible breakage usually meant any exciting work was too risky for a real actor, so it was usually done by stunt people whose faces had to be hidden. With *Hook*, because we could suspend Robin Williams on safe heavy cable, he could do his own flying stunts and the wires could be 'painted out' by the computer experts later. It made a more believable adventure for the audience and, of course, some fun days for us on the set with Robin 20 feet in the air!

"We went even farther with *Flubber*," he adds. "I might tell you about that later," he says impishly. "Now, if you want to talk about how we created a new market for tennis balls, we could talk about my second film with Steven Spielberg," he smiles.

Hook, which won Dean Cundey an A.S.C. Best Cinematography Award Nomination was only the beginning of the relationship with Spielberg. On the next picture, they literally made stars of half a dozen, 65 million-year-old animals. *Jurassic Park* has become a landmark collaboration between various filmic mediums. "With today's advanced technology we were able to bring 'flash' and 'fantasy' even closer together to tell a story no-one believed did happen, yet reacted as if it could," Cundey says. That devilish look appears once again. "Although," he adds. "DNA cloning is a reality. Some mad scientist could bring these predators back, one day."

Disregard the controversy over the subject matter of Michael Crichton's book and look at the logistics, *Jurassic Park* was still a monumental effort in patience, something Cundey is known for. "Really," he laughs. "I must be a better actor than I thought!

"Actually, it isn't as much patience, as it is the fascination of making never-before-possible visuals work," he adds, getting serious. "*Jurassic* became a study in finding the best technique to carry on the 'reality' factor. We had model dinosaurs, puppets, and computer generated images. Our biggest challenge was finding the strengths and weaknesses of each technique, and blending them together as seamlessly as possible."

At times, this was a Herculean effort. "Five years before, we had to lock the camera down and involve extra people in seamless duplication of actors in *Big Business*. We also had to use part of the scenery, a wall for example, to provide identification and differentiation marks for opticals. For *Jurassic*, ILM's Dennis Muren had created a new technique which allowed us to shoot without locking off the camera. We could now use the Steadicam.

"Actually, we created a whole new market for fluorescent tennis balls on this picture," he laughs. "By placing them in specific geographical points within the set, we were able to give ILM markings for their characters and measurements for the camera movements. The Gallimimus stampede was a perfect example.

"We shot it outside, in bright sunlight. The direction and the density of the sun and other important movements were recorded carefully and given to ILM. Using this information and the visual references of the tennis balls we had placed every ten feet, effects could lay in the dinosaurs. All they had to do was 'grow' grass over the tennis balls.

"Remember the water slide sequence in *Romancing the Stone*," he says, shaking his head. "I once said that was the biggest logistical challenge of my career. I now take it back! *Jurassic* had another throw-away that caused a few sleepless nights!

"There was a little sequence where the Raptor chases the children through the kitchen," he begins, slowly. "That took weeks of heated discussions. First, we had to find places to hide the equipment and the crew so they wouldn't be seen in the reflective surfaces of the stainless steel walls. Then we had to create bright light and dim light without moving the equipment. The simple act of having the children turn the lights off was a nightmare.

"The next challenge was to find which element worked for which part of the shot. We had to make the creatures look their best wherever they were and with whatever they did. Rubber puppets had to be lit carefully. Like actors, we had to find the 'best side' of the face. We knew the puppets could interact with the humans, but their jumps would be mechanical and their facial expressions non-existent. That meant choosing which cut would be 'real' and which would be CGI, then, blending them together as seamlessly as possible.

"Of course," he laughs, "we just had to make it even more complicated. Someone," he says ominously, "decided it would be great if we had 'almost' collisions between the children and the Raptors.

"Basically," he adds, with a sigh, "it became the old tool – light pieces of the monster to focus the audience's attention. Never give them a really good look at the creature, just tease them emotionally."

Dean Cundey had a great time doing just that in his next "creature feature," the delightful live-action version of the children's cartoon, *Casper*. "He was a very friendly ghost," he laughs. "Sometimes, too friendly and too real! We had these huge Casper cutouts as stand-ins for lighting and physical placement. At times, our 'operators' got a little devilish, and we found ourselves being haunted by our 'little' friend. We even started to talk to him!"

Casper went way beyond *Roger Rabbit*, where audiences knew the characters were interacting with cartoons and *Jurassic* which had multi-dimensional animals. *Casper*, however, had three-dimensional cartoons with the character-istics of humans. They talk, emote, even interact by touching and playing together. "The idea was to get the audience to think of them as actors, not effects," says Cundey.

For *Casper*, Cundey joined a creative team which included producer Steven Spielberg, director Brad Silberling, and ILM and Amblin Animation effects teams helmed by supervisor Dennis Muren, "in an awful lot of pre-production hair pulling," he laughs. "We'd come a long way," Cundey adds. "Now cinematographers could create light and effects teams could move animated characters into and out of that light. Cinematographers could now capture the image with far less complications and more creativity.

"In *Roger*, we had him picking up tools, even running a file through his ears. To do that, we had to have puppeteers handle the file from an elaborate overhead rig. It was difficult, because we had to get the puppeteers high enough above the shot to keep them out of frame. That meant the lights had to go on the floor.

"In *Casper*, all we had to do is use a real prop, and duplicate it in the computer. To try to manipulate food in the big food fight scene would have been impossible," he adds. "Imagine all of the little wires! Instead, we placed real food on the table, then had the computer duplicate it and make it 'fly.'

"One of the techniques that most successfully ties fantasy or animated characters into the real world, I think, is the 'hand-off' of an object or prop from a real person to an animated one," he says. "The computer has greatly enhanced our ability to do that. On *Roger Rabbit*, we would take an object, a gun for example, and put it on a rod held by a puppeteer. The actor would hold it and maybe 'hand it' to a non-existent cartoon character which was being manipulated by the puppeteer. The animated character would be added later, but the animator was restricted to moving the object.

"On *Casper*, we specifically designed props and objects so they could be added in as CGI elements later. This meant we could have the object handled by the actor in the real world scene and then when handed off to the animated character, the object could be computer generated along with the character. Now the animator has complete freedom to animate the character and object any way he feels is best or entertaining for the scene. We looked for many opportunities on *Casper* to do that. All kinds of things were created with that in mind. Of course, we still end up 'flying' objects on wires and rigs, anything from small household objects, to people, robots, and entire cars. And, for *Flubber*, it was all of the above.

"We took rig work in a completely new direction for this picture. Once again, Robin Williams was off the ground, both hanging on wires and in a flying car. The wire work has become pretty familiar territory to him and us now, and because he is so good at it, and a willing victim, the work was about his comedy more than the effect. However, the flying car took us to some new heights, no pun intended.

"The car, this time a 1963 Thunderbird convertible as opposed to the Model T from the original *Absent Minded Professor*, was mounted on an amazing motion base. The base, originally a technology designed to manipulate flight simulators for training commercial and military pilots, was adapted to our needs. Six large eight-foot long hydraulic cylinders could move the full-sized T-bird in six different directions about six feet in each direction.

"When placed in front of the bluescreen and occupied by Robin Williams, the result was not only a new technological step for visual effects, but also a laugh-a-minute for us. I manipulated the car's attitude in space using a 'Waldo' (a scaled down version of the base) hooked to the real base by a computer, as it went from cruising flight to aerobatics maneuvers. Robin manipulated his own attitude, which usually went from funny to over-the-top. When the bluescreen is replaced with cloud plates and moving backgrounds generated by the computer, we have a new and hopefully even more believable twist on a classic."

It is no secret that Dean Cundey has become the king of the fantasy film. He has taken every picture he has shot into unknown territory, pushing the envelope in special effects – bringing other-worldly characters into the audience's real world. "Hey, I've also taken real characters into another world," he adds. "Well, at least a weightless world, through director Ron Howard's eye via *Apollo 13*.

"It was a challenge, and a change," he says, soberly. "There was less a feeling of fantasy and more of a feeling of creating a very somber reality for an incident that really and truly happened. An incident that the whole world witnessed via their television screens.

"For me, the challenging aspect of the picture was finding the subtle and subconscious cues the audience needed to believe they were watching reality – the same kinds of things they saw on their television during the event. Watching the sunlight moving in the inside of the real space capsule video and film footage, and the real weightless sequences provided just some of the things we had to duplicate.

"The amazing weightless sequences David Nowell and the second unit shot added tremendously to the believability, but also to the difficulty of matching the lighting and mood. In order to best match, and because I felt that David would have a lot to accomplish in too short a time, I had the art department build the set that was going to go inside the 'weightless' airplane on a stage at the studio. I then asked them to build a mockup of the airplane's fuselage around the set so we would know what kind of space the second unit would be dealing with. We were then able to prelight the set to match the ones we were using for the majority of the capsule interiors and also solve any difficulties in advance. As a result, the weightless material cuts in perfectly with the scenes we shot at the studio. A great job by David and his crew."

Where will Chapter Five in Dean Cundey's life take place? It might be as a director; it will definitely be as an innovator. Before he began *Flubber*, Cundey and Ray Stella, his camera operator for many years, shot a straight-to-video project called *Honey, We Shrunk Ourselves*, with Cundey directing and Stella as cinematographer. "We developed a process for putting the visual effects together initially on our Mac computer system," he says. "See, I told you it was a better computer! It was another study in stretching the technological possibilities, and something that helped us a great deal on *Flubber*."

Working closely with son Chris, Dean Cundey has developed temp comp (for temporary compositing) techniques and systems for previsualizing the effects. It also takes the elements shot for the effects and puts them together for the editor to use in making creative decisions.

"This way the director, editor, and studio can make the creative choices in editing without the high cost of doing the finished visual effects before they might even be needed. If you decide to eliminate a scene or shorten it, you haven't spent the time and money to have an effects house make the effects. They have to do only the pieces you need for the finished film. And all the techniques and tools of high end effects work are available on the Mac, if you know how to use them effectively," he takes a breath. "Now, aren't you sorry you haven't become a convert?!"

Cundey, gets serious, or at least tries to. "We've also put together a new on-set digital video assist system that does much of the same in allowing the director, cinematographer, and visual effects people to evaluate, in real time, the effects as they are being done. Just another example of trying to keep ahead of the technology and make it serve the creative process," he smiles.

The phone rings, again. Dean Cundey looks much too comfortable in his over-stuffed chair to scramble across boxes and bags. He's just taken a long stroll down memory lane. "I like it busy and challenging," he says, "you get more done. The tools and toys, that's the perks and the fun. Sometimes," he adds.

******

American Academy Award Nomination *Roger Rabbit* – **British Academy Award Nomination** *Roger Rabbit, Apollo 13* – **A.S.C. Nomination** *Hook, Apollo 13* – **Cable Ace Award** *Tales From The Crypt* – **B.S.C. Award** *Roger Rabbit, Apollo 13*

"A great deal of work happens between scouting and shooting and it can be a very tedious process. In the end, if any of that behind the scenes work shows in the final product, then I think that work has been for nothing."

Originally from Torquay, a small coastal resort in the South west of England, Roger Deakins A.S.C., B.S.C., has always loved movies and joined the local film society at an early age. Any idea of actually working in the industry seemed very remote. "I always thought of being a painter I guess," he remarks, with a thoughtful smile. "All that Bohemian intro-spection! But I was soon drawn into photography. I loved observing life and being able to capture what I saw with my camera. It was just what I had been trying to do with paint."

When Deakins heard the new government sponsored National Film School was opening outside London, he saw his opportunity to move into film making. His years in school were interesting, but "fairly uneventful," he says. When he left, he started working as a cinematographer. "I couldn't get any work as an assistant, so calling myself a cameraman made me feel better, even though it still took a long time to get any work.

"I eventually managed to establish myself shooting industrials and rock concerts but it was documentaries I really loved. My first real opportunity came when I was asked to film the war in Rhodesia for the African National Congress. For a few weeks, we clandestinely filmed the effect the white separatist regime was having on the black African population, before we were discovered not to be the tourists we purported to be."

Soon after this experience, Deakins was sailing off around the world. "I heard that Associated Television (now Central Television) wanted to put a film crew aboard one of the entrants in the Whitbread Around the World Yacht Race," he explains. "It was really to be a film about people confined in small spaces and under the stress of such a long voyage. I told the producers that, since I was from Devon, the home of sailors, I was the perfect choice for the job. I even claimed I had spent my whole life on boats, though it was hardly true. In fact, at the time I couldn't even swim and had sailed on a yacht only once! And, I had been very seasick then."

So, for the next nine months Deakins and sound recordist Noel Smart sailed from Portsmouth to Cape Town, Cape Town to Auckland, Auckland to Rio, and Rio back to Portsmouth. "It was quite a trip, but also frustrating as far as the filming would go," he explains. "Often, the most dramatic times to shoot were also the most dangerous for the boat itself. We were after all members of the ten-man crew. At one point, the rudder broke as we were surfing down-wind in a particularly heavy sea somewhere in the Southern Ocean. Noel and I were part of the watch on deck, so we had to trim the boat and make things safe before we could record anything. Interviews became commonplace because the events in question were very present in all our minds.

"The great thing about documentaries," he explains, "is that you learn to be conservative and you learn, almost instinctively, when to shoot and what material is really important to tell a story. We could only carry a relatively limited amount of stock on our yacht due to weight considerations. We had to be really sure that what we shot was worth it. Of course, nowadays, you might have an endless amount of video tape – the nature of such filmmaking has changed a lot, I guess."

After this experience, the same television company sent Deakins to Eritrea where the People's Liberation Front was waging a separatist war against Ethiopia. Along with a journalist and a sound recordist, Deakins hitched rides on supply trucks into the liberated areas of Eritrea and spent some six weeks filming the new society that this independence movement was creating. Eritrea finally became independent from Ethiopia in 1994. Other documentary projects in Sudan and India followed.

While at the National Film School, Deakins had shot a variety of films for student directors. These fellow students would show the films around. This meant his work was brought to the attention of producers and production executives. One sample led to a drama series for television called *Wolcott*, about a black detective working in London's East End.

"It was shown in two, two-hour episodes," he recalls. "We shot for about 13 weeks and, at one point, were averaging six and a half minutes screen time a night. The producers loved it of course, but friends in the industry told us to slow down," he laughs. "If we could shoot that much and at night, wouldn't they expect everyone to do it?!"

Soon, after that, Deakins teamed up with *Il Postino* director Mike Radford, to shoot a feature film called *Another Time, Another Place*. The two had worked on various documentaries together, and Deakins' work on *Wolcott* convinced the director that he was ready for what was the first dramatic feature film for both of them.

"It was a wonderful project and still one of my favorites," Deakins smiles. "The story centers around three Italian prisoners of war who were to spend their captivity working the land on a small farm in Scotland. The farmer's wife is seduced by the exotic nature of these captives and their stories of the outside world."

Working with a small budget and subject to the vagaries of the Scottish climate, the filmmakers had to create the illusion of changing seasons, the oppression of the endless highland winter, and the magic of the coming of spring – important to the story.

"One day, we managed to do three seasons starting with artificial snow in the morning. Then it rained, so we shot an autumn scene. In the evening, there was this beautiful soft sunset. So, we shot a summertime scene. I guess that's where my documentary experience really came in handy."

Another Time, Another Place was received well, especially at the Cannes Film Festival, which gave Radford the opportunity to tackle a cherished project. The next year (1984), the director and the cinematographer were shooting a film of George Orwell's classic view of the future, *1984.*

"I vividly remember the day in Twickenham Studios when we shot Winston Smith, played by John Hurt, writing in his diary '4th May 1984.' That was it, it really was the 4th of May 1984! I think it was a beautiful film. Sure it was dark and depressing, it was, after all, about brainwashing. About the eradication of any desire for free speech by the eradication of any words or language that made such a concept possible. But I still think of it as beautiful.

"Mike and I talked of several approaches to this story," he says. "Black-and-white was our first choice, but commercially unacceptable. So we looked for ways to desaturate the negative. Very late in pre-production our laboratory, Kays as it was then called, suggested simply removing the bleach bath during print processing. This, they suggested, would leave developed silver crystals within the final prints. That, with the right timing, would lead to a partial black-and-white image." (This silver acts as a catalyst to the color couplers and is bleached out during normal processing. It is a process something like ENR in its effect.)

"We only had a short pre-production left to test the effect of the process on color and contrast ratios," he adds. "I remember the color of many sets and costumes being altered at a very late stage. This allowed for this overall de-saturation. Production designer Allan Cameron exaggerated the color of some interiors so that the final effect would be a creamy yellow. To our eye, they would appear a vivid yellow. Much of the real testing was done as we went along. Something I don't advocate," he adds dryly.

"Everywhere in the film, large Telescreens look down with messages from Big Brother. We wanted to have a brown sepia look for them. We also wanted the scan lines of a contemporary TV set. To do this, we re-photographed all of our playback material off a small area of a television. This exaggerated the scan lines. Also, we made the playback prints rich in color to allow for our 'bleach bypass process.'"

Deakins went on to do a third film with Mike Radford, *White Mischief*, a film set in the colonial days of Kenya. He continued shooting films in the UK, including *Pascali's Island*, with James Dearden; *Stormy Monday* with Mike Figgis; *Defence of the Realm* with David Drury; and *Sid and Nancy* with Alex Cox.

"It was *Sid and Nancy* that really brought me to America for the first time," Deakins explains. "The film was shot in London at first, then Paris, followed by New York for a few weeks, San Francisco, and in a studio and on locations in Los Angeles. The film is photographed in an almost documentary style with a lot of work at real locations such as New York's Chelsea Hotel where much of the climax took place.

"We went very quickly and simply. Much of the film is handheld which gave Gary Oldman and Chloe Webb, who played the leads, freedom to improvise and really be those characters. The lighting was very naturalistic with a lot of practical work, as opposed to traditional film lighting. This also helped to give the actors freedom to move. Even when we shot on sets, I often lit with a couple of fluorescent tubes which hung in the shot and provided our only light source.

"I guess I was a little nervous about coming to America at first," he admits. "In England, I had established a tight working relationship with my crew. I had worked with the same gaffer, John Higgins, on all but one of my films. Also, and this comes from my documentary background, I almost always operate the camera. I was hesitant as to how a new crew would take to this. Well, *Sid and Nancy* broke the ice for me, and in fact, I met an electrician on that film, Bill O'Leary, who has been my gaffer on every American picture that I have shot since."

For Deakins, key people who know the way he works and can help produce the end product he is looking for quickly are all important. He likes to work fast, simple, and with little discussion. "Feature films generally work at a fast pace these days," he acknowledges. "If I have to explain why and how I want something every time the set-up changes it leaves me, the camera operator, less time to communicate with the director or to think. Besides, I really like the team that I work with and will take them with me on projects wherever and whenever I can. Sometimes you cannot have all the crew members you might want and you meet new people. Generally, I love to tackle different problems from film to film with people that I have a history with."

The 1990 production *Mountains of the Moon*, a film shot mostly in Africa is, he says, "very dear to me." He had formed an intimate relationship with this richly visual continent while shooting documentaries and also the features *The Kitchen Toto* and *White Mischief*. "We didn't carry a lot of equipment for *Mountains of the Moon*: two Arriflex BL cameras, one small dolly, a pretty small generator, and a basic lighting package. I don't think we even carried a small jib arm, just a small

Chapman dolly and 100 feet of track." Deakins smiles gently. "We may have had a back-up 2C camera," he concedes.

The story, about the Victorians' search for the source of the Nile, is a feature but it documents a fascinating part of the early history of the exploration of Africa by white Europeans. Richard Burton plays a man who was perhaps the greatest of the Victorian explorers and it is his obsession with finding the source of the River Nile that is at the heart of this film. The film re-enacts two expeditions made by Burton's character during the mid 19th century. It centers on the conflict which broke his friendship with his partner on both expeditions.

It isn't hard for Deakins to pick out one of his favorite scenes. "One of the most ambitious was of the explorers' discovery of a lake they think is the true source of this great river. In fact, it was Lake Tanganyika, far away from the true source, Lake Victoria.

"The scene they saw was of this caravan moving up over this rocky landscape. This lake spread out in front of it. Burton was at this point very ill and being carried on a stretcher. Most of the other members of the expedition were also in bad shape. The director, Bob Rafelson, wanted a total of seven or eight shots and he wanted them all at sunset," he adds.

"I told him that I thought we could do it if we planned our shots carefully and did the whole scene in the last hour of sunlight. It was impossible to fudge that look during the day, as we were in a completely open area of desert and I remember the days being blindingly hot. We laid out and rehearsed about five different dolly shots and other camera angles and were ready to shoot by 2:30 in the afternoon. Holding Bob back from shooting until 4:30 when the light was right was the hardest battle of all!" he adds.

Although solid films like *Long Walk Home, Thunderheart, Homicide, Passion Fish,* and *Secret Garden* followed, the 1992 film *Barton Fink,* directed by the Coen brothers, and *The Shawshank Redemption,* directed by Frank Darabont, really put him on the map. "*Shawshank* was a realistic and a poetic film at the same time," he explains. "No, you can't believe the film's ending. Life just never happens like that. But you want to believe in it."

To show the contrast of life inside the prison and the world outside, Deakins and his team planned two radically different visual styles. "We wanted to make prison life feel like a slow grinding hell," he explains seriously, looking up at the sky. "Something like the unrelenting interruptions to the beach silence when those planes go over too low, too loud, and too often," he says, dryly, showing something of the quiet humor that his crew swears hides inside his long frame.

"When Morgan Freeman's character escapes, we wanted a completely different look and feeling to the film. We shot the main prison yard and some interiors in an actual abandoned institution in Mansfield," he explains. "Then our designer, Terry Marsh, built a composite cell block set within a local warehouse, which housed the personal cells of our main characters.

"The hardest lighting challenge was to maintain a consistency of look from set to set and location to location. This is probably the toughest thing on any film. I didn't want the conventional blue, cold light look or harsh backlighting with shafts of fake sunlight piercing heavy smoke. I wanted the kind of light that naturally seeps through small barred windows set in oversized stone walls. A soft, cool, gray light. Something quiet and naturalistic, which I guess is my style, if you can call it one.

"When we were doing the main location prison interiors, we had something like 55 12k HMI lights rigged on huge scaffold towers outside the windows. The windows were themselves covered with an industrial plastic diffusion, since film diffusion materials would have just cost too much in such a vast quantity. We also had some par lamps bounced in the ceiling, in places where we needed to bring light further inside the interior as if it were coming from the window sources. I know," he smiles, "it was a big rig. But when you are shooting 12 hour days, this cell block had to be under total control. The natural light was wonderful but you couldn't use it before 11:30 A.M. or after 3:00 P.M."

Deakins and his gaffer, Bill O'Leary, lit the cell block with maxi-brutes with blue gels on them to match the color of the HMI lighting that he was using on location. To rent HMIs for use on the set would have been very expensive. This set had to remain ready for shooting as weather cover for a large portion of the schedule. Deakins, for the most part, used 5293 stock and used no filtration on the camera to "correct" the color balance. This gave him the overall cold, grey look of the film, "with some judicious printing at the lab," he says. "People say you can just correct for the 85 filter in the lab and it makes very little difference if you use one or not, but I have always believed that you get rich, cold shadows if you shoot without the correction." Deakins shot the outside world with long lenses fully corrected, even adding a little more warmth through filtration.

When anyone finds out that Roger Deakins did *Shawshank*, the sequence they seem to most enjoy is where Morgan Freeman's character, Red, finds "the box." "It was a difficult scene in many ways," he shrugs, preparing to explain the challenges once again. "In the main shot, we see Red wandering down a field and towards us into a small wood. The camera cranes down to his level and it follows behind him as he passes. Red exits the bushes and stands staring for a moment at the huge oak tree surmounting the field before him.

"The location was a considerable distance from any road and we needed our Giraffe crane, which has a reach of 32 feet, to do the shot. I also wanted to make the shot at about 10 A.M. since we were facing East and I didn't want the sun directly down the lens or the overall shot too top lit. I wanted Red to be walking into the sun at the head of the shot and the tree dramatically back lit at the end. Also, I needed a low sun just to reach into the woods, between the trees," he explains, as another plane overhead drowns his words.

"As it was, I had to use a stop pull during the shot, opening up inside the wood and closing towards the end to silhouette, a little, this grand old tree on the hill top. It looks like a simple shot. No way! Given the location and the soggy condition of the ground, it turned out to be quite a pre-rig so I could shoot in the right light and complete the day's work."

The rest of the scene was also blocked out to use the light to the best advantage. He shot Red opening the box beneath the tree during the mid day hours which allowed dappled light through the branches. The shots of Red walking through the countryside in the opening part of the scene were done earlier and later in the day. "I think exterior scenes can be the hardest to do at times," he explains. "Obviously, if the scene is of any length, matching from shot to shot within the scene becomes the greatest challenge. Just to create the right look for the scene can be hard, too. A small second unit can often wait days to get the perfect moment but the first unit seldom, if ever, has such a luxury. Generally, you have a certain amount of time on a particular day to do a scene and you have to make the best possible use of the light you have."

The Hudsucker Proxy and Dead Man Walking brought Roger Deakins and Tim Robbins together again. "Tim played the lead character in the Coen brothers surrealistic 'industrial comedy' and went on to direct Dead Man Walking," he explains. "I really wasn't sure about doing another prison movie, but I had had a good time working with Tim, so I read the script. Well, Dead Man Walking was just wonderful. It was so different from Shawshank but, in it's own way, had a similar feeling for the characters. "I saw it would be very different visually." Since it was based on a true story, Robbins wanted to do nothing to break the feeling of reality or intrude on the audience's relationship with the characters.

"We shot location work in Louisiana, based out of New Orleans, during some of the wettest weather imaginable. Following that, we did the later interior prison scenes, including the execution, on a set in New York," he explains.

Tim Robbins and Deakins felt that a major challenge would be bringing a sense of progression to the many interview scenes between the two main characters played by Susan Sarandon and Sean Penn. "We had all these conversations between Susan and Sean with this wire mesh between them. It tended to be very distracting," he explains. "Tim wanted this feeling of the barrier between them breaking down as they grew to accept each other for who they were. So we played the first of these scenes with the camera backed up and the mesh in focus. This made Sean hard to see and his character more removed. At one point, we even played a hot light on the wire mesh, as though sunlight were hitting it, obscuring Sean's character completely. Later with longer lenses and slowly tracking the camera close to the wire, we progressively revealed Sean to Susan and to the audience. We even used pieces of larger mesh wire for some close up shots.

"Still later in the film, the two are separated by a cell block door which in the real building had had a fine wire mesh window for communication. This we changed to plexiglass with holes to speak through. We did this in part to use reflections to heighten the bond which now existed between the characters."

After the confinement of *Dead Man Walking*, Deakins turned to the re-creation of battle in the Gulf War story *Courage Under Fire* with director Ed Zwick. "The battle sequences were definitely the most difficult of the film," he concedes. "We had two different stories. One involved Meg Ryan as the captain of a downed helicopter, the second involved Denzel Washington as the tank commander who mistakenly fires on some of his own men during the chaos of a night battle.

"In planning the film neither Ed or I wanted to do blue screen for the sequence of Meg's helicopter crashing," he remarks. "I brought up a technique I'd used on *Air America*. There, we had used the shell of a helicopter mounted on a hydraulic gimbal and driven atop a flatbed truck. For that film, we built a road directly into the jungle to simulate crashing into tree tops. In the end, for *Courage Under Fire*, we built a road alongside a desert escarpment so that riding along in our helicopter/truck the landscape going by gave the feeling of flying through the dessert. Even so, we shot much of the action in a real airborne Huey with the actors. There is still only so much you can fake."

Another interesting technique used by Deakins on *Courage* involved exposure and processing. "We wanted the hot dry dusty look of Iraq but winter in El Paso, Texas, is not that – not that year anyhow. After testing everything from flashing to filtration, I settled on a technique similar to that used by Conrad Hall on the film *Tell Them Willy Boy Is Here*. Shooting on 5293 stock, I overexposed some two and a half to three stops but then underdeveloped the negative by one stop. The result was a negative that was still overexposed by one and one half stops and required printing at some very high printer lights. The effect on the final image seemed to be a desaturation of the colors and a lowering of the contrast somewhat, turning our location into something resembling a hot dusty desert."

In direct contrast, the tank battle, comprising fifteen allied tanks attacking the Russian tanks of the Iraqi lines, took place entirely at night and for this Deakins required an opposite visual approach. "We wanted this part of the film to be graphic and colorful, a kind of vibrant hell, I suppose. I knew that the end of the battle would be lit by the fires of the burning tanks and enemy lines and therefore have an orange look to it. I also knew that the tank commander's view of the battle and that of the gunners would be through the green of the night vision equipment.

"Today, the interiors of American tanks are illuminated by blue light but in the past the light was red. Red would add to our hellish color scheme and we felt the departure from reality was in this case justifiable. For practical reasons and aesthetic ones, I selected to illuminate the beginnings of the battle with a low, cold moonlight effect generated by three Major Musco lights set in parallel to one another. For this initial tank 'charge' we had multiple cameras working at all times, even a high and wide air to ground, so large HMI units of some kind were the only option for such a huge area of operation.

"Bill O'Leary came up with a great solution to the flare effect at the beginning of the scene," he adds. "He found a rock concert lighting company in El Paso who created a truss of lights which looked like a spacecraft from *E.T.* when it was suspended from an 180-foot crane above our tanks."

Deakins had some very different battles on the Academy Award nominated *Fargo*. "The night driving shots were the battles," he says. "They look easy on screen but they were a real challenge, and not just because of the cold," he adds adamantly. "How do you light a car chase at night in the middle of nowhere? Where are you going to put a 'moonlight' source and then do you move it from shot to shot? Those were just a few questions I asked myself in the very beginning.

"Then I realized that I could use the darkness to my advantage. After all, the film cuts to daytime at the same location and we are then surrounded by blinding, snowy white landscape. The change from black to white would be a nice effect."

In the story, kidnappers are stopped by a police officer. They kill the officer but are seen by a couple in a passing car and a chase ensues which ends in the death of these two onlookers. "'Moonlight' would have given a background to the scene," Deakins says. "It would give it a sense of location but would have probably been less threatening. Besides it was totally impractical given our schedule and resources. So, what you have to do is make an asset out of a reality, just as you do on documentaries."

This was only part of the solution however. "You can't really light a sequence like that with real car headlights alone," he continues. "Especially as I was not willing to shoot on the higher speed stock. I really wanted deep blacks," he adds dryly. "For the most part, our added lamps lit the scene and these varied from shot to shot. When the picture car was free running we used 12 volt lamps from the aircraft industry. When the car was being towed, we could use conventional 1k Fresnel lamps. After the crash of the passerbys' car, we used narrow beam Par lamps to send a simulated headlight effect out across the snowscape. Interior lights and brake lights were also boosted to give exposure for the slower speed of the stock, the 200 ASA 5293."

Just a little challenge, and again, far different from Deakins' next movie. For *Kundun*, he spent five months in Morocco doing Martin Scorsese's faithful recreation of the early life of the Dalai Lama, Tibet's spiritual leader. "I had never done anything like this film before," he explains. "The experience was something more akin to my work in documentaries than in the mainstream feature world. I am still surprised that the film was made, and by a major studio."

Kundun was shot on locations in the Atlas mountains and on sets constructed within a stage that also had to be built with a definite purpose in mind. "It was hardly a stage, just a big shed with a tin roof really. When we started work in July, it was 120 degrees in there and by the time we finished in December it was close to freezing. The roof had no place to rig from and would support very little weight anyway, so Tomaso Mele, my Italian key grip, was faced with a very interesting challenge. In effect, huge sets had to be lit entirely from the floor. Large 'goal post' rigs spanned the larger spaces, a task made more difficult by the almost total lack of scaffold available to us in Morocco."

The cast of *Kundun* was almost exclusively made up of exiled Tibetans and this gave Deakins the feel of shooting a documentary. "We were basically recreating the old Tibet, which sadly is being obliterated by the influx of Chinese culture," he explains. "For the Tibetans, it was their culture and many of them had sacrificed a great deal to be with us in Morocco and to be a part of the film making process. I think most of them found it all very confusing at times. It was a truly remarkable project and one on which it was an honor to work.

"I guess the most difficult scenes in *Kundun*, from a technical point of view, were some of the night exteriors," Deakins continues. "Moonlit night exteriors can be hard anywhere, but this time, I had no Musco light as an option. In fact, I didn't even have a crane as an option. Our next restriction was that all the equipment came from Rome and that was the minimum of a nine-day trip to where we were, beyond the Atlas mountains in the town of Quarzazate.

"Knowing that the schedule was liable to change throughout our stay, I had to be prepared for most things, at relatively short notice. This precluded bringing anything in at the last moment and of course, added considerably to the rental cost of any equipment we had. I already had a hefty stage package of lighting, which was, at any one time, either rigged or being rigged for shooting on our large interior sets. Besides, my gaffer Bill O'Leary and I prefer to use an HMI source to do 'moonlight.'

"The solution was to augment our small daylight location package of HMI lighting to accommodate our larger night exteriors. Bill also pointed out that we would need a larger HMI package anyway, to shoot a location interior in Casablanca that came up later in the schedule. Also, in terms of manpower, of generator capacity, and for many other reasons it seemed the right way to go.

"To cut a long story short, we ended up ordering 10 12k units and 5 6k HMI Pars, which were to be brought over from Italy, to arrive before our major night shooting and to remain until the end of our schedule. The truck left from Rome in the middle of a French lorry drivers' strike! Our truck from Rome had to pass through France on it's way to the ferry for Tangiers and no trucks were moving! Thankfully, the lamps arrived at the last minute and with a little overtime, we were rigged and ready to shoot.

"I offer this as just a brief glimpse of all the many practical considerations that impose themselves upon the way a set may be finally lit. A great deal of work happens between scouting and shooting and it can be a very tedious process. In the end, if any of that behind the scenes work shows in the final product, then I think that work has been for nothing."

After *Kundun*, Deakins returned home to Los Angeles. He immediately began prep for his next film, *The Big Lebowski*, which was being directed by the Coen Brothers. The Moroccan trip had gone a little over schedule, and he had a lot of catching up to do.

"It is difficult to finish a project that might have been just about your whole life, for many months, and then immerse yourself in another straight away," he adds. "It is not just about lighting, the whole way of relating to a project is often very different."

"In this case, the two projects could not have been more different. *The Big Lebowski* is all you would expect from a Coen brothers film – and more. It is a dark comedy of botched crime with a tapestry of very strange characters.

"Not being in the company of the Tibetans every day was quite strange at first. As you might expect, they are very gentle people and very, very quiet. It is hardly the same on a Hollywood set."

******

American and British Academy Award Nomination *Shawshank Redemption, Fargo* – **B.A.F.T.A. and A.S.C. Nomination** *Fargo* – **A.S.C. Award** *Shawshank Redemption*

"Politics is part of the process. You need to be political, and that isn't a dirty word. You also need to be pragmatic. There are extremists and prima donnas on every project. People do get pissed off. You need to be skilled with people. There is a give and take. Getting the image is what is important."

Stephen Goldblatt A.S.C. still walks around his new Northern California home, trying to memorize where the furniture is placed. Goldblatt and family bought the house over a year ago, but with the rigorous shooting schedule on *Batman and Robin* he has had little time to really enjoy his surroundings. He may have had weekends off during the long shoot, but he wasn't always free to make the short flight from Burbank North. The gray in his close cropped hair and neatly trimmed short beard is well earned. He is a man who gives 250 percent to every project he shoots.

Goldblatt may have been working in the States for many many years, but his demeanor will always belie a very different background. A native of South Africa, he began his visual career as a still photographer for The London Sunday Times organization.

"London in its heyday was wonderful," he smiles. "I was just 20 and already obsessed with the content and look of still photography. I had that underlying desire to make the visuals striking, whether I was shooting The Beatles or wildlife in Zambia."

His striking portfolio won him a spot at the Royal College of Art Film School where he made more than a few friends, including director Tony Scott. "All I wanted to do was shoot," he recalls. "They could become directors – I wanted to create the pictures. Sure, I made a lot of mistakes, but that's the way you learn. I learned that if I under-exposed or over-exposed, or whatever, the world wouldn't come crashing down on me. We were students."

The three years he spent making mistakes and learning were his post graduate art school. "Everyone came to look at our work and offer us jobs," he smiles. "David Hockney graduated right before me. I guess they thought there might be more of that kind of talent there.

"My first job under the English Union system, (an organization harder to join than that in America) allowed me to shoot the documentary format," he recalls. It was not exactly what he wanted to do with his life. "Fortunately, the UK system was part of the Common Market," he explains. "British cameramen could work anywhere in Europe, without fear of reprisal or expulsion, so I worked in Holland, Germany, Italy, France, and Spain, as well as England."

Goldblatt chose to return to shoot in South America, oftentimes getting out of a situation by the skin of his teeth. "There were three of us in that hot and sticky climate," he recalls. "Me, a sound person, and a director. I quickly learned to do everything from loading mules to securing the 16mm film for transport. The cans may have come back red with rust from the moisture, but we never lost a foot of film."

It was an avalanche set off by dynamite in Peru that brought Stephen Goldblatt to his senses. London, and a career in commercial production suddenly felt far safer. "Commercials weren't 'commercials' back then," he says, obliquely. "They were more intelligent products. Advertisers and agency people worked together to produce a better quality of material. There were problems, of course, but people were hired to do what they were supposed to do – be creative. For three years Goldblatt was deeply involved in experimenting with product spots from dog food to perfume.

Goldblatt's first feature, called *Breaking Glass*, was a musical. It, too, was based in the English artistic sensibility. "When director Brian Gibson and I talked, it was about what we were going to do more than what we were going to use to do it," he observes. "It is beyond the words but part of the subtext. I think the American movie industry can be obsessed with 'the face,' when there is far more to the project."

It was the 1983 film *The Hunger* that helped Goldblatt get the attention of the movie-making public. Joining with his old film school chum, Tony Scott, he made a picture with extremely outrageous photography, "for its day," he adds quickly. "There was a kind of competition between the top commercial cinematographers," he admits. "Each of us tried to outdo the other with lighting and camera techniques. We used smoke, one source lighting, and a few techniques that are considered 'mild' today."

Goldblatt believes that the kind of lighting used in commercials and exploited in innovative features like *The Hunger* really changed the way features were being shot. "We began to reinvent the wheel," he says simply. "I remember this one continuous shot of Catherine Deneuve, which started some 30 feet away from her and came into a close up.

"I started with diffusion off to the left of the lens, out of frame. As the camera made the dolly in toward her, I brought the diffusion in closer and closer, until it just hugged the edge of the frame. By the time we got to the big close up, the diffusion frame had traveled 30 feet, but the light had remained the same. It made a tremendous difference and was the cutting edge of creativity back then. Today, it isn't that unusual to move the unexpected."

Goldblatt tried to continue that theory with the Barry Levinson/Mark Johnson picture, *Young Sherlock Holmes*. "Some of the picture worked, some didn't," he says simply. "I loved the stained glass man and the flying bicycle. To make that flying sequence, we used a construction crane (about 200 feet high) and a wire expert to fly the plane. We lit from underneath and shot at night. I think it worked well."

The glass man was another story. "It was the first time that ILM's Dennis Muren used CGI on a 'normal' scene," Goldblatt explains. "Dennis went out on a limb and told me to shoot the sequence with rudimentary motion control; he would put the glass man in after. The shot, commonplace now, was a historical first for both of us."

Those beyond-the-limit techniques Goldblatt used on these films caught the eye of one of the most powerful people in the industry. When Francis Ford Coppola saw what he wasn't afraid of doing, he ask Goldblatt to work with him on a film called *The Cotton Club*. "There was a lot wrong with this project," he admits. "Like no script, no money, and no sets while we were shooting. Yet those challenges really pushed us beyond the limits.

"I began my love affair with real theatrical lighting on this picture," he adds. "My gaffer and I went to Broadway lighting houses and brought back primitive computer boards," he recalls. "Using cassette tape storage for the information, we rigged the whole Club to these boards, from backstage to stage and up front. We even hooked the practicals and theatrical lights to them. By recording the set-up of the lights and color settings, we could change the look at a moment's notice. That was vital, especially with the dis-continuity important to this picture.

"Sure, using dimmer boards is commonplace today. We couldn't have done *Batman Forever* or *Batman and Robin* without them. However, in 1984, the technique was unheard of, on feature films."

Goldblatt's forward thinking and lack of fear came in handy on *The Cotton Club*. "When you've escaped an avalanche by the skin of your teeth or done some of the crazy things I used to do on documentaries, surviving Coppola's changing attitudes was very easy," he laughs. "So much of this picture was done off-the-cuff, that I expected the chaos every day when I went to work. What's more – I enjoyed it! If something was 'simple,' I wondered what was wrong."

Although the project is infamous for its behind-the-scenes chaos, *The Cotton Club* is also known for some of the most stunning visuals of the era. "They were stunning because we never knew what we were going to do until we did it," he laughs. "Take the much talked about love scene between Richard Gere and Diane Lane.

"All I knew was that Francis wanted to use photographer Man Ray's style," he explains. "That meant shadows against the walls and extreme tight shots. So, I put an open arc light far behind the window drapes. This projected the pattern on Diane Lane. I think I even added a lava lamp!" he laughs. "Anything that would project the pattern we wanted! At that time, I was ignorant enough not to know what I 'could' or 'couldn't' do."

For Goldblatt, it is always use-what-you-have or what-makes-it-simple. "Get caught trying to do a run down a hospital corridor? Throw a blanket on the floor and sit on it. Have someone pull you down the hallway. It's a great invention – the blanket dolly!," he interjects.

"Thirteen years later, on *Batman and Robin*, I got caught in a similar situation," he says, coming back to the off-the-cuff lighting on *The Cotton Club*. "A problem surfaced which I wasn't prepared to handle. So, I had to come up with something quickly. I did a very 'low-tech' effect – shooting light through water and a plastic tube, wriggling the light around to make a blue flickering light."

It is amazing that Stephen Goldblatt could get such stunning work done in the chaos. "Politics is part of the process," he says simply. "You need to be political, and that isn't a dirty word. You also need to be pragmatic. There are extremists and prima donnas on every project. People do get pissed off. You need to be skilled with people. There is a give and take. Getting the image is what is important. If the shot is too expensive, let's say, I see it as my job to work with what I can. It is simply good for the movie. I find ways to be cheaper somewhere else, and not fight if at all possible. However, there are times when you have to put your foot down. If you know what will work, and you are sure it is the only way, then you have to stick to your guns."

The ability to make those choices is one of the things that helped Goldblatt in making the action packed *Lethal Weapon* movies. "I think I brought something very different to these pictures," he says, without a trace of ego in his voice. "I was a British resident, newly established in Los Angeles, doing something that was so very American – yet, it was completely foreign to me."

His lack of pre-conceived notions of what "America" and "Los Angeles" were was probably one of the things that drew director Richard Donner to him. As with any project he works on, Goldblatt plunged himself into the development of the story. To this day, he will work on special salary considerations for pre-production, so he can be involved in the process as early as possible.

"I am never a passive contributor," he says dryly. "When we were prepping the first picture, I had some special feelings about certain sequences. The scene where Mel Gibson confronts the would-be suicide, for example, was shot on the roof above the restaurant where I would have breakfast every day. I was struck with the whiteness of the building and the blueness of the sky above Hugo's and knew this was the place where the scene would look spectacular.

"Fortunately, Dick Donner loves to have everyone contribute. He likes people's involvement. And, he gathers his crew from those who are not passive but outgoing and creative."

The sequence was really Goldblatt's interview with Donner. He remembers bringing in a photograph from *Life* magazine of a totally unmarked woman who had jumped from the Empire State Building. "Dick and I discussed the shot when we met. We really worked it out together," he says. "What we did really became famous in its way for the times.

"To get the reality of the story – not reality itself, mind you, because that isn't what these films are about – we trained an actress to free-fall from a Condor. Three months after we had done the main shooting, we spread a canvas painted with a false perspective and lights over an air bag. After she jumped, we saw her fall – saw her as a real person. When she touched the canvas, the shot was over and we cut to the interior of a car.

"We used a helicopter to shoot the sequence," he recalls. "Because we needed to change the camera speed from 18 frames per second to 24 frames, for the speed of the flight, it was necessary to dim the lights on the interior of the room. To make sure it worked, I was the one on the dimmer board – under the sofa, mind you, watching the helicopter's flight!

"I told you, I like to get involved. If the shot is flying, I'm up there. Wherever we are going to be, I'm there to make sure the visuals follow through with the plan. That is part of my responsibility.

"I think the opening sequences with the car stuff are extremely innovative," he continues. "Barring a few wide shots, they are all rear projection. Dick wanted to do them in real cars, but if there is one thing I hate the most, it is car work. It is tedious and you can't get the performance you want," he says, dryly.

Goldblatt's opinion prevailed. The long sequence was done with plates. For him it was simply a matter of finding the best way to shoot them, work out the camera moves, and follow through with a little enhancement at Technicolor before projection. "I did a lot of plate work when I was shooting *Outland*," he explains. "So, when it came to *Lethal Weapon 2*, I knew what to do.

"There is nothing worse than 200 people watching an electrician trying to adjust a Mole light in a car in the middle of the night," Goldblatt says. "That tedium aside, car shots can really drain the spontaneity between actors. To put across the wonderful camaraderie between Mel Gibson and Danny Glover, we couldn't shoot on the streets. So, in pre-production, I shot a lot of street plates. I then put them through the ENR silver process, making the blacks real contrasty. When they were projected in rear projection, the extreme blacks and high contrast was washed out, bringing the shots back to a more 'normal' look. This then allowed us to put Mel and Danny in a car on the stage, and give them the freedom to do what they do best – play off each other."

To get the feeling of the streets, Goldblatt's operator Ray de la Monte told his dolly grip to move him around so that he didn't know what was coming. His reactions to the sudden movements were the same reactions passengers in a moving car would feel.

According to the timer on *Lethal Weapon 2*, this was the first time this process for rear projection was done. The final effect was so startling that it caught Spielberg's eye. He went on to use the same technique on *Always*.

Goldblatt's next and probably favorite picture, *For the Boys*, might have the legacy of being a big picture that didn't catch on the way those involved expected, but it contains some of his most artistic work. "I've done films that are far more complicated, but I think these shots are far more artistic," he says.

"Two scenes stick out as my all-time favorites," he explains. "The opening scene, where the boys are screaming 'Eddie,' (James Caan's character) and the party sequence where Bette sings in flashlight lit darkness.

"We used real flashlights, some 300 of them. We replaced the front glass with frosted glass and used special batteries.

Of course, working with Bette Midler was also one of the reasons he enjoyed the picture. "I love lighting women," he says, his eyes twinkling and a shade of a smile playing on his lips. "That is my favorite thing! Bette was amazing and so much fun."

Goldblatt's rules for lighting women also apply to men. "You light for the good of the story," he says. "You find a way to make the lighting dramatic and believable. Sometimes that means you have to cheat – and cheat quickly. When you go from a wide shot to a tight shot, it is important to change the direction of the light for the close-up. Sometimes that means fading out the key and fading in a hand held softer light.

"I love working with operators like Ray de la Monte," he adds. "We've developed a system of signals. After a shot, Ray will give me a signal behind his back. If he doesn't like what he saw through the lens, I will quietly ask for another take. Sometimes," he says with that twinkle, "it requires going to an actor or actress. 'If you are looking in that direction and the camera comes in here, your nose looks big. Now, it's your choice – a big nose, or a different eyeline.' I try to do it lightly, and with a smile. Sometimes it works, then there are those who...."

It is obvious Stephen Goldblatt has his favorite pictures and favorite stars. *For the Boys*, so far, is at the top of his list. *The Pelican Brief* is also right up there. Being able to shoot this story with one of the most popular female stars of the time in the visually beautiful New Orleans was important to Goldblatt. More important, however, was working with "one of the nicest people I've ever met," he adds quickly. "*The Pelican Brief* is another of my favorite films because of director Alan Pakula. I will go farther than I've ever gone for a man like that.

"He is a man with all the money he could want and a solid reputation in the business. Yet he still retains that boyish enthusiasm of someone new to this complex world we work in. I remember scouting with him in Washington. We were in a park just across from the White House. I came up with what I thought was an interesting idea and he actually jumped up in the air with enthusiasm! Now that's the way every director should be. You get a lot more out of a crew when you work with them, support them, and respect them."

One of the challenges on *The Pelican Brief* was the decision to shoot the story in sequence. "As much as possible," Goldblatt adds. "This allowed us to make sure the character transitions were real and the story development would ring true." Pakula and Goldblatt are committed filmmakers. For them, the written word is important. It must be supported in every way possible.

The decision to shoot in sequence also helped Pakula and Goldblatt keep control of a very complex story. Both knew all too often editing or out of sequence shooting can leave major gaps in a character's reality. By moving the shooting from A to B to C, they were able to make sure the character's growth moved in the same direction.

"Just as a well crafted story keeps the audience's attention, well crafted visual moves hold their attention as well," he says. "Each of the transitions in this picture was carefully planned. The film grammar supports the story and holds the audience's interest.

"If we had a wide shot for one exposition, we would cut to a tighter shot for the next. If one was surreal, the next would be angry or exciting. A writer's job is to guide the emotions with words, a cinematographer's job is to do the same with visuals."

Sometimes that job is an exercise in technique, other times it is an exercise in patience. Usually, it is a combination of both. "For me, one of the most stunning visuals in this picture is in the opening sequence," Goldblatt says. "We did it at the end of the picture, while Alan was in New York editing. It was my chance to go out with a wonderful pilot and second unit DP and work as a second unit director."

To get the stunning visuals of pelicans flying over the beautiful but endangered swamps of Louisiana, Goldblatt, second unit DP David Nowell, and pilot Bobby Zee flew to the location to work out where the sunrise would be. "We then did the G.P.S., giving us a best guess for altitude and angle, and found a place to land," he explains. "Then, it was a matter of taking off at pre-dawn and flying toward the light, hoping we would be in position when the sun was absolutely right.

"Skill isn't always the amount or type of lights you use, it is also knowing how to get the right exposure for the shot. With this sequence, we decided on a double 85 filter on the camera, and keeping close control of the direction with spot readings off the water. It was worth the challenge!

"There is more to making a movie than lights, cameras, and lenses," he says. "There is also composition. That was a key element, in this picture. The anamorphic format allowed us to weave over half a dozen characters and their stories into single shots. It also allowed us to follow the natural development of the story.

"Writers take audiences through emotional steps, so do cinematographers. We plan the transitions with the director. If one scene is wide, we try to make the next tight. If one is high and sweeping, even surreal, we try to make the next angry and exciting. Take a look at the opening – it was sweeping vistas of endangered marshes. The dissolve? To the crowd outside the Supreme Court. Each transition does a specific job. We don't have to go from close up to close up. Unless, of course, it is right for the story."

The logistics of *The Pelican Brief* were nothing, however, compared to what Stephen Goldblatt took on when he began shooting the *Batman* series of pictures. "These were by far the most physically challenging projects I've ever worked on," he says, still trying to recover from what feels like non-stop pressure on two consecutive movies – he did *Striptease* between these two blockbuster films.

When Goldblatt signed on to do *Batman Forever*, he had few preconceived notions about the comic book feature. "All I knew was that I wanted to increase the color palette," he says. "By giving each character a color signature, we were able to enhance the comic book atmosphere and bring a more surreal subtext to the story. Nothing about this picture was going to be subtle!"

Rather than go for the anamorphic, wide screen format he had used on *The Pelican Brief*, it was Goldblatt's suggestion to go for the regular 1:85. This way he could use the height of the shots to advantage. "In New York, for example, we were able to light whole streets from top to bottom, taking full advantage of the made up colors we decided to use to enhance the story.

"We really played with color in these shots," he adds. "You could call it an interpretive look! We had an awful lot of gels out there – strawberry for the city of Gotham, other gels for different characters and places."

For Goldblatt, one of the key elements in a picture, whether it is a drama like *The Prince of Tides*, or a comic book adventure like *Batman Forever*, is the actors and the characters. "The trick is to draw the audience into the story," he explains. "In *The Pelican Brief*, it was from the devastation of the marshes to the death of those who oppose the horrible acts. In *Batman Forever*, we used transitional moves to draw the audience into the characters and their words and actions.

"Take the scene where we first meet Kilmer as Bruce Wayne," he continues. "In the character of the millionaire tycoon, he is always on the move, so we kept the camera moving with him, to draw the audience into his words. When we first see him, he's on several phones at once. We started to draw the audience in by using a Technocrane, moving down and around the desk, framing him with his two aides. The shot takes over two minutes and it's always moving. By the time the camera settles, everyone knows all they need to know about Bruce Wayne." Unfortunately, the scene was cut from the picture.

Of course, movement doesn't always have to be smooth to implant an idea in an audience's head. If the character is evil, an aggressive and angry movement can support the story. "We had fun with the Riddler's lair," Goldblatt recalls. "The camera was as angry as the character. We used the widest lens possible, an 8mm, on many of the shots. What you see through that lens is something like a fisheye – it is so distorted, it is unsettling. Add a little distortion in the set design, and you have a wonderful image for Riddler's character.

"The lighting added to the effect," he adds. "We used computer boards and rock-and-roll lighting, of course. We built close to 100 lights into the set, creating pools of light. Since they were pre-rigged to the computer board, all the operator had to do is play the controls, dial in the moves, and add the density of color. Complex, but highly effective. Of course, now that I've almost finished *Batman and Robin*, this job feels like we were at the elementary school level. Ask me in a year or two, and I'll tell you if the new one was high school, or college. Right now, it feels like post graduate!"

When Stephen Goldblatt walked onto the set of *Batman and Robin* he knew he was going to face one of his biggest jobs yet. Fortunately, he had had about four months of pre-production preparation and testing for the newest epic. "We needed every minute of it," he explains. "We were going for concepts and challenges never faced before."

One of the first tools he called on was the now sophisticated dimmer board. "I knew when I first started using an unsophisticated board on *The Cotton Club* that this tool would help us go farther and faster," he laughs. "I just didn't know how important it would be in a future project. We literally could not have done this picture without this equipment."

An inherent problem Goldblatt and team knew they would encounter going into this picture was the inability to get several of the film's biggest stars on the same stage, at the same time. "With George Clooney on *E.R.*, we knew we could have him with us for three days – Friday, Saturday, and Sunday," he explains. "Arnold could give us only six weeks. That meant working out of continuity – with the two rarely on the set at the same time. This necessitated visiting sets ten or 12 times, instead of the normal two or three. We were constantly using doubles to shoot backs, over the shoulder shots, pieces of a body – anything where the face didn't count.

"It was essential that all our lighting be computer controlled. Too many lights were going to be too far away and inaccessible to change during a shot. This way, I could control the light exactly for first and second units. Of course, Jamie Anderson (our second unit cinematographer) was encouraged to make changes if he felt he needed them. However, we still were able to bring things back to exactly where they were, no matter what.

"I guess we used more boards on the Museum set than any other set in the picture," he says. Created on Stage 16 at Warner Bros. Studios, the Museum took up more than 200 feet, had a vaulted ceiling, large windows, and a variety of museum artifacts, including a huge dinosaur.

"Fortunately, we were able to put most of our lights right into the set," Goldblatt explains. "After all, this is a museum. It had to have lighting inside. We just used larger units than would normally be seen in a museum. Given the size of the room, the movie lights looked like practicals. The fixtures focused on the various exhibits were anchored at about 60 feet above the ground. With that kind of throw, high powered movie lights gave us just enough illumination for the exhibits and for patterns on the floor.

"We then added framing projectors like Source Fours and Shakespeares to focus on specific areas or cut light off other areas. We also had high intensity but low voltage pin spots on the showcases. To light the ice shards, we created an overhead grid of about 40 NATs. Since the stage floor was built up, we were able to enhance the shards, some of which reached 20 feet, by laying in programmable lights and fiberoptic lasers. This gave the 'ice' the shimmering effect.

"Since the floor was supposed to be covered with ice, we added high intensity searchlights to special effects drums which revolved around the set. This gave us the cold blue-white rippling effect off the surfaces.

"Outside the set windows, we set a series of color scrollers on a board. The slowly changing colors enhanced the interiors. They were far away, but worked extremely well with the size of the set.

"Fortunately, everything was programmed to the dimmer boards, so once we got them right, we could keep the lights going as long as we wanted."

To create a constantly changing environment, Goldblatt and the various production teams had a motorized mirror rig installed. This allowed Goldblatt to sweep Xenon lights through the skylights and focus them on the museum floor.

To keep Mr. Freeze in the forefront of the visual action, Goldblatt had Schwarzenegger's outfit rigged with an autopilot system which controlled half a dozen NAT lights. They tracked his movements around the museum. "The transceiver was on his costume," Goldblatt explains. "The lights would follow him everywhere. It worked great for several of the other characters, too. In the shots where characters are racing around on skates, we were able to program the lights into the computer instead of having a follow focus operator attempt to track them.

"In addition to the skating sequences, the programmable lights worked great for our pseudo hockey game. If we put a transmitter in the bottom of a hockey stick, the light would follow the stick wherever it went."

Since so much of the action takes place on the Museum floor, Goldblatt and rigging expert Earl Wiggins designed a special tracking rig for above. "We put two tracks along the ceiling and had the camera crane hung from above. This enabled us to cross the whole set quickly, even spin the camera in a 30-foot circle and go up and down, going virtually anywhere. We could get close, but stay out of the thick artificial fog that was supposed to be coming off the icy floor," he explains.

"It also allowed us to bring Mr. Freeze into the scene with the theatricality he deserved. Well, sort of," he smiles. "We wanted to show the whole museum, then track into Mr. Freeze's face – as wide as possible to as close as possible. The problem – the rig couldn't come to a dead stop. So, we shot everything in reverse! We started on his face and moved back. That meant he had to walk backwards up the steps – and all the actors had to make their moves in reverse as well!" Goldblatt stops for a moment, his eyes flashing. The shot might have been complex, the logistics just a little high pressure – but the results were amazing – and fun!

"If you can't have fun with it, then projects like this aren't for you," he says. "We knew going in everything would require extra effort. You just have to take it a shot at a time, and pray you have covered all the bases."

Ask Stephen Goldblatt what other sequences stick out in his mind, and that dry laugh and understated English humor take over. All of them and none of them at the same time is the gist of his answer. Everything was high pressure and high gear. "The most difficult set was the Gotham Observatory," he says, still trying to sort the shots out in his mind. The set, built to full scale at the docking area of the Queen Mary in Long Beach, California, contained a 20 ton fully operational hydraulic telescope. The enormous set undergoes a major transformation from the site of an elegant party to an iced over habitat. When Mr. Freeze takes over, the telescope becomes a freeze gun focused on turning Gotham into an iceberg.

"I think the most interesting part of lighting this set was the use of 'cosmic projections,'" says Goldblatt, thoughtfully. "After all, this is a planetary observatory. We should be seeing planets and comets. During pre-production, I went to New York and looked at the projectors made by a company called Electronic Arts. After testing, we decided on the French projectors known as Telescan Mark 4 Chameleons. Instead of working like regular projectors, the image is directed into a mirror which can send it anywhere, even distort it or change the scrolling speed or color from a lighting board."

With production designer Barbara Ling's help, Goldblatt was able to have 40 projectors built into the set. To supplement the look, he positioned two larger PIGI projectors, which light from HMI arcs, into the set. "When everything was in place, I realized we couldn't get the exposure level above a T1.4. To get it to a T2.8, we had to have several of the gray walls painted white. Of course, that created another problem. The ambient light and parts of the projected art washed the effect out. We had pastel instead of dramatic. The only solution was to go back to the gray walls and boost the lamps.

We would just have to go four points lighter on the printing lights."

Unfortunately, that didn't solve Goldblatt's problem completely. "We ended up rigging a massive amount of what could be called 'negative fill,'" he explains. "We attached these large rolls of black material to parts of the set, pulling them down when we needed to counteract the bounce back we had been getting."

That left Goldblatt with the finesse part of lighting this huge set. "We had a ring of 12 NAT lights put into the high ceiling and did the rest from the floor," he explains. "We added blue gel to 2ks, focused on the huge ice shards and hit Kino Flos under the telescope platform. We got the 'zapping' effect from neon lights designed into the barrel of the telescope.

"Since the set was so huge and there was so much activity, including the use of a massive amount of ice smoke on the floor, we had a truss designed into the top of the set. A 40-foot revolving arm had a camera set on one end and a counter balance on the other end. Also, a Technocrane was mounted on a Titan crane to give a very long reach into and around the set.

Goldblatt stops to think for a moment. "Actually, maybe that wasn't the most challenging shot," he says with a smile. He pauses for breath, searching his memory banks for another "unique" Batman shot. He sits back, scratches his short beard, and takes a deep breath, ready to launch into another shot when the phone rings. He comes back to earth. He's not in Northern California anymore! He's trying to relax at the Universal Hilton, taking a break from the timing session of *Batman and Robin*. "That call is probably to tell me they are ready for another round," he says as he reaches for the phone. He listens for a minute, nods his head, hangs up and takes a deep breath.

"This is our second go at it," he says, a little edge coming into his voice. "I have one more session and then they are making 5000 prints. It's incredible, the pressure put on releasing a film at a particular time these days. We finished the picture three months ago, and they want it out – now! Three months for over 1000 difficult shots with wire and pimple removal," he says, the trace of his understated humor coming back.

"You have to be very, very good with exposure these days," he says, seriously. "There is no time for major corrections. The most you can get away with is four points – that's only half a stop. If something is wrong in the initial photography, it goes, ready or not. It's no longer the 'show' that is being emphasized. It's the 'business.' It's scary, that kind of pressure.

"I know one thing that I am looking forward to seeing," he adds, as he gets ready to go to the second of his three timing sessions. "They are going to make several Technicolor Dye transfer prints. It will be the first time in 25 years that they use an updated version of this old technology on a new film. I'm told the color will be amazing. If it looks as great as expected, all the pressure will be worthwhile," he sighs, the weight of trying to deliver a perfect print so quickly showing just a little.

Rumor has it, another sequel is already in preparation. At this point, asking him if he is going to do it is tantamount to begging to have your head chopped off. Give him a little time, and he'll be ready to get started on day 301, or whatever the number is, of the highly successful and challenging *Batman* series.

******

Academy and A.S.C. Award nomination *The Prince of Tides, Batman Forever*

"When I started, it was just about getting images. We weren't afraid of making mistakes. The idea was to use what we could to get to the heart of a scene. We wanted to get into the conflict within the character. It was our way of best serving a movie, a story. There was more time to develop a look. We would watch the blocking, and begin to sift through an infinite number of ways to do the story."

Emmanuel

Getting Emmanuel Lubezki A.S.C. to sit down and talk about his career is close to impossible. People around him say he is shy. "Not when I'm around Cuaron," he laughs, referring to his longtime friend and director Alfonso Cuaron. "Our sets are low key and intense, but there is a lot of affectionate banter. Cuaron and I tend to be vocal. He tells me my lighting is terrible, I tell him his blocking is silly. I guess it is our way of showing how much we care about each other!"

It isn't artistic temperament that makes this thin and wiry young man pull his long hair and bounce around a set, it is a passion for life and his work. "It is also a little frustration," he adds quietly. "I still think in Spanish!"

A native of Coyoacan, a small middle-class community of intellectuals and artists in what used to be the suburbs of Mexico City, Lubezki (better known to those around him as "Chivo" – a name given him in private school) learned to be heard while playing in the city streets. His parents, a psycho-analyst and psychologist, allowed him to follow his instincts and create a world he was comfortable with. They would capture his interest by telling him tales of family history, including the great adventures his grandmother had while touring as a featured actress in the Yiddish theater. "Although I never had a chance to see her work, the stories and that world fascinated me," he says. "Maybe that's where the seed of interest in making pictures began."

While growing up in this artistic community, he developed a fascination for the work of some of Mexico's famous still photographers such as Alvarez Bravo and Graciella Iturbibe. When visiting his uncle in Pittsburgh,

Pennsylvania, he expressed an interest in still photography. His uncle bought him a 35mm reflex camera. And the rest, as they say, is history.

"As soon as I got back to Mexico City, I joined a still photography club," he says. "I would shoot anything I could using black-and-white film. I was learning the basics, from development to the relationship between speed and the iris. Frankly," he adds, "most of what I shot was pretty bad!"

Although few people made a living as still photographers or even as artists in Mexico, Lubezki was determined to follow that path for his future. In the early 1980s he found one college in Mexico, Centro Universitario de Studio Cinematographico, that specialized in still photography and film, so he set his eye on that for his continuing education. "It was a five year course, given by people who were more interested in the documentary filmmaking done in Poland, Russia, and other European countries than they were in making feature films.

"I knew they were going to accept only 20 students out of the hundreds who applied, so I did what seemed to be expedient on my application test – I lied!" he laughs. "I watched the films they showed me and told them what I thought they wanted to know about the people and the pictures. What I didn't say was that I also admired American directors like Woody Allen, Coppola, Scorsese, Ford, and Spielberg," he smiles.

After joining the select few students to enter the school, he found out everyone else had done the same thing! "It was an instant bond," he says. "We were the first generation at this school who wanted to do fiction instead of documentaries."

Although the college system in Mexico is inexpensive – about 200 pesos per year ($10.00) – there was no lack of equipment. As soon as he began his studies, he had hands-on experience with Super 8mm and 16mm cameras and as much film stock as he could use. "We made a lot of mistakes learning our craft," he says without shame. "That was what it was all about. Learning."

His first project, a three minute Super 8mm movie, was done with five other students. They wrote the script – a story that took place in a room lit by a candle. "I thought I was hot," he laughs. "We all did. There we were, in film school, shooting a picture the way we wanted.

"The first day and first take, I kneeled down with the meter hanging around my neck and crashed it to the ground. It exploded in a thousand pieces! I had to buy another – which wasn't easy in Mexico. Someone actually had to send to Los Angeles for a replacement. It was expensive, and painful. I learned how to treat my equipment well early!

"As for the picture, well that was another story! We decided to put some gels on the lights, to simulate candlelight. Of course, our eyes got used to the gels quickly and we found ourselves adding more of them as the night progressed. By the end of the shoot, there were seven layers of gel in front of the lights. Obviously, the first shots didn't match the last. Another great lesson learned early!"

Lubezki began paying attention to his professors, real artists who loved the work and realized that teaching was one of the only ways to make a living at what they loved. He spent time asking questions, exploring techniques, and breaking rules. For two years, he was in heaven.

"I learned from my teachers and my friends," he adds. "Alfonso Cuaron, who was two generations of students above me, called me to be his gaffer/focus puller/electrician/best boy on a film noir project. He taught me a lot about approaching a story from the camera's point of view."

For a while, everything went smoothly. Lubezki tackled more complicated projects. "Then, one day, reality set in when I realized there would be nothing – no tools, film stock, or time to play – when I got out of school," he says. He began investigating the film "industry," if that was what it could be called, in Mexico. "Most of the work done there was really awful," he says. "The scripts were poorly written and designed. There was no concept behind the lighting. All they did was put lights up so they could see the actors.

"The projects were made by cheesy producers, doing 16mm or straight to video on short schedules. They were filling the demand for movies to show the illegal immigrants in the states who could not go to the movie theaters, in fear of being picked up and deported."

It could be a start, for Lubezki, as long as he could control the story and maybe the light. His idea, get together with a few friends and write a script. "It took one night to write and three weeks to make," he laughs. "Because no one else would produce, that was left to me!"

One of Lubezki's cohorts, Luis Estrada was able to round up several well known Mexican actors to perform in *El Camino de Largo*. Suddenly, there was a little money behind them, a studio of sorts, even offices, and equipment. Soon, the decision to shoot on film instead of video. For about six thousand dollars, they had a movie. When they finished, they took the project to DuArt to make a 35mm blow up.

"Instead of going into the illegal theaters, the project was sold to the Mexican Institute of Cinematography. The film was distributed in Mexico, not the States."

And, what about school? "Oh, I got fired!" he laughs. "I was working too much! I didn't want to go to classes, I wanted to use the equipment and facilities. They said it was time for me to leave and make room for others who wanted to learn! Cuaron was fired at the same time," he adds.

Emmanuel Lubezki was now out in the real world and doing quite well. The studio, "if you could call it that," he adds, liked the first project. They asked for another. Luis Estrada wrote a project called *Bandidos*. "It was our chance to use the equipment," Lubezki says. "We had BL3s with Zeiss high speed lenses, a Tulip crane, and a few HMI lights.

"The problem was getting the crews to do what we wanted them to do with the equipment we had," he explains. "We were the kids who had strange ideas about movie making. Diffusion? Bounce? They were foreign words to some of these men. At that time in Mexico, things were done a little differently," he explains. "One person does the job of lighting and moving the equipment. In America, the jobs are split. That means communicating with more people. An adjustment."

Cornered, he dug his heels in and eventually prevailed. "I was lucky to meet a forward thinking gaffer by the name of Fernando Moreno. He was one of the few people who understood the art and craft of making movies. I learned a lot from him. We explored new ways of making real movies."

Along with a few friends who really cared about their projects, Lubezki began to change the rules and use the equipment in an artistic as well as utilitarian way. He was on his way, working in non-union films and low budget video television projects. "Union? In Mexico? There are only seven cinematographers in the union in all of Mexico," he explains. "Someone had to die to get in. We were determined to be the generation who destroyed the archaic system. It was time to grow up."

Since so much of the work was done out of this system, Lubezki had no trouble getting work. Between feature and television projects, he did commercials. "They were more restrictive," he concedes. "But they were work. They had smaller budgets and took less time, but it was a learning experience. For a while, I did a lot of second unit work with one particular director. Since he worked with different cinematographers, this allowed me to watch, listen, and learn.

"During the two years of Chrysler spots, I was able to put some of those lessons into my work. It was a challenge, working on what was called a 'stage' and finding ways to light cars without equipment. There was no such thing as a Fisher light," he laughs. "We created big sources and bounced lights, unheard of at the time. It was here that I fell in love with stage work."

However, that wasn't always possible. Most of the feature work, both first unit and second unit, "for some wonderful Mexican cinematographers," he adds, was done on location. "Lighting exteriors in Mexico is extremely difficult. The exteriors are just plain ugly. The part of the country we worked in was high in the mountains and close to the equator. There the sun goes up fast, and the shadows are ugly. Scheduling was vital."

Lubezki's work was being noticed. *Banditos* had been a success. The writer, Luis Estrada, wrote another script called

Love in the Time of Hysteria. This time, Mexican financiers gave them 150,000 dollars to shoot the picture. "In our first discussions, we talked about doing the film in black-and-white," he says. "However, we knew the investors wouldn't go for it. Instead, we decided to make color, or the lack of it, a focal point of the visuals. Cuaron's favorite color was green; so we ended up with green. The upside of using color is the way it visually emphasizes aspects of a story. The downside is that some people don't look so great next to this particular color. Fortunately, we didn't have that problem here.

"The story is of a designer who is a Casanova in the AIDS era," Lubezki explains. "One of his conquests, a nurse, wants revenge. She changes the results of his blood tests, and suddenly he thinks he has AIDS. He becomes confused. He meets a woman who has been betrayed by a man and they decide to end it all together. The last scene was to be shot in our Empire State-type building in Mexico City.

"The problem, a five week shoot that we had to stretch to six weeks because we needed more time for the chase sequences. We simply had to give up some of the equipment we ordered to get the extra days to shoot scenes where friends try to stop the two from suicide and explain that the test was okay, that the whole thing was a joke."

The crew was caught in what looked like a no-win situation. They needed to shoot this scene on top of the Torre Latino Americana Office building, which housed a large tower and many pieces of communications equipment that powered the city system. However, the tower was too dangerous for a shoot. "We made a compromise," he admits. "We used a helicopter to shot the actors on the roof at night. By using a 1.4 stop, we could have the city lights glowing in the background. Then we made a smaller mock up tower on a safer building for the love scenes and shots on the tower. The trick was to make everything match."

Lubezki's work on this feature won him praise and an Ariel Award nomination, the Mexican equivalent of the Academy Award. Mexican filmmakers began to notice the changes people like Emmanuel Lubezki were making. Now some craftspeople were using light to fit the characters and to create atmosphere – radical moves. "So was the way we shot things," he says. "For *Love in the Time of Hysteria*, I did some radical framing, with very little head room in the shots. The characters' position in the frame changed as they got deeper into trouble. This move from center created a loss of equilibrium."

Lubezki then went on to team up with another well known Mexican director, Alfonso Arau, for what became almost a cult picture – a definite cross over from strictly Mexican audiences to international significance, *Like Water for Chocolate*. "Originally, I was offered the second unit," he says. "However, there was a problem with the first unit cinematographer and it was suggested that I take over. I was a little afraid," he admits. "I thought they could bring in a great European DP they could afford and I could learn something. However, when I saw the producers were firm, I rose to the challenge."

Set during the Mexican Revolution period, the film follows three very different young girls as they grow to be women, as the world is changing around them. "It was an exciting period, when traditions were being broken and the world was changing very quickly," he says. "Fortunately, the locations chosen were farther North and closer to the border. The light would be better. Shooting in winter also helped us, since this provided a less aggressive and toppish light. One of my first thoughts was to find a look for each of the women and maintain that emphasis throughout the whole picture, even as their worlds changed."

Using food as the underlying theme, the story is a very sensual, passionate, and both harsh and striking look at old traditions and archaic views on intimate relationships.

The biggest challenge was the two different looks. Half of the story takes place during a time when there was no electricity. "The difficulty was in how to light these sequences and make them look like they were lit strictly by fire," he explains. "We began the picture without furniture, simply because it hadn't arrived and we couldn't wait. So, we used a simple table and painted everything black, shooting dark. This set the tone for the whole film.

"If there was light, it would be coming from a window. We used no fill. It was my contrasty version of a Vermeer painting," he adds. This set the look for the whole movie. Critics thought the project was too dark. "That didn't matter," he shrugs, "I felt that most Mexican cinematographers shot too light."

To capture the stunning visuals with the best possible equipment, Lubezki and Arau made a deal with Arriflex and used the new BL4 cameras. "We even got a bigger Tungsten package and 12k HMIs for the exteriors," he says, happily.

"Arau understood the cinematographer's challenges," Lubezki continues. "We were able to schedule the exteriors for the best times of day, cheat the actors around when necessary, and frame extremely tight to enhance the claustrophobic feeling of a house with no escape."

Another major step in changing the approach to a Mexican production was an extended shooting schedule. Production gave them eight weeks – "which stretched into 12, and then ran out of money," he says sadly. "We simply faced too many roadblocks while shooting in the desert and border towns. If it wasn't weather, it was availability of locations, or other challenges that happen when you are out of the controlled studio situation."

Unfortunately, while the project was on hold and waiting for the money to finish and release, Lubezki had to leave for another commitment. "Still, I really enjoyed the film and felt I did some of my best work with these sequences."

Another cinematographer took over, shooting several scenes that took place on the American side of the border. The look was quite different. "He never even called me to ask what lights I used or why I had chosen certain lenses," Lubezki says, sadly. "Since the sequences were of another era, the looks didn't have to match. It even helped, a little, that they looked different."

When Miramax acquired the project, they shortened it, re-edited it, and added more red and yellow color to the visuals. "By the time they called me, the IP (Interpositive) and

IN (Internegative) were so warm, there was nothing I could do. In a way, it was okay. The manipulation helped blend the two looks."

Still, challenges, manipulations, and schedule aside, the project won Lubezki his first Ariel Award. He was beginning to show the Mexican (and American) movie making community what aggressive changes could be made in their products.

Things began to get a little boring – more unusual visuals, more award nominations. Lubezki's next two Mexican projects won him his second and third Ariel Awards. *Miroslava*, the story of the Mexican equivalent to Marilyn Monroe, details the actress's tragic life and death from an overdose at the top of her career. "We used food to tell the story in *Like Water for Chocolate*, here we decided to use props," he explains. "Perfume bottles, a napkin, her passport, served as memories that would trigger flashback sequences."

The enjoyable part of shooting this picture was the period. "This time was earlier in the 1940s, when Mexico had a film industry," he explains. "That meant re-creating the studios, the stages, and the magnificent homes. We shot in both black-and-white and color, depending on the part of the story.

"How did we get the money to do such lavish locations and work? Easy. The above the line cost isn't as big in Mexico. Even the biggest stars don't demand so much that it has to be taken away from other departments. The money is more even, so you can split calls and get to shoot at the best times. It's a luxury I miss, even today."

Lubezki's next Mexican production was very different from anything he had done before. Done in the early 1990s, *Amber*, taken from a stage play, takes place in an imaginary place, on an imaginary river. "It was a big theater play," he says simply. "The idea was to keep the stylized look of the stage and create a jungle (both location and stage elements) in the same vein.

"On location, we were lucky. Many of the sets from *Medicine Man* were still available," he adds. "They had destroyed part of the jungle and made a road, so we used it to get in. The challenge, matching the real exteriors to what we had already created on stage for the first parts of the shots.

"This was the first time I lit everything with Tungsten lights," he adds. "Even the exteriors. It gave the whole movie the amber look of its name."

Emmanuel Lubezki got his first taste of American film-making between these two Mexican pictures. He shot a small picture called *The Harvest* for a producer by the name of Jason Clark. Clark liked his work and recommended him for an American comedy called *20 Bucks.* This led to *Reality Bites*.

Reality bit Lubezki in more ways than one on both pictures. "Mexican directors shoot for the story, while I found American directors like to shoot for coverage and editing," he says. "I was used to moving from A to B to C. In America, I found we were going to move from A to B and then A to C. It was television style, even in features. And, it was a change and a challenge.

"In addition, I learned something else the hard way on *Reality Bites*. Permits. In Mexico, you can go into the streets and hang things wherever you want. When we got to this wonderful street location in Houston for *Reality Bites*, I was ready to hang silks. However, we didn't have 'permission' or a condor, so I ended up shooting without the softening elements."

Fortunately, Lubezki is quick on his feet and had learned to deal with elements in Mexico. "Again, it became a matter of scheduling the shots for the right time of day," he explains. "Something that isn't as easy in America as it is in Mexico. I was used to working in an environment where costs were more evenly divided. In Mexico, to get the best shots possible, we would often work split days, shooting certain sequences in the morning and breaking until late afternoon or evening to get the rest. Here, that is rarely a viable option. It is simply too expensive."

These two pictures were Lubezki's trials by fire. When he partnered, once again, with director Alfonso Cuaron for *A Little Princess*, he was ready for anything. As with *Love in the Time of Hysteria*, Cuaron and Lubezki chose to use a green color to impact the picture. "It is the story of a little girl brought up in privilege in India, who is suddenly thrown into a harsh world at a very disciplined school," he explains. "We went with beautiful colors such as orange and yellow and a few reds for the India shots, then contrasted them to the harshness of the school and this new world by using the green pallet. Production designer Bo Welch gave us sets dressed in a green, and costume designer Judianna Makovsky used fabrics in the green family," he continues.

They used color to manipulate the emotions. "What saves this little girl from her harsh reality at the school is her dreams," he explains. "In the scenes of her memories of time with her father, the colors are bright. When she finds out that he is dead, we bled the bright colors away and infused the shot with the green of reality."

To emphasize the world overwhelming this little girl, the team also worked with false perspective. "Oversized doorways, larger-than-life banisters, anything that would make her look and feel small and insignificant," he explains. "Lighting these sets was interesting," he explains. "We used Tungsten lights for most of the picture."

For Lubezki and Cuaron, *A Little Princess* was a chance to do an American movie their way. "It was back to telling the story through the point-of-view we chose to use," he says. "In this case, through the camera as her point-of-view. Cuaron likes to cut things in his head and does long takes to accomplish what he wants. We had the luxury of planning moves carefully – then we improvised when he started to ignore the boards.

"We wanted to do the unusual," he adds. "There is a touching scene where the little girl tells a friend about her memories of India. Since the two are locked into their own rooms, we needed to go from room to room to reveal the story. Or, did we? Instead, we decided to use the adjoining wall as a wipe, literally sweeping across the open wall with the camera. With the last wipe, instead of bringing in the two girls or emphasizing one, we transported the little girl's fantasy of the two of them together, in a safe and beautiful environment to India. We went to a shot of the great temple and to a beautiful waterfall, then to a shot of the two girls standing on a beautiful statue.

"This kind of situation is a perfect example of working together to cut a project before it gets to the cutting room," he explains. "It made the visuals stunning and supported the emotion of the story in the best possible way."

Lubezki's unorthodox approach to color and visual style won the young cinematographer a 1996 Academy Award nomination for *A Little Princess*. Now he was supposed to top himself with every new project. "The pressure was on," he admits, "although I didn't really have the time to deal with it. I went into another project, with Alfonso Arau (*Like Water for Chocolate*). This time we needed to create a very stylized look for *A Walk in the Clouds*.

"Although the story was grounded in reality, we wanted each sequence to look like a matte shot," he explains. "It is possible that we went too far," he laughs, "but at the time, it worked for our picture.

"To get this look, we created extremely stylized visuals with very warm lights and more sources. My favorite shot is when the women stomp the grapes in this huge barrel. Fortunately, we were able to work with the shooting schedule and do the shots the way we used to do them in Mexico – half day and half night, saving the grape stomping for the sunset. That way, we had the back light we wanted and the atmosphere to make the shots as beautiful as they were."

Lubezki's next picture was anything but a stylized drama. He was now thought of as a mainstream cinematographer, up to the challenge of any major studio picture. "So, what did I take on but a Robin Williams project!" he laughs. "Bo Welch introduced me to the director, and he liked me immediately. When the offer came, I was nobody's fool. You don't turn down Mike Nichols and Robin Williams, especially when the project is a new version of *La Cage au Folles* called *The Birdcage*. It is a hilarious comedy and I wanted to make everything I could out of it.

"One of the toughest things about this picture, aside from trying to second guess Robin Williams's movements, was making long scenes of people sitting in a room look interesting," he says. "This was not a picture where we wanted a stylized look to over power the comedy. This was a picture where reality was important. We didn't want to do anything to take the audience out of the story."

Fortunately, Mike Nichols likes to block scenes with his actors. This gave Lubezki the time to create lighting to fit the sequence. "Although we had a great relationship, it wasn't like Arau or Cuaron," he says. "Mike comes from a theater background, so staging is very important to him. Lighting comes second."

The Birdcage was Emmanuel Lubezki's first experience with high key comedy. Although Mike Nichols wanted him to use his creativity, he did not want to feel the sources. It might not have looked it, but the sequences were far more complicated to light than some of his other projects. "This time I was prepared," he laughs. "We had a few scenes I knew would be the kind that stick out in the audience's minds long after they left the theater. I had all the permits needed to hang anything I wanted anywhere on our Florida locations.

"When we got to the big scene between Robin and Nathan Lane, where they discuss how to represent themselves to their son's future wife's parents, I had a great system of silks and lights prepared for the outdoor table location."

Unfortunately, Lubezki hadn't counted on the Florida sun to throw a monkey wrench into the plan. First, the script girl fainted from the heat, then Mike Nichols got a case of heat stroke. While Nichols was recovering in his trailer, Williams came to Lubezki with a little "problem" about sweating. "Robin was great," he says. "He wanted to know what he could do to help, as long as we cooled the shot down a bit.

"Now I had to turn all the lights off, get rid of the silks, and anything else that would reflect the light," he laughs. "Instead of shooting a single camera, we set up two cameras and went, a capella, as we said. What we saw was what we got. The only thing I could do is throw a silk over a fan somewhere, and hope the image would work on the screen!" It just shows that, when you master something in movie making, life has a way of throwing you a curve."

The Birdcage featured several rather outrageous sequences done in a gay club in Florida's most notorious entertainment district. "So many of the wonderful dance numbers never showed up in the final cut," Lubezki says. This was one of the first times he worked so hard on a project, just to see the struggle end up on the cutting room floor.

"It doesn't matter," he says, smiling. "It was a great experience and I got to pick Broadway lighting designer Jules Fisher's brain! He got my head out of the traditional movie lighting and into a whole new world of varilights and visual effects.

"Jules didn't have time to work on the project, but his information was valuable. This allowed me to work with John Todesco, who was the theatrical lighting consultant on Stephen Goldblatt's first *Batman*. Together, we created the club's mood. We set up an elaborate lighting scheme, which included varilights, consoles, and extremely intricate computers.

"I had a blast, timing the lights to the music and lighting these wonderful actors," Lubezki admits. "Gene Hackman and Diane Weist were marvelous. I think the other highlight scene from this picture was their 'escape' from the club. Who wouldn't laugh hysterically, seeing Gene Hackman dressed in drag! It was hard to concentrate on what we were shooting," he admits.

"One of the biggest challenges was lighting Nathan Lane as a woman. He looked terrific, but we had a few elements to deal with, like his make up. It kept changing with the Florida heat. Still, we had to do a 'glamour lighting,' so that the audience would believe that Gene Hackman's character could fall for this woman."

Lubezki went from working with one comedic lunatic performing in front of the camera, Robin Williams, to a certifiable creative lunatic behind the camera. "Cuaron and I went at it again," he laughs. "This time it was his slightly bent version of the classic novel *Great Expectations*. Trust me, the only similarity is in the title! Alfonso went completely insane! His appetite was huge. The first story boards were the size of the yellow pages. There were birds, fish, young children, water shots, everything imaginable. I had no idea how we were going to capture everything." Fortunately, Lubezki has dealt with this kind of creative genius before.

"At the end of our pre-production period, Alfonso had a revelation. He wanted to shoot the movie in anamorphic," Lubezki says. "How do you explain to a crazy person that everyone wants to shoot anamorphic now and there were simply no lenses available?" he adds, affectionately.

Fortunately, or unfortunately, Panavision was able to pull a set of Primo lenses for him at the beginning of the shoot. By the second week, he realized he didn't like them and traded the Primos for an E-series of lenses. "The toughest part was to adjust the brain to using anamorphics," he says. "It wasn't the framing, that came easy. All I had to do was make sure my lights weren't in the shots. It was the lighting package itself.

"To get the proper stop for the critical stock and focus, we had to add units. Doing this without time to test was brave," he admits. "The first day's shots were shocking. All I kept thinking about was how to survive! We were trying to do an anamorphic picture without extensive testing or a faster stock. And we were trying to add a lot of camera movement and fluidity, something extremely difficult with the bulk of the anamorphic system!"

In the middle of the picture, Cuaron and Lubezki looked at each other in a mutual understanding. One of the things that saved them was the fact that this film was not really supposed to have one set style. "It was a case of doing what we wanted to support the strange story," he says. "Hang a consistent lighting style throughout the picture. We had grown past that – just look at what we did with *A Little Princess*. Throwing the book out the window altogether was simply the next step."

The first part of *Great Expectations* begins in Sarasota, Florida. To set the tone of the location, Lubezki decided to light everything with Tungsten units, inside and out. "We really took a lot more risks on this film," he admits. "It's not a pretty picture. We used the harsh noon light and kept the harsh aggressiveness of the locations. The subways were great," he says. "We used what was there – even foregoing fill. The color changes worked great for the story.

"When we did use lights, it was again Tungsten with a few HMIs. It was important to me to give the story support by enhancing the mood with lighting, or the lack of it," he explains. "There were more than a few times when Cuaron and I really came to blows. It went beyond loving screaming. It became creative differences, major.

"There is a scene in the kitchen, where Cuaron wanted the actors in silhouette but I wanted to see their faces. We had our usual friendly 'discussion' – he said I didn't have the guts to do it his way.

"Since Cuaron was the director, I gave in. Before I lit the shot the way he wanted, I had him sign a paper saying he authorized this daring scheme of lighting!" Lubezki laughs. "Good thing, too, because the lab called the next day in a panic. They couldn't see the actors. At dailies, we saw the same thing. 'Whoops, we went a little too far,' was what came out of Cuaron. He couldn't admit he liked the look, but that we pushed it just a little too much!

"We went back to the same location and added a little side light, just enough to see their faces. Unfortunately, Cuaron wasn't satisfied with the performance he got. We went back a third time.

"That's one of the wonderful things about working with a director like Alfonso Cuaron," he says, seriously. "He will push a DP farther than anyone else ever would. He will take more risks. And, if they don't work, it isn't a problem. He simply goes back to do what he does best, and lets the DP work out the kinks."

When Lubezki was shooting *The Birdcage*, he instinctively knew that the scene between Robin Williams and Nathan Lane, plotting their actions as husband and wife would be the one sequence everyone remembers. "In *Great Expectations*, I thought it would be a scene in a hotel room, where Ethan Hawke's character, a struggling painter, gets to paint the emotional love of his life for real.

"She (Gwynneth Paltrow) comes to him in the middle of the day and tells him it is his one chance to paint her. She takes off her clothes and poses, as he moves to his easel and starts drawing. I wanted it sensual and filled with tension," he explains. "So, we set up a completely naked light through the windows. We used hard back light and bounces from Ultra Dinos. As she moves through the room, this creates shadows and patterns.

"We did it hand held," he adds. "That way, we could keep the tension and focus on what was important. Because we didn't want to show her completely naked, we kept only pieces of her body in focus – naked shoulders, hands.

"At a certain point in the story, she simply picks up her clothes and leaves. This is the climax of his life – he can't have her, but he can have her painting. We closed the sequence with one shaft of hard light, with him centered and alone in the middle of the room. It is a beautiful shot.

"The process of creating images is much more difficult today than it was even when we were doing *Love in the Time of Hysteria* or *Like Water for Chocolate*," he says, sadly. "There is a lot of additional pressure because movies are so expensive. You have little time to think, to prepare. It has become 14 or 15 hour days, then dailies, and a few hours of sleep – if you can get past the worries. It is tough just to keep moving.

"That's one of the things that I don't like about mainstream movie making in America. We may have the tools, the money, and a band of great actors, but the time is so short and pressured. In Mexico, there is less money and not as many tools, but just as fine actors. The films aren't a product but an experiment. You try things and hope they work.

"When I started, it was just about getting images. We weren't afraid of making mistakes. The idea was to use what we could, to get to the heart of a scene. We wanted to get into the conflict within the character. It was our way of best serving a movie, a story. There was more time to develop a look. We would watch the blocking and begin to sift through an infinite number of ways to do the story.

"It was more than soft bounce or direct light – stylized or natural. Determining contrast was philosophical. It was what was best for the moment."

Lubezki's next mainstream American picture is going to challenge him even more. For *Meet Joe Black*, starring Brad Pitt, he will have to top the complex club lighting in *The Birdcage*. He has to work with a location that might just rival the complexity of Batman, a set that is about eight football fields in size!

"Yes, I like working in America because of the tools and the ability to live well doing what I love to do. However, there is still something intriguing about shooting in Mexico. You can put your whole life into a project that might never get distribution. You can't live on what you make, but your soul can be fed by what you do.

"Of course, that can also happen in America. The trick is finding a balance – a lot like lighting. You need a studio willing to invest in your creativity and a director who will let you walk on the edge. So far, I have been lucky to find both. I can only hope this trend continues and I can still find scripts with real stories and characters who give me the inspiration to walk on the edge, with whatever way I choose to shoot."

******

1992 Ariel Nomination *Love in the Time of Hysteria* – **1992 Ariel Award** *Like Water for Chocolate* – **1993 Ariel Award** *Miroslava* – **1993 Cable Ace Award** *Fallen Angels - "Murder Obliquely"* – **1994 Ariel Award** *Amber* – **1996 Academy Award Nomination** *A Little Princess*

"I got into lighting because I wanted to help create that 'magic' moment when the audience is not only entertained, but moved, informed and, hopefully, changed in a positive way by what they've seen and experienced. My job is to create a visual environment that best supports the connection between the actor and audience, an environment in which that magic can occur."

Jo Mayer

The neighbor's dogs sun themselves in the middle of the narrow road in front of Jo Mayer's house in the rustic Topanga Canyon area of Los Angeles. Her bird, Barney, tries to make conversation as he watches her sort through lighting plots for one of her current assignments. She sifts through several film and television projects that she has in development. Mayer admits that she is at a crossroads in her career. Lighting for stage and television was, and always will be, a fascinating part of her work. However, she has a lot more to say – and that means putting on another hat or two – a producer's or a director's.

She's well-suited to the intricacies of putting a project together. A Smith College graduate at the age of 19, Jo Mayer's original direction was toward the complexities of the social sciences – actually a double-major in economics and sociology. Right after graduation, she went to work on Capitol Hill as a researcher and speech writer, then later as an economist for a major research firm. While at Smith, she was also involved in lighting theater department productions. Stage lighting fascinated her and she found herself "moonlighting" as a lighting designer for productions around the Washington, D.C., area.

"Secretly," she says, "I had wanted a career in the theater since I was 14. I would go to Saturday matinees at the American Conservatory Theater. I remember sitting in the balcony of The Geary in San Francisco watching a production of Chekov's *The Three Sisters* starring Michael Learned as Masha. Toward the end of the play, Masha's lover Vershinin leaves and she knows she'll never see him again.

"At that moment, Ms. Learned's 'Masha,' stumbling away from her departing lover, let out a cry of such pain and sorrow that the entire audience caught its breath. We were all suspended in the emotion of the moment, no one moved or made a sound. I decided then and there that I wanted to be part of this magic process. Going into the theater would have been my first choice from the start if I'd had the courage. I knew, though, that my parents wouldn't approve and I wasn't sure I could make a living at it. Going into the social sciences was a safe, and distant second, career choice."

Juggling these career paths became difficult and she felt she needed to choose. When she got an offer to teach at the University of Michigan's Department of Natural Resources, she felt the decision had been made for her. Ironically, the first person she met in Ann Arbor was the business agent for the I. A. Local. Soon, she was working on all of the shows coming through town.

One of the groups that came for a month-long residency was John Houseman's Acting Company (a touring repertory company originating from Julliard's Drama Division, headed by Mr. Houseman). By the end of the semester, she had left the worlds of academia and government behind to become the assistant stage manager and tour lighting director for the company.

Mayer became the protege of the resident lighting designer, David F. Segal. He taught her to work with the elements available. She basically became Segal on the road, following through on the lighting plots provided for the various theatrical venues.

"David does beautiful work," she says warmly. "He taught me to be creative and use my imagination to support the play with the equipment available. His work for The Acting Company reflected the wonderful things he had done on Broadway and in theaters around the world.

"We did a production of Shakespeare's *Edward II* with a simple setting of red carpet and red drapery. He used a lighting design similar to what one might use for dance rather than drama. It facilitated the piece's movement and flow. He also gave a distinctive look to the actor playing Edward by using a follow spot softly focused on his face. This gave him a regal glow wherever he moved on stage. He showed me how to create scenery with lighting."

For two and a half years, Mayer toured throughout the country lighting the Company's productions. "You learn to adapt. You help draw the audience's eye to what you want them to focus on. The key to lighting is visualizing what you want to see. I know I'm not treading new ground when I say that lighting is both art and craft," she says smiling, "but it is important to understand that lighting is a form of artistic expression.

"It is also important for me to understand the emotional and psychological aspects of a piece as well as the historical, literary, and visual allusions which may be employed. Just as actors make a mental inventory of interesting 'characters' they observe in real life, it is important to make a visual inventory of scenes in your everyday life. Museums, libraries, and galleries are obvious sources of inspiration and research.

"Perhaps less obvious is using your own store of emotional memories that you can translate into visual expression. When I was a kid growing up on the San Francisco Peninsula, we had an unobstructed view of the Coast Range Mountains. Every afternoon fingers of fog would crest and roll down the side as the sun set over the ocean. The mystery of the fog, the warmth and color of the setting sun, the reflections off the ocean are memories that have served me well on several projects.

"I don't want to give short shrift to the craft part of the business," she continues. "To me, 'craft' refers to tools and techniques. You need to get all the information you can from equipment manufacturers and trade journals. If a production has the budget, I will order the latest gear. More the norm, though, is what is available and what is affordable, a best-of-the-rest situation. If you know the specs, you will have a good idea of what might do the job and what won't. Experience, of course, makes this process easier.

"Whether it is theater, tape, or film the art/craft approach is still the same. You visualize what you want to see and choose appropriate tools and techniques for the job. It is possible to take a show from theater to television to film without losing the original look and feel. Any number of actors have successfully translated

their stage triumphs into equally successful films. Same performance using different techniques adapted to the medium.

"For example, a drama presented in a large Broadway
proscenium theater might be lit primarily with lekos. They are
long-throw, specifically focusable lights that help delineate the
actors and scenery in a way that allows even those in the back
row of the balcony to clearly discern the action. The actors'
make-up may be exaggerated and their gestures broader to
project their character's expression and intent to the back of the
house.

"If that same play were to be done in a small off-off
Broadway house, the basic unit might be a shorter-throw,
softer, six-inch fresnel. The actors' make-up and body language
would be less exaggerated to reflect the intimacy of the theater
and their proximity to the audience.

"If the play was being taped in a multi-camera, pedestal
boom studio situation, the basic unit might be a 2k ten-inch
fresnel keylight hung off a grid with softlights filling in downstage and smaller fresnels on hangers set off the downstage
corners as eye lights.

"If the same play was to be filmed in a single-camera
studio situation, it might be desirable to do much of the lighting
with fresnels and softlights on stands. The result – same vision,
different tools and techniques."

Jo Mayer came into the business with only one stage
lighting course. All of her knowledge has come from doing and
working with people who were willing to share their experience.
"My first production in Washington was lit with reflector bulbs in
juice cans (tomato juice cans to be exact!) controlled by rotary
household dimmers. I created little light plots and cue sheets and
made mental notes of what design ideas worked and what did
not work. I still make sure I have accurate records of all my work.

"I've always been envious of people who can breeze in
and kind of wing it," she says ruefully. "Careful planning,
preparation, and attention to detail are crucial for me."

When she was touring with the Acting Company, the
sponsor at each stop was supposed to provide a minimum
lighting package. Mayer would call them the week before to find
out what 'minimum' meant to them! "In the midst of constant

travel and set-up, I had to develop a workable plot regardless of the kind of equipment provided," she explains. "I had four hours to get the lighting rigged, so my design choices had to work. There was no time to change them. The only lighting equipment we carried were some inkies, two R-40 strip lights used in *The Robber Bridegroom,* and clip-ons used for running lights – all of which came in handy on more occasions than I care to remember!

"My time with The Company was a fantastic learning experience that would have been hard to duplicate anywhere else," she says. "We would mount our new productions for the season at the Company's summer residency in Saratoga Springs, New York, working with Broadway directors, designers, and choreographers. Once on the road, we adapted to all kinds of theater spaces and all kinds of crews – union, student, prison work-release. . . ," she stops, chuckling at the memory.

"In many places, I was both the first woman stage manager and first woman lighting designer these crews had ever seen. Sometimes they would act like they didn't know what I was talking about. So I would borrow a wrench, scamper up a 20-foot A-frame, focus the light, scamper down and casually ask if there were any questions. Funny how it would all seem to make perfect sense after that!

"David Segal taught me to treat crews in a business-like, respectful manner. Never yell, never react with visible anger, keep everything on a strictly professional level and people will rise to the occasion.

"In my entire experience with the Company, there was only one stop where I had trouble keeping my cool. For some reason, the stagehands in this town related to each other with their own brand of physical bravado. Punching someone really hard was their way of saying hello! The union business agent was missing his two front teeth and halfway through the run the board operator came in with his thumb bandaged and splinted. When I asked him what happened, he said he'd been playing a game with the crew where someone dares you to keep your thumb on the table while they take a swipe at it with a hammer. Apparently, he'd won!

"In any event, by the end of a miserable week's run, I just wanted to load out as quickly as possible. The crew was messing around as usual and I finally snapped. I picked up a wrench, got in the business agent's face and told him in a quiet, firm voice that if he didn't get his crew moving, I was going to knock out the rest of his teeth. He smiled, gave me a hug, and got his men moving double time. If I'd only known the solution at the beginning of the week!

"One of my favorite memories with the Acting Company was a performance of Chekov's *Three Sisters* at a small state college in rural Oklahoma. The whole town was excited that we had come and couldn't wait for the show. They had very little lighting equipment and there wasn't enough room for all of the scenery, but it was one of the Company's best performances. The audience reaction was emotional and overwhelming – it was a great reminder of why I wanted to be in this business in the first place!"

There came a point in Jo Mayer's career when she realized the charm of touring was growing thin. "When I started to think of the Ramada Inn as home, I realized it was time to come off the road," she laughs. Returning to New York, she became a freelance theatrical lighting designer, eventually lighting more than 90 productions. In addition to her own work, she assisted top designers Tharon Musser, Jennifer Tipton, and the late Arden Fingerhut.

She became increasingly interested in television work. "Someone I knew at NBC called someone at ABC and recommended me for the soaps," she recalls. "ABC was expanding their schedule and needed more lighting directors. They wanted to try training a lighting designer with a theatrical background rather than television engineers stuck in a single mode of lighting, as they had in the past."

It was a whole new world. Instead of a two-hour production, repeated nightly, Mayer was now thrown into shooting a complete script – a one-hour show – each day. "A one-hour prime-time dramatic show might take five or more days to shoot," she says, still amazed at what soaps turn out.

"From the beginning, due to good planning, we were given enough equipment and enough crew. What we didn't have was a lot of time! We had, at most, six hours from 3:00 A.M. to 9:00 A.M. to get the job done. I learned to make instant decisions and to think fast on my feet. Fortunately, I had the opportunity to observe such veteran lighting directors as Howard Sharrott, William Itkin, Mel Handelsman, and the late Everett Melosh. They generously shared their knowledge and experience, making my transition from theater to television much easier than it might have been."

There were still big differences between lighting an ABC soap and lighting for the theater. "In the theater, you watch the rehearsal, design the lighting, order equipment," she says. "You give the plot to your master electrician and his crew puts it up for you to focus."

When you are doing a soap at ABC, it can seem a little chaotic. At the top of the light call, you walk in and see the jumble of equipment left from the day before – usually, from an entirely different set. You have to figure out how to get each unit where you need it, as quickly as possible.

"On *One Life to Live,* the original lighting package was based on the saturation concept – 2k fresnels placed at five-foot intervals on every pipe in the studio, with 2k and 6k dimming circuits hung just above. Ideally you could zip through and light a set without having to move a lot of equipment from one part of the studio to another. For the most part, the system worked quite well.

"We had a 17-foot dead-hung grid on 5-foot centers. With additional cross-bars equipped with swivel chesboroughs, we could place a unit precisely where we needed it. The camera aisle ran down the length of the studio with sets on either side and both ends. We ran two lines of softlights down the length of the studio for fill. The 2k 10-inch fresnel was the main unit for cross-keying, back lights, some set and exterior accents. We also had a full compliment of 1k fresnels for eyelights, keylighting tiny sets, or hallways and set lighting accents. Broads, scoops and cyc units were used for backings with lekos, pars and 5ks used to simulate different kinds of window and exterior lighting.

"When I started on the show, we were still using tube cameras. We had to light at 125 footcandles to achieve the F4 iris setting the producers wanted. It was a lot of light. I always focused with sunglasses," she laughs. "It wasn't an affectation it was a necessity. Depending on the camera, you might be lighting at 45 to 50 footcandles for an f4 setting or even less. With the advent of better camera equipment, some soaps are lighting at 20 to 30 footcandles now. Finally no need for sunglasses!"

When asked what other major differences there are between soap and theater lighting, she pauses, laughs and says, "Well, we never had to worry about a sound boom waving around the middle of a theater!

"In the theater," she explains, "sound augmentation was provided by unobtrusive floor, body, or hand-held microphones. On most soaps, audio is picked up by a retractable boom arm on a wheeled pedestal. The microphone at the end of the boom arm should ideally be no further than two feet from the actor who is speaking. That means the boom arm needs to follow the actor around the set.

"If there is more than one actor in the scene, a second boom will often be added. To prevent the booms from shadowing the actors or the set in a particular camera shot, key lights are brought in from upstage so any shadows will fall downstage out of camera range. Eyelights are hung low-enough to get underneath the boom. Still, no matter how well-planned, there are always situations which require major compromises for both lighting and audio.

"Another big challenge for me, coming from the theater, was anticipating what the camera would see," Mayer continues. "Or, I should say, what five cameras would see. We had five cameras shooting every scene. We would have upwards of 400 shots per show and the lighting director is responsible for making them all look great!

"We needed to provide pleasing lighting for the actors while maintaining appropriate set lighting consistent with the mood and tone of the scene," she adds. "We also had to be judicious in the use of color. In the theater, most lights are gelled and color blended based on what is seen by the naked eye. On tape, as in film, you have to be aware of color temperature, as well as how a particular color will register on camera.

"There were two lighting directors on One Life to Live who would light every other day. "On my 'meeting,' I would see the director and go over the shots and the actors' blocking for the following day," she explains. Due to time constraints, we would light to the acting marks, keeping in mind the shots and the boom, the actor(s) who would be standing there, time of day in the set, special light cues or lighting requirements that had been requested.

"During my time on the show, I had a couple of different partners," she adds. "Fortunately, we agreed on how the show should look and tried to maintain a consistent visual style from day to day. Since we would shoot approximately 260 episodes a year, the everyday routine allowed the lighting, camera, audio, and video departments to work as a team, automatically solving problems which might halt production on other kinds of shows."

As the soaps soared in popularity and producers and writers looked for ways to expand their productions past the same four walls, remote shoots came in. "We did a lot of single camera remotes which allowed me to experiment with film lighting. I would haunt the equipment rental companies looking through the dusty shelves in back," she laughs. "I found some miniature 18-inch square gold and silver leaf reflectors, mounts, some strange little battery powered sun guns and other grip oddities they had forgotten they owned. These little throw-aways came in very handy on a couple of occasions."

Mayer's first remote took place in different locations around a railroad yard. One scene had the two stars jumping off a bridge onto a small, open, sand-filled rail car moving underneath. The jump shot worked fine, but the rest of the scene in the moving sand car presented several problems. "We were losing optimum sun position," she recalls. "Once the car started moving, we had to start shooting immediately or we would run out of track before the scene was done.

"There was almost no room to light the actors' close-ups once the camera operator, director, and I were in the car. The oddball grip mounts worked like custom grips on the side of the car with the diffused sun guns on top. The 18-inch reflectors and a piece of foam core anchored in the sand completed the rig."

On another remote, in New Paltz, New York, Mayer faced a somewhat different problem. "We were on some boulders jutting off the side of a mountain, shooting a good guy/bad guy confrontation," she recalls. "This area was popular with mountain climbers and featured a 100-foot drop past our little outcropping. We only had enough portable power for a couple of small HMIs. Because of wind, lack of space, lack of time, and the real possibility of people and gear falling down the mountain, there was no way we could use any regular-scale grip equipment. Once again, those little 18-inch reflectors worked perfectly. Big and sturdy enough to do the job, small enough to be used in the space available.

Over the years, shooting schedules changed and so did the time lighting directors like Jo Mayer had to prepare a show. "There would be a dry rehearsal the actors, in a downstairs rehearsal room from about 7:30 A.M. to 9:30 A.M. Camera blocking followed, with a break for lunch at 12:30 P.M. After lunch, a dress rehearsal was followed by producers' notes and the taping of the episode. When I first started, we would tape the show as if live. As soon as we started taping, we would stop only during the scheduled commercial breaks. This stricture was eventually relaxed to allow additional takes if necessary. The value of this system was that I had the opportunity to fix and touch-up during blocking, knowing I had another opportunity after run-through.

"These days, they block and tape, scene by scene, from the top of the day," she continues. "You have to try to anticipate every problem, knowing there won't be much time to fine-tune. Still, there are some very talented lighting directors creating terrific pictures under constant pressure and often trying circumstances."

The years of long hours took their toll on Mayer, who decided it was time to move on to something new. She moved from soaps to Good Morning, America. "The 5:30 A.M. call was like sleeping in after so many years of 3 A.M. calls. I joined the show at an exciting time," she says. "We had a new co-host and a new set. They wanted to have the set feel like a New York loft. We had several different interview/performance areas, which included specialized kitchen and weather map areas in the sets.

"On *GMA* the goal was to create a lighting design requiring minimal refocusing day-to-day. We needed a look that would make the hosts and guests look great, provide the kind of ambience they wanted for the set, and have enough built-in flexibility to accommodate musical performances, demos, etc."

Although the kind of lighting equipment used for both soaps and talk shows might be the same, Mayer points out other distinct differences. "In soaps, the camera is rarely straight on to the actor and usually emulates the height and position of the character to whom the actor is speaking," she says. In a show like *GMA*, the opposite is true. The talent address the camera directly and are photographed full face at eye level.

"Also, since everyone has lavaliere mikes, you don't have to worry about lighting around a sound boom. All key lighting was diffused and brought in on hangers as low as possible. The height of the keys was just out of the top camera frame when taking wide shots from one end of the studio to the other. Set lighting was much the same technique as on the soaps.

"Speaking of the set," she continues, "when it was first designed, I noticed that the breakfast nook was distinguished by a narrow room divider that looked like a porch-rail supported by two columns with an ornate arch on top. The columns were so tall, I knew the arch would never be seen because we would shoot off the top of the surrounding set.

"When I spoke to the set designer, I asked if he could cut it out of the design before the set was built. He assured me it would be hinged for removal later. Unfortunately, the shop built the arch and columns as one piece. It was a real headache to light around, but the director insisted the arch had to stay.

"When that director moved to another show, the first thing I did was get permission to saw off the arch. The set decorator put a big red bow around it, we loaded it into a cab, and left it with the doorman in the director's apartment building, making sure the tag with the guy's name was prominently displayed!"

Mayer's work on this show garnered her Emmy nominations for 1988 and 1989. However, since the *GMA* sets generally remained unchanged for years at a time, the lighting challenges were minimal once the standing sets were lit.

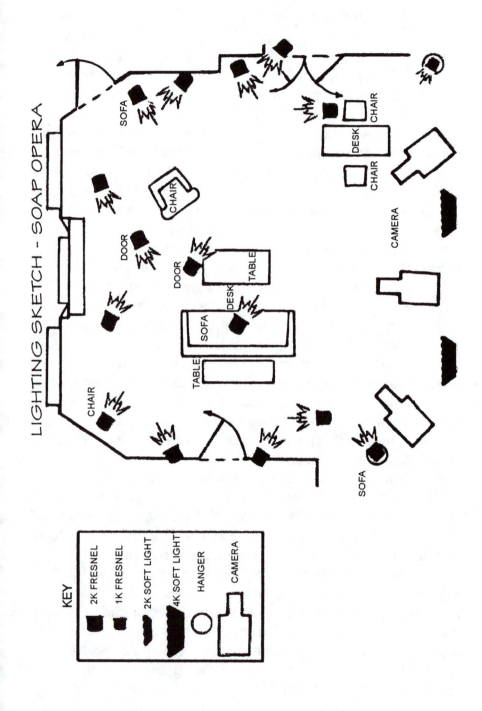

LIGHTING SKETCH - SOAP OPERA

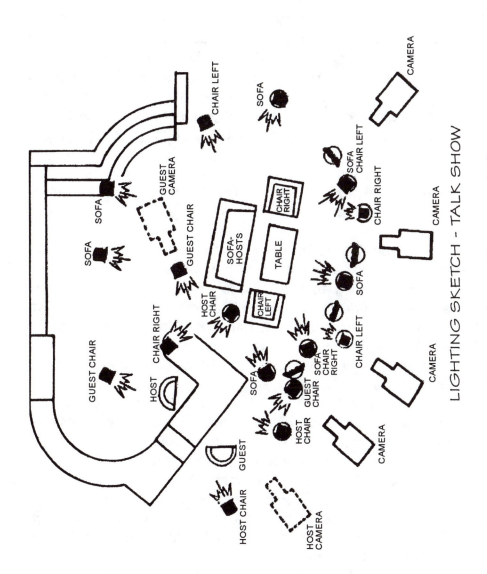

LIGHTING SKETCH - TALK SHOW

In 1989, Mayer moved to Los Angeles to try her hand at sitcoms. "On soaps, you don't necessarily have the time to employ a lot of the grip equipment (flags, silks, nets, cutters, etc.) that are commonplace in film," she says. "Once again, I was very lucky that I had the opportunity to learn about film lighting technique from some very generous DPs like Alan Walker, Donald A. Morgan, George Spiro Dibie, and Tony Askins."

When Alan Walker began doing a multi-camera comedy show called *Grand*, the veteran lighting director brought Mayer in to work with him. The two worked hard at creating the show's filmic look.

"Although the show was shot on tape, the producers wanted it to look as much like film as possible. We used Tiffen low-con filters and an iris at f2.8 to soften the picture and allow us more latitude in contrast ratios without losing detail. We wanted to give the show a naturalistic look using as many motivating light sources as we could. The low-cons allowed us to make the windows and practicals comparatively bright without distorting the video.

"Our wonderful production designer, Garvin Eddy, and his assistant, Jerry Dunn (now a production designer in his own right), knew exactly what we needed to make the concept work. They provided us with sets that were not only architecturally interesting, but contained contrasting and textured wall treatments and trim, with set dressing and practicals that provided the detail and accents needed to pull the picture together. In video, it is important to have bits of contrasting color within the shot to make the pictures pop.

"We installed a dead-hung pipe hung on four-foot centers at 16-and-a half feet. We had so many sets coming in on a weekly basis that there wasn't room for them all! We had some constructed on wheeled wagons containing their own light grid which would be rolled on during the show.

"Keylighting on hangers was brought in just above the set walls," she continues. "Set lighting was separate. In fact, we made judicious use of flags, fingers, dots, cutters, black wrap, and art card to minimize any keylight or ambient light hitting the walls.

"We also made foam core hoods for softlights and employed the usual assortment of nets and silks as necessary. We needed both control and flexibility so we installed a dimming system using socaplex cabling. This allowed us to power the self-contained wagon lighting quickly, and gave us the one-to-one dimming capability we wanted."

Although Alan Walker went on to other projects after the third episode, Mayer stayed on. In that short time, he had given her a crash course in how things worked in Los Angeles, and invaluable insights from his years of lighting and photography.

By the early 1990s, sitcom lighting had begun to change. At least Jo Mayer and a few others were trying to change it. "I was surprised to find out that there were both filmed and taped multi-camera sitcoms that were being done on D.C. powered stages with little in the way of dimming," she says. "This was nothing new to the guys who had come up through single-camera film, but it was a serious problem for me."

Theatrical dimming systems have been in existence since the turn of the century and that was my tradition! I felt I couldn't do the kind of lighting I wanted to in a multi-camera situation without the flexibility of a dimming system. Although they are commonplace now, asking for an AC dimming system on certain lots, just a few years ago, was a very big deal.

Some old-timers thought it was unnecessary, new-fangled technology that would cause nothing but trouble. Fortunately, as more and more DPs on major films started requesting dimming systems for their time-saving flexibility, the issue became moot."

When Jo Mayer is asked if she can be demanding, "Certainly," she replies. "I want the show to look as good as possible and I can be a real stickler for details. Generally, producers will hire the crew I request. The people who work with me know that I value their contribution and that I couldn't do it without them. When I first came to Los Angeles, some of the crew people thought I was a little too meticulous, but they went along with it anyway. In the end, they could see that all the little details added up to a much improved look. Do I still drive them a little crazy sometimes? I'm sure I do, but I want the results to reflect our best efforts."

Mayer gets very quiet. Outside the house, the dogs start barking loudly and run down the road out of ear-shot. It is very quiet – just the rustle of leaves. In this little hamlet, hustle and bustle are a rare phenomenon. It is a place for peace and decision-making – a place to get away from the frenzy of the studios and the freeways.

"I got into lighting because I wanted to help create that 'magic' moment when the audience is not only entertained, but moved, informed, and, hopefully, changed in a positive way by what they've seen and experienced. My job is to create a visual environment that best supports the connection between the actor and audience, an environment in which that magic can occur."

For the past six or seven years, that is what Jo Mayer has tried to bring to the sitcom world. She has done many pilots and series including *Grand, Phenom, Local Heroes, Franie's Turn, The Wayans Brothers*, and the second season of *Davis Rules*, for which she received an Emmy nomination.

"The television business has changed considerably in the last few years," she reflects. "I have worked on some very special projects with some highly creative and accomplished actors, writers, and producers," she says. "They've been willing to take artistic risks and tweak sitcom conventions. We put a lot of care and energy into *Grand, Davis Rules*, and *Phenom*, my favorite projects, and it showed.

"Today, an increase in the number of broadcast venues has created an increased demand for programming. Due to changes in the industry's financial structure, there is also increased financial risk for production companies. Does a company want to try something risky and new, or go with something based on a formula that has worked before?

"Personally, it is disappointing to work on a series that can't get through the first 13 episodes without rewriting *I Love Lucy* storylines. The audience may still laugh and the show might succeed, but the spark of originality is missing. I enjoy working on projects that have the potential for more than just a couple of obvious yuks. Although there are some wonderful shows on the air, those that are original, well-written, and well-produced are in the minority.

"I'm still interested in lighting original, creative projects, but I've come to realize that it is time for me to move from creating the environment to creating the project! The skills that I have learned through designing and lighting are highly adaptable to the challenges of producing and directing. Although I'm not planning to give up lighting in the foreseeable future, I am excited about expanding into new areas of opportunity."

She has also formed a production company to find, develop, and produce the kinds of stories that she hopes will create the magic that inspired her to become a part of this industry in the first place.

******

1984 Adelco Award *The Beautiful LaSalles* – **1992 Emmy Award Nomination** *Davis Rules* – **1988, 1989 Emmy Award Nominations** *Good Morning, America* – **1981, 1983, 1985, 1986 Emmy Nominations** *One Life to Live*

"I never went to school for this. I just picked things up as I went along. There is nothing wrong with looking and listening, but a solid foundation is just as and even more important. I guess, violating the 'this is the way it is' rules stirred things up. For the most part, the newer lighting designers were stretching the limits as well. I just became the focus of attention."

Donald A. Morgan

The traffic in the air is fairly light, the streets below uncrowded. It is a pleasant morning's ride past Burbank Airport to the small but active industrial park where the Axel stages are located.

Drive inside the padded main stage and all noise disappears. Follow the click of metal against metal to a small electrical closet in the corner to find two jeans-clad legs protruding from the darkness.

"Be with you in a minute," comes from the closet depths. "We've got Yanni coming in for a few weeks of rehearsal before his national tour, and we aren't up to full power yet."

A moment later, tool belt looped around his waist, electrical cord and plugs in hand, six time Emmy Award winning cinematographer, Donald A. Morgan steps out of the closet, a smile on his face. "What? You mean the tools? You forget, I started out in electrical. It's like a bicycle, something you never forget."

Morgan tries to find a quiet spot in the midst of the new facility. Axel is his second behind-the-scenes endeavor. Down the street, Shades of Light, his first production studio, is booked solid for months in advance. "It's just another form of expanding what I do," he comments when queried about the facilities.

"Don't mistake these businesses for disillusionment with the industry. I will always want to be a lighting designer and cinematographer. But someday, when *Home Improvement* does go down and there isn't a quality show available, I'll be here doing what I love. It will just be in another venue."

Although Donald A. Morgan has been in the business for over 25 years, he still has the enthusiasm of a kid in a candy store. He might be dissatisfied with the way the content of the multi-camera format is going (camera equipment for film format is changing to pedestal versus the conventional tried and proven three man with dolly process), but his enjoyment of capturing the elements for the small screen hasn't wavered. "Laughter is part of life," he says. "Being able to make it look real is and always will be a fascinating part of the art of cinematography."

He settles into the corner of a couch and glares at his pager as it beeps just as he begins another thought. He checks the message, apologizes, and reaches for his cell phone. "Even when I have a day off, I don't have a day off," he says.

The call is about a new pilot he will be shooting. Details about new film style lighting on this half-hour comedy. He throws the cell phone on the coffee table and settles back to explain his career.

Morgan began as a graphic arts/architecture major, then segued into printing. "Who knew working with color separation would come in handy years later, when I began lighting shows like *Good Times*?" he laughs. In the mid-1970s, young people were flocking to the West Coast to "get into the business." Morgan wanted to be a musician, however, he had to eat. So, he "worked" to pay the rent and "worked" for his soul in the evening. That all changed, when a roommate introduced him to television. He began in the mail room of KTTV, a local station in Southern California. "What I learned about f-stops and light measurements in college helped me immensely in television production," he says.

However, he learned that making the rounds with a cart wasn't always about delivering mail. "Running mail through a major studio is a great way to meet industry people," he adds. Television comedy was just starting to bloom. "I saw Norman Lear (*Maude, All in the Family, Silver Spoons, The Jeffersons*) almost every day. It was also the era of big musical variety specials, i.e., *Barishnikoff on Broadway, Soul Train.* Back then, we worked with only four stages for all of this sitcom production. So, when one show wrapped in the evening the stage would go into turn around. Which meant we would wrap out the existing sets and replace them with an entirely new show on the same stage." It was a great training ground and the way Morgan admits he developed his speed.

Soon, Lear's company offered him a solid job with a certain future, working in the computer room. "What excited me was being on stage. The first time I saw what lighting consultants George Schamp and his brother Tommy could do with a cold, blank stage something clicked," he recalls. "Whatever it took, I was going to learn lighting."

In the 1970s, television stations had a successful system going. Their staff could work a variety of jobs. One day Morgan would be a gaffer and the next an electrician. "This is a great way to develop a basic knowledge of what goes on during a shoot," Morgan stresses. That knowledge, he believes, should extend beyond the mechanics. In his position as a Director of Photography, he bids the job, or at least informs the production manager what the costs will be. "That is where money and people managing skills can come in," he says. "Even when I am teaching my lighting class at UCLA, I have learned to have patience and be more tolerant with my students. This all stems from helping my children with their homework."

At Metromedia Studios, various lighting designers worked with their in-house staff. This is where Morgan watched George Spiro Dibie (*Barney Miller*) create a new sitcom style – softer and more diffused light – and saw how Bill Klages and John Rook lit variety and award shows.

"I began to realize that the hard light used on a KTTV shoot wasn't the only device available," he says. "We worked on stages that were about 70 by 100 feet with typical television lighting. When we did *Three's Company* or *The Jeffersons*, the standard positions for the old Norelco pedestal cameras was two facing straight in and two from the side. Shadows on the back walls, even harder shadows if they wanted to get light into the eyes, were also typical. We shot with two-inch tape. Both camera and tape stock needed a lot of light. With 200 footcandles, we would often fry the actors." Today Morgan and other multi-camera cinematographers average about 60 footcandles. "A lot less heat, but no less light because they use more units, at a lower temperature.

"When the visiting lighting designers came in, they added a few things that would finesse a shot," he says. "It was more than the standard 2k for back cross, 5k to throw light farther away, and 10ks to pump in even more light. That was hard light, which translates ultimately to a harder video look.

"Suddenly, there was a little color. John Rook would put a hole the size of a quarter in the middle of a gel on the front key and it would create a white center light for the actor's face and have color drop off at their shoulders, a beautiful effect for concerts and variety shows. And, there was the antitheses of these tools – soft light. By using diffusion, frost, and a front row bounce fill for entire sets, I began to see what had been wasn't written in stone."

Morgan began to experiment in his mind. When local television shows working out of KTTV needed a lighting director for interviews, he would try something a little different. "Having the power to say 'bring this up' or 'take that down' was a great feeling."

When he went back to the meat and potatoes shows, however, it was the traditional lighting on a pipe system that is still used today. Because of the way a stage was, and still is, laid out, the lights were rigged to a series of rails with counterweights. This enabled the networks to bring several different shows into the same set and re-light each for the style that they felt fit the product.

For many, the piping system is cumbersome. (This rig is of overhead pipes dead hung – flush to the ceiling, no catwalks or greenbeds.) Once a show's sets are cleared from the stage area, the pipes are literally lowered to the deck via counter weights and pulleys, and the lighting designer can hang any types of lights he/she wants anywhere he/she wants them.

"Then they are pulled back up to the ceiling," Morgan explains. "You better have your lighting plot right, because it takes time, energy, and money to bring the pipes down or move the furniture to get a manlift or ladder in to make a change."

Turn around time was usually two days. A show shot on a Tuesday would be broken down as soon as the lights were turned off. A grip crew would come in and take the lights off the pipes. Electric would then come in and drop them to the floor, rearranging the lighting according to the plot for the next show.

"When the map was finished, we'd fly the lights up and bring the sets in," Morgan explains. "By Thursday, we'd have a completely different rig. That's the way it was," he says simply. "We didn't know from dead hung or greenbeds (wood rafters wide enough for crew members to walk on), where we could move one light without disturbing the rest. Both of these other techniques were used on features. Even touch on the subject of change and your standard answer was 'this isn't a feature set' or 'we don't do it that way.'"

This was the first time Donald A. Morgan came up against what is often called the "old rule." For the most part, the "veterans" wanted to stick with what worked. Fear of the unknown was in control. "Things were changing rapidly in front of the camera," Morgan concedes. "Who knows? Maybe once the format became familiar, some of these people would look up and realize there was another way to do things.

"Today, if I had the time, I would put beds in," Morgan concedes. "Not only are they helpful when dealing with the boom's position, they also allow you to finesse the lighting on a standing or swing set. However, because of the urgency of so many projects, we don't address the idea unless we know a show is going more than 13 weeks."

In the burgeoning era of multi-camera television, the idea of finesse was a dirty word. It wasn't just the Norman Lear shows (*Three's Company*, etc.) that followed the edict "brighter is funnier," everyone had adopted that idea. "The Schamp brothers came from that bright Kinescope background," Morgan adds, snapping off his pager as it sings once again. "Overall contrast might be okay, as long as the shots were also overall bright."

Suddenly, the "situation comedy" began to fill the airwaves. Lear's company began producing shows like *Maude* and *Hot'l Baltimore*. "The basic lighting tree was back crosses, hard light from the key coming in center stage, Juniors in the center, and two Juniors facing the doors," he explains. "You had a flotilla of light that was head high with two slots for the booms. That's all we knew how to do. True, the actors could move wherever they wanted without a really bad shadow. We would balance them out as much as we could, and still let Norman see the joke."

Morgan admits he was young and eager. His mind didn't stop. While out on a location with lighting designer Bill Klages, he began to see what single camera lighting meant to a shot.

"I started to think what if," he says. "I would watch the old black-and-white movies, to see how they lit their actors. I saw Cookes on the back walls and dramatic-type lighting without the light actually hitting the walls. That's what I wanted to do. I wanted to find a way to accommodate both the 'old guard' and still give a show a little edge by lighting the faces."

Morgan got up the gumption to begin drawing his own plots. One day, he handed his sketch to Tommy Schamp. "Tommy took one look at it and sort of growled," he remembers. "'It can be great on paper, kid, but it doesn't mean shit until you get out there and do it,' he told me. I thought I was doomed. That is, until, a few weeks later. I was walking across the lot and Tommy slapped a lighting plot on my chest. It was for my new show!"

Morgan's immediate reaction was to put his plan into play right away. Not only would he take light off the walls and give the actors' faces more attention, he wanted to show the production designer's sets as well. To him, that element is as much a part of the story as the performance. "It had to be done carefully," he admits. "*Another Day* starring Joan Hackett and David Grogh was my first baby. Was I going to stick with the *All in the Family* style, never coming in full face, always half, and lighting for side upstage only? That way, the light and shadow dictated the actor's position. Or, was I going to take light off the walls?"

Morgan found a happy medium. Not sure what he could get away with, he began taking light off the walls and still kept the hard key in front. He also began to develop his own style of interaction with crew and cast. The division between the way tape and film production is today hadn't yet developed. Today, a lighting designer for a tape show is often confined to a booth or in a truck outside the stage. That designer has little interaction with the actors or cameras. Multi-camera film cinematographers are right on the floor, as the single-camera feature cinematographer was in the early days. They can work with the actors and will also assist the director in camera placement, angles and lenses.

"Wherever we parked, we still interacted with the cast," Morgan remembers. "I remember one of my first conversations with Joan Hackett, who comes from a stage background. She was concerned with her look. 'Whatever you do, make me look good,' she said. I took the time to show her where her upstage key would be and what we were doing for our basic lighting concept. She picked up on the multi-camera style immediately. It became a cooperative effort."

"After 21 episodes, *Another Day* went off the air. Producer Norman Lear had created a new and revolutionary show called *Good Times*. "Did I feel pressure? Of course," he laughs. "Was there additional pressure because I was the first black man to helm an all black show? Not at that point. When Norman Lear created *Good Times* and turned it over to me, the color of my skin was not a factor. The environment at his company was wonderful. There was no such thing as color or religion or even the gender factor. If you worked hard, showed an interest, and had the talent you moved up. You moved around. In my area, we weren't pinned to one job. We were electricians four days, then lighting designers three days. We learned the intimate details of our equipment. I've always been grateful for that background experience."

While floating around KTTV, Morgan had watched many different directors and cinematographers work The Paulist Productions shows, deeply dramatic and emotional, often featured directors like Delbert Mann. Each of the in-house lighting designers was given one of these shows to light. "It was like a student project," Morgan recalls. "This is where I could try the 1940s stuff. I would mold walls and hard light cross key, but wrap it around to where it was the three-quarter fill you would see on a Paramount feature."

Because of the Union, when film companies came in to use the facility an in-house lighting director would have to be available. Morgan would watch John Alonzo light projects at 100 footcandles. *China Syndrome's* James Crabe worked with low light and did hand held moves. Although the stock they used was more-or-less a secret, Morgan still asked questions and got answers. Answers that helped when he went into *Good Times*.

He wasn't the first lighting designer on *Good Times*. Several had contributed to the look. At the same time he was doing this comedy, he was also working on another show at the same studio. *Different Strokes* might have been on the same lot, but had a totally different rig. "At first I began *Good Times* using what was there," Morgan comments.

The major difference Morgan began to make was in lighting the actors. "Was I able to light black faces because I had a better knowledge of the differences? Yes and no," Morgan comments. To him, the question isn't offensive. Too often he has found that denying there is a difference is tantamount to reverse discrimination. There is a difference in lighting on black faces and it has less to do with pigmentation than with reflection. Oftentimes, lighting people will be more concerned with the color factor, forgetting the range of pigmentation in make-up encompasses a wide color palette.

"When lighting black people you need to learn more about *light*," Morgan says. "'Highlighting,' to be exact. It is how and where you place or bounce the light that makes a difference.

"At the time, spun glass was being used as a diffusion filter. (Spun glass is no longer allowed, it is far too dangerous). "Tommy taught me to use tough spun," he says.

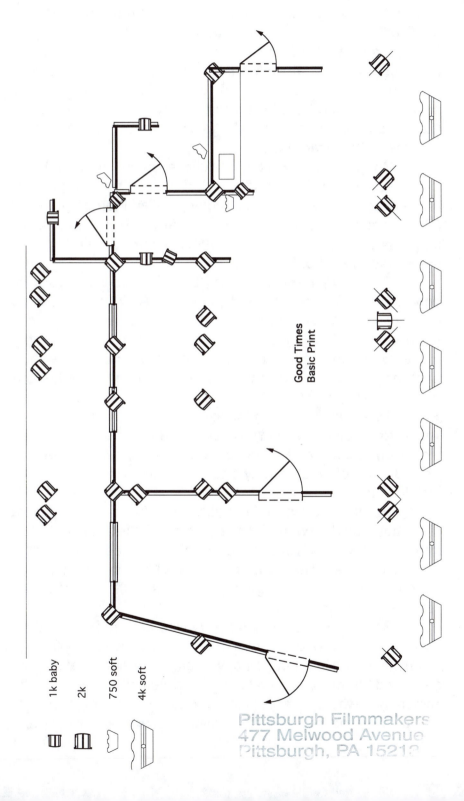

Good Times
Basic Print

1k baby

2k

750 soft

4k soft

"Another black lighting designer was also experimenting with the filter. Walt Glover worked with back crosses and hard light. The spread was the trick. Tough spun needed 80 footcandles from up stage. What he would do is tighten in on the hard light. By giving the set only 70 footcandles of hard light, he could really make the black skin pop." Although he would still like to use the tough spun, Morgan has moved on to using a 216 filter. "It's softer and bigger," he says.

Morgan was definitely making a name for himself. "At the time, Norman Lear had left KTTV, and Tommy Schamp had moved over to Universal. Schamp called Morgan. If he left KTTV immediately, he could get his card at Universal. Again, Morgan took the chance. He quit his staff position at the studio and moved onto a major lot.

That is when reality hit him full in the face. Things were done quite differently on a Union lot. "At 7:00 A.M. on a Monday morning, Morgan showed up at Universal to do a show called *Silver Spoons*. He was to replace a cinematographer who had decided to get out of the business. The show had been set up. Morgan was expected to continue the look that had been established.

"I was a kid out of a fairyland," Morgan admits. "I didn't know from politics. I didn't know from egos. All I knew was what worked for me. As I looked at the swing set of a boat, all I could think of was Tommy's words. 'Don't listen to anyone, just do your thing.'

"What I saw would probably work for a single-camera shot, but wouldn't work for the boom. I asked the gaffer to strike several units." Suddenly, the air was filled with tension. "I set the lights." That was the gaffer. "I am in charge," was Morgan's answer. The gaffer left in a huff. Morgan had stomped on his territory.

Morgan inadvertently made waves on yet another show under his care. *Gloria* was one of the first shows to do off-stage segments for each show. "I'll never forget our first location. The gaffer and key grip came up to me and asked where I wanted the camera and where I wanted the truck parked," he laughs. "Up to that point, I had never been involved in camera placement. If

(For cards outside the US please affix a postage stamp)

BUSINESS REPLY MAIL

FIRST CLASS MAIL   PERMIT NO. 78   WOBURN, MA

POSTAGE WILL BE PAID BY ADDRESSEE

DIRECT MAIL DEPARTMENT
BUTTERWORTH-HEINEMANN
225 WILDWOOD AVE
PO BOX 4500
WOBURN MA 01888-9930

At Butterworth-Heinemann, we are dedicated to providing you with quality service. So that we may keep you informed about titles relevant to your field of interest, please fill in the information below and return this postage-paid reply card. Thank you for your help, and we look forward to hearing from you!

What title have you purchased? |⎵⎵⎵⎵⎵⎵⎵⎵⎵⎵⎵⎵⎵⎵⎵⎵⎵⎵⎵⎵⎵⎵⎵⎵⎵⎵⎵⎵⎵⎵⎵⎵⎵⎵⎵|

Where was the purchase made? |⎵⎵⎵⎵⎵⎵⎵⎵⎵⎵⎵⎵⎵⎵⎵⎵⎵⎵⎵⎵⎵⎵⎵⎵⎵⎵⎵⎵⎵⎵⎵⎵⎵⎵⎵|

Name |⎵⎵⎵⎵⎵⎵⎵⎵⎵⎵⎵⎵⎵⎵⎵⎵⎵⎵⎵⎵⎵⎵⎵⎵⎵⎵⎵⎵⎵⎵⎵⎵⎵⎵⎵|

Job Title |⎵⎵⎵⎵⎵⎵⎵⎵⎵⎵⎵⎵⎵⎵⎵⎵⎵⎵⎵⎵⎵⎵⎵⎵⎵⎵⎵⎵⎵⎵⎵⎵⎵⎵⎵|

Institution |⎵⎵⎵⎵⎵⎵⎵⎵⎵⎵⎵⎵⎵⎵⎵⎵⎵⎵⎵⎵⎵⎵⎵⎵⎵⎵⎵⎵⎵⎵⎵⎵⎵⎵⎵|

Address |⎵⎵⎵⎵⎵⎵⎵⎵⎵⎵⎵⎵⎵⎵⎵⎵⎵⎵⎵⎵⎵⎵⎵⎵⎵⎵⎵⎵⎵⎵⎵⎵⎵⎵⎵|

Town/City |⎵⎵⎵⎵⎵⎵⎵⎵⎵⎵⎵⎵⎵⎵⎵⎵⎵⎵⎵⎵⎵⎵⎵⎵⎵⎵⎵⎵⎵⎵⎵⎵⎵⎵⎵|

State/County |⎵⎵⎵⎵⎵⎵⎵⎵⎵⎵⎵⎵⎵⎵⎵⎵⎵⎵⎵⎵⎵⎵⎵⎵⎵⎵⎵⎵⎵⎵⎵⎵⎵⎵⎵|

Zip/Postcode |⎵⎵⎵⎵⎵⎵⎵⎵⎵⎵⎵⎵⎵⎵⎵⎵⎵⎵⎵⎵⎵⎵⎵⎵⎵⎵⎵⎵⎵⎵⎵⎵⎵⎵⎵|

Country |⎵⎵⎵⎵⎵⎵⎵⎵⎵⎵⎵⎵⎵⎵⎵⎵⎵⎵⎵⎵⎵⎵⎵⎵⎵⎵⎵⎵⎵⎵⎵⎵⎵⎵⎵|

Telephone |⎵⎵⎵⎵⎵⎵⎵⎵⎵⎵⎵⎵⎵⎵⎵⎵⎵⎵⎵⎵⎵⎵⎵⎵⎵⎵⎵⎵⎵⎵⎵⎵⎵⎵⎵|

email |⎵⎵⎵⎵⎵⎵⎵⎵⎵⎵⎵⎵⎵⎵⎵⎵⎵⎵⎵⎵⎵⎵⎵⎵⎵⎵⎵⎵⎵⎵⎵⎵⎵⎵⎵|

☐ Please keep me informed about other books and information services on this and related subjects.

(FOR OFFICE USE ONLY)

BUTTERWORTH-HEINEMANN IS ON THE WEB – http://www.bh.com/

US1

they were going to get me, that was my Achilles heel. Fortunately, the camera operator was a friend. He called me over and literally walked me through the shot."

Suddenly, Morgan's desk was covered with books. After years on a lot, he began to learn the job of a cinematographer. Placement of the camera was a good part of the job description in the real world. Even here, he began to be innovative. Now he was doing wild things like wetting down the street to take the f-stop down. This helped the video, since tape didn't have the latitude to keep in the proper range. On the set, he used a lot more bounce light, overhead fill light, and tried to add Muslin as a top light. He still kept the traditional front keys.

Word got around. There was a black cinematographer on the back lot and he was making trouble. "I had graduated from the protective world of Norman Lear's school and into the firepit," Morgan admits. "I never went to school for this. I just picked things up as I went along. There is nothing wrong with looking and listening, but a solid foundation is just as and even more important. I guess violating the 'this is the way it is' rules stirred things up. For the most part, the newer lighting designers were stretching the limits as well. I just became the focus of attention."

Part of the problem was that Morgan had violated the system from another direction. He came in from the outside. At this time, the Union had a stranglehold on the industry. You had to be a member to work on a major lot. To be a member, you had to come up through the ranks. In fairness to those in control, this was a leftover from the old studio system where employees were protected, jobs secure.

However, this did not allow for growth. The industry was changing as fast as the equipment was being developed. Faster film and tape stocks, better and lighter cameras, sharper lenses were giving the younger people alternative ways of shooting. The "settled" crowd was not as receptive to change. When young up and comers like Donald A. Morgan began to strut their stuff, the "old boys' network" closed ranks.

"I was told that if I was to be let into the Union, I would have to start as a Class 1," Morgan explains. That meant

Morgan would have to be a loader for a period of years and wait until a spot as an assistant, then as an operator would be available.

That wasn't acceptable and, for the most part, the Universal hierarchy was behind him. Donald A. Morgan and a few of his contemporaries were changing the face of television. "The business agents weren't user-friendly at that time," he comments. "'That's the way it was done, and we aren't going to change it. If we let you light, then you will be knocking one of our boys out of a job.'"

For a while, Morgan would set up a show and someone else would take over. There was the vague hope that someone would bend. Finally, things came to a head. The Union threatened to close down Universal if he continued to work.

Morgan left Universal and went to work at ABC, despite the fact that another maverick by the name of George Spiro Dibie was just coming in as President of the Union. His efforts at modernization began to crush the old Union's stranglehold. Not in time, however, to help Morgan stay at Universal.

"In a way, the move to ABC was better," Morgan admits. "There were a few people who were changing the face of lighting. Richard Hissong on *Soap* and Allen Walker on *Benson* were among the first to do away with the front key light. They were putting soft light across the front downstage of the set."

Walk on one of those sets and the first thing you would see was that the 2ks rigged to stirrup hangers were gone. Instead, bigger and softer lights like Mole Richardson 4k Tungsten lights had been brought in. Instead of using the standard five Juniors, these lighting designers were using two Juniors and three soft lights side by side. They would then blend the light with egg crates and teasers to keep light off the walls.

"When I saw this, I almost shouted that it was about time," Morgan laughs. It was then that Morgan knew he didn't have to censor himself or hold back. His first show for ABC was a variety special starring Rodney Dangerfield. "Even before I put one light in, I had to pass a test," he recalls. "I was told that they had to see 150 footcandles on the chart. I did it my way."

A chart is a simple device that tests the registration of cameras. Before a show is lit, each camera focuses on this black-and-white device. The video man tells the lighting designer how much he wants and the lighting designer puts it in. "My challengers came in and took a look at the chart and the lights I had used and reacted," Morgan recalls. "There was no way I had given them 150 footcandles. I didn't back down, but challenged them. As they stepped up to the chart, their meter read 150 footcandles on the nose."

Morgan's challengers backed off and he was able to work with some of the newer, outside cinematographers. "George Spiro Dibie was doing *Barney Miller* at the time. He brought an incredible energy to these shows," Morgan says. "He also brought color, filters, and a device he created called the 'Dibie net.' This device is located behind the camera lens and softens the image captured on film."

Morgan set up a new show called *Mr. Belvedere* and Dibie took over. For the pilot episode, Morgan, the new kid on the bloc, shared a 1985 Emmy for multi-camera television lighting.

He began to be noticed for his lighting on every kind of skin tone. "I learned to finesse dark skin on *Good Times* and perfected it a little more on *The Jeffersons*," he says. "It became more than highlighting, it became a matter of the mixtures of light."

Maybe it was because he lived with the subtle differences all his life. Or, just maybe, because he had an open mind and treated each character as a unique entity. He always felt that actor Robert Guilliame wasn't lit as effectively as could be on *Benson*. When he took over that show, he worked out subtle changes to make the star stand out. "I added a hard back light and rim light for separation," he explains.

"White cinematographers weren't learning as much about tone and pigmentation as they should have," he adds. "For the most part, their only experience with the radical differences in black faces had been on dance shows. When

John Rooke lit big specials, like the *Live at the Apollo* shows, he stuck to only certain colors. That was his background. George Spiro Dibie's multi-camera look came from a different source – a filmic source. What he did with color couldn't have been done on a dance show. I just found a way to blend the two styles."

It is more than an actor with a different make-up job. It is texture. Morgan took his earlier idea of highlighting the next natural step and he carried that extra punch to another challenging show called *The Golden Girls*. "Older faces have different problems than black faces," he concedes, "However, in theory, the same changes hold true for both. Tape people put up a major resistance to the natural film techniques like softening the camera. Going to a faster stock is also another possibility. That, too, met with resistance."

Morgan and his fellow mavericks began to look at things in a radically different way. "What was good for the story and the actors was more important than an arc is an arc and that's what we use."

When Morgan took control of a set, no one could change it. Many walked out, but even more began to watch what he and a few others were doing. The changes came rapidly. Morgan began lighting a variety of different multi-camera shows and even segued into the afternoon venue, lighting local news, Olympic projects, and one of the top-rated soap operas, *General Hospital*.

"I watched Ted Polmanski take his soaps to the limit," he says. "He used to experiment on shadow and highlighting. I logged his techniques, vowing to try them when I had time."

In the late 1980s, Morgan's work became even more radical. The style he set for *Bagdad Cafe* won him a second Emmy nomination. It was different, it worked.

Soon his innovations were showing up on other shows. "Chip cameras had finally come in and we could go down to one inch tape and 150 or 125 footcandles," he explains. "When we did *227*, I began to experiment and play a little more. Now I was using soft light in front and hard light in the corners. Light was off the walls and there was a space at the top. I played with hard light that you couldn't see. This helped make the brown skins pop without the glow. Too often, people miss the ability to use the reflective value of these faces."

It was no secret, Donald A. Morgan was hitting his stride. There wasn't a challenge he wouldn't take down or a new tool that he wouldn't try. People were watching Morgan. Among them was David Zakaroff, the production designer he worked with on *Mr. Belvedere*. "We had a rapport," he says. "I didn't do anything for him that I wouldn't do for any other production designer. I have and always will feel that part of my job is to light so that the designer's sets look as good as the actors. Not all lighting designers feel the same way."

Zakaroff's recommendation brought Morgan into a Windancer/Disney pilot called *Home Improvement*. Morgan admits that he went into the pilot in a more or less mechanical mode. He knew he couldn't pick the scripts, or the sets and locations. He focused on giving the set as much depth as possible, and making the people look as good as possible.

Five Emmy Awards and six years later, Don A. Morgan is still on *Home Improvement*. The cast and the lighting designer might be the same, but the lighting tools and the plot are a world away from the first show. "When they pulled the lights down from *Carroll and Company*, I knew I wanted to re-rig the set in another way. Not only from the show that had occupied the stage, but from other shows that were on the air.

"I decided to go with a different type of front light, a bounce light. It seemed like the right time to move away from soft light. Using front bounce, I found I could create a nice strip and volume of soft light, like what commercial cinematographers use when they light cars.

"On movie sets, they do it with 12-by-12 grifflons. I'd learned about this when I watched Vilmos Zsigmond light a set at a seminar," Morgan continues. "He put up a 12-by-12 front bounce in the far back of the front of the set. He then used three 5ks as an overall base light. That overall soft look would be a great front fill. He then made the background outside the windows pop by using 4ks and 5ks right on the backings. The windows jumped out and the front filled with a nice blue color.

"Even when I substituted foam core for grifflon, I knew the set would handle the lens on a 2.8mm setting. And it would be great, almost like a commercial table top shoot without a small product in the foreground."

As the show progressed, Morgan became more and more daring. It was as though he was trying to defy the edict that there was movie lighting and there was television and multi-camera television lighting. The levels needed might be going down to 50 or 60 footcandles or even lower, but, the amount of units didn't decrease, in fact, they began to increase.

"If I had my way, I would be working with greenbeds instead of pipes," he admits. This would allow us room to make subtle changes. Instead of interrupting a rehearsal or moving the furniture around in the set to accommodate a ladder, a member of the grip crew can climb up into the beds, walk across the crossbars and move a light in minutes. It is easier to finesse a shot with greenbeds."

The lack of accessibility hasn't stopped Morgan from finessing *Home Improvement* and the other shows under his direction. Where there is a will, there is a way. The smaller units help.

He still uses a basic back cross, but with 4ks. Only he has them boxed down because they have to have a longer throw. He adds smaller units like 2ks, Babies, and Tweenies for a more subtle look.

His ability to integrate movie tools into a multi-camera production is one of the keys to his success. The "un" multi-camera feeling has made his contemporaries focus on his work. "How did he do that?" usually precedes an award nomination.

"We have one of the staple movie tools on the show every day," he explains. "We even light for the jib arm and crane or remote head. The idea came when I began to discuss one of the standing sets and sequences for the show. On every episode, there is a conversation between Tim and his next door neighbor. We found that the jib arm was the best way to get the camera over the fence.

"By going back to the roots of lighting, hard light, but creating it with soft light, we are able to move the jib anywhere and not make a shadow. We now have front bounce and, instead of hard light as cross key, we go with 2k lights. They have enough punch, yet are still soft enough to wrap around the booms and jib arms instead of bouncing off them. No boom shadows means freedom of movement. Now we can get great eye lights, we can even move a camera directly into the front of a light and not see a shadow."

The theory being the "mist" from the soft light will travel around the hard surface of the arm instead of landing on it and bouncing off. It is like a plane flying through a cloud. "It really only works with this kind of formula," he comments. "Other lights might be soft and smaller, but they project a harder shadow. And, although the 4k is great, it takes up too much room. If you can control the soft light it is great. If you can control both soft light and fill, that is truly the key."

Cinematographers and gaffers alike have told Morgan he couldn't control this kind of lighting. He's made them eat their words. "The idea is controlling it enough so that it doesn't reach the corner of the set," he explains. "That's where grips are so important. They can hang blacks at certain, sometimes ridiculous, angles. The rig may look nuts, the blacks may be in crazy places, but the result is specific. It's basic physics. The farther away the duvetine is from a unit, the sharper the cut is going to be. Now you can have downstage fill that doesn't reach the walls.

Whatever Morgan is doing, it's getting noticed. His shows are consistently beautiful and completely different. Sometimes it is hard to believe they aren't done on film in the traditional movie style. In 1993, his "Bye By Birdie" episode on *Home Improvement* featured a variety of times of day. The shots went from a 4:00 A.M. look to after midnight. Early morning dawn, early morning, daytime, a clean show within the show, evening and night all had different looks.

"Each had a light cue within the segment," he explains. "The idea was to zero the camera off at specific points. By focusing on specific areas of the face or the set, we could then plot the lights above to coordinate with the time of day."

He would have shots go through a diagonal, giving the faces two different looks. There was a cool and a warm side.

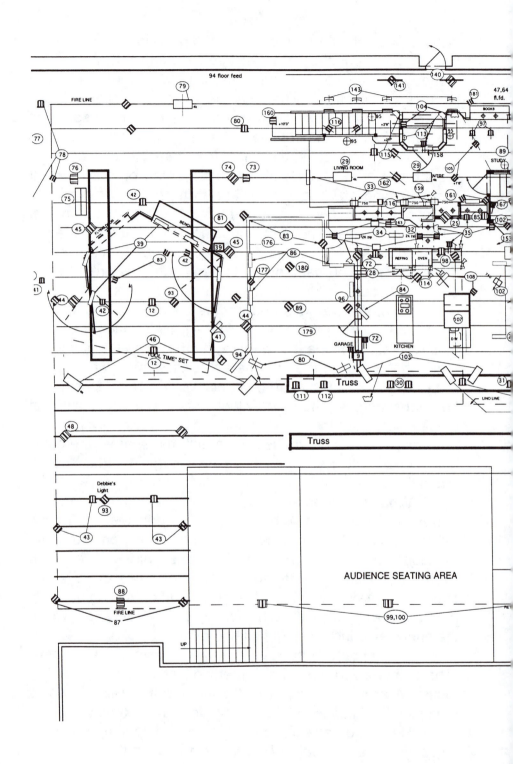

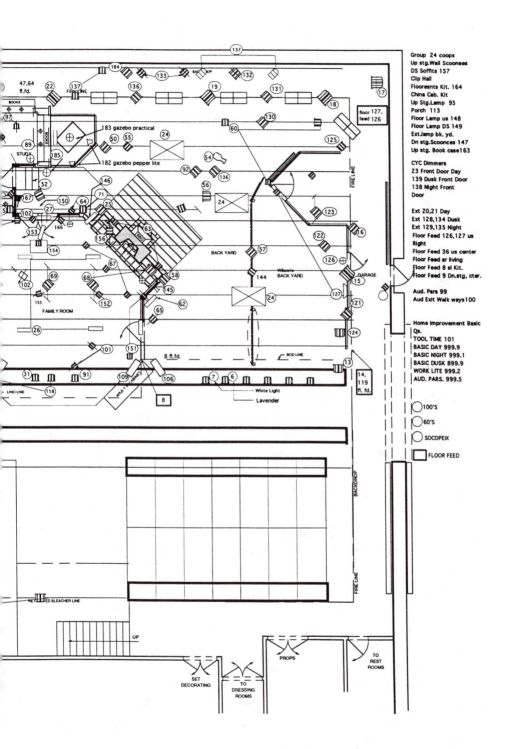

Group 24 coops
Up stg.Wall Sconses
DS Soffits 157
Clip Hall
Flooresnts Kit. 164
China Cab. Kit
Up Stg.Lamp 95
Porch 113
Floor Lamp us 148
Floor Lamp DS 149
Ext.lamp bk. yd.
Dn stg.Sconces 147
Up stg. Book case163

CYC Dimmers
23 Front Door Day
139 Dusk Front Door
138 Night Front
Door

Ext 20,21 Day
Ext 128,134 Dusk
Ext 129,135 Night
Floor Feed 126,127 us
Right
Floor Feed 36 us center
Floor Feed sr living
Floor Feed 8 sl Kit.
Floor Feed 9 Dn.stg, cter.

Aud. Pars 99
Aud Exit Walk ways100

Home Improvement Basic
Qs.
TOOL TIME 101
BASIC DAY 999.9
BASIC NIGHT 999.1
BASIC DUSK 899.9
WORK LITE 999.2
AUD. PARS. 999.5

100'S
60'S
SOCOPEIX
FLOOR FEED

He would flatline at 3200. Top and fill would be a 217, and he would warm the sun with a 159. "The trick is to make each side just off-axis of the other," he explains. "As long as they are complimentary, they work."

"In the middle, you could see the difference. However, each segment worked quite well. We simply reversed the process for nighttime and dusk. This can be done with any color combination or range, as long as they are each on the opposite side."

Television comedy is no longer a two-dimensional medium where bright and tight is more important than character and story. Even though the physical dimensions are two-dimensional, the vision has to clearly appear as multi-dimensional. "The farther away you go, the warmer the shot looks," he explains. "Give a shot more depth and the shallow falls away."

That is what Donald A. Morgan tells his students at UCLA. "Today, there is no right or wrong to lighting a show," is one of the first things he says when he begins a class. "It is what works for the situation.

"If you have a 5k at two feet and no diffusion, you are going to have a problem. Not only will you fry the actors, you will create a look that wouldn't be accepted even in the first days of television comedy. You need depth – and you can get it in any way that works."

Morgan was nervous when he was first asked to teach a class at the UCLA Film Department. After all, he learned everything the hard way. No one stood up in front of him and gave him a lecture. Did he have a right to tell the younger generation what to do and what not to do when he is an advocate of "do what works?" Six Emmy Awards and a lot of common sense says the younger generation can learn from his experience.

"I got lucky. I found mentors. Today, they are out there, but harder to find. Besides, there are far more tools at our disposal. You have to know the intimate details to survive."

Donald A. Morgan has a storehouse of knowledge about shooting multi-camera film and tape production. He is still adding to it every day. However, his focus has shifted from television comedy to a variety of other photographic interests. Part of the shift is a natural progression in the growth of a creative mind. Another part is the state of the product available.

Home Improvement is one of the last surviving "real" comedies. It is family oriented. It deals with all phases of the human drama. Audiences relate to Tim Allen and his television family. They have all been in similar situations. "You can't say that about many of our comedy programs today," Morgan admits. "The content isn't what it used to be.

"At some point, we all have to make a choice. Do we work on something we don't believe in just to bring home a paycheck, or do we look in another direction and enjoy the challenge that might bring?"

For now, Morgan is putting 150 percent into *Home Improvement* and a few other reality stories. He is also putting another 150 percent into the two studio complexes his company has built. Here, he is his own boss. If he chooses to shoot a project, it is on his terms. He can experiment as much as he wants. So can the other cinematographers or artists who work at his facilities.

That's not to say that if and when *Home Improvement* has finished its run, he won't take on another show. However, he has the option. "There are so many other venues," he says. "Areas where we can get to work with things like the Vision 320 stock. I've wanted to use it on *Home Improvement*, but the production won't allow it. There's always something coming along that is considered experimental. Sometimes it works, sometimes it doesn't. No matter what you are doing, you always have to find time to push your own limits."

******

Six time Emmy Award Winner for Multi-Camera Television Productions *Home Improvement, Mr. Belvedere*

"I want light that works for the story. I like to start in the very background and work my way up to the foreground. It's like a puzzle. I very seldom know what I am going to do way ahead of time. I have an image of what I want it to look like. I go for the contrast, then take a reading. That's when I know the stop."

Donald M. Morgan A.S.C.

February 27th, 1996, Century Plaza Hotel. Over 1000 attendees have just finished an elegant dinner and are applauding the winners of the 11th Annual American Society of Cinematographers' Awards. Actor/Director Charles Haid opens the envelope for best Miniseries and reads Donald M. Morgan's name. The applause is overwhelming as Morgan walks up to the stage. This is an unprecedented event. As of 1996, Donald M. Morgan A.S.C. is the only cinematographer to have won four A.S.C. Awards.

"I hope I didn't look as uncomfortable in my tux as I felt," laughs Morgan, as he settles into the comfortable couch in his San Fernando Valley home. Look around the livingroom and you will see few things that say "Hollywood." There's a saddle on one shelf, other western memorabilia scattered around. Photographs are plentiful – but speak more about the family man than the cinematographer. Morgan may not be comfortable in a tuxedo, but he is a man who is very comfortable with the way his life is going.

Donald M. Morgan is a great example of perseverance. A man who has followed many paths, there were times when he could have taken a wrong turn. He admits to having made a lot of mistakes in his life, but he's always managed to learn from every one of them.

"I failed, miserably, at a lot of things before I got into cinematography," he says. "I started out wanting to be a bronc rider, hoping to follow the rodeo circuit. I was lousy at that. I tried driving on the race car circuit. That didn't work either. For a while, I wasn't sure where I was going or how I would end up," he says ruefully.

That all changed when he ran into a man named Nelson Tyler. "He had just designed a new helicopter mount that allowed the operator more stability. The moment I saw it, things came into focus. One ride in a helicopter and I was hooked," he laughs. "They were older helicopters, hopelessly under-powered. By the time we put the Tyler Mount, a camera, camera operator, and director inside, it was at maximum weight."

Eventually, Morgan was the rightful resident of the operator's seat. "On my first or second 'real job' as an aerial cameraman, they put a plank on the helicopter's rudders and I took a 9.8mm lens, laid under the helicopter, and shot a car going around a test track in Detroit." He shakes his head in amazement. He knew it was crazy then, he knows it is crazy now. But, ask him to do it again – and he'll say yes without a second's hesitation. "Don't tell anyone," he whispers, "but I did the same thing a few years ago on *Terminal Velocity*!"

Fortunately, Donald M. Morgan got into the heart of the movie business when there was still an air of making the "impossible" happen. Like Morgan, his contemporaries were living fast, having fun, and willing to take a gamble on their future. "A group of us were working at Producer's Studio (now called Raleigh) in Hollywood," he recalls. "We all wanted to make movies of our own, so we started a pot. When we had enough money, we shot a picture called *Win, Place, or Steal.* The director picked me as the cameraman, Jack Green (*Speed*, *Twister*, 20 Clint Eastwood pictures) was my assistant! Each day, we would go out with a different crew.

"*Win, Place, or Steal*, starring Dean Stockwell, Russ Tamblin, and Alex Karras actually got released!" he adds. "Don't ask me what I did when I was shooting! I don't remember now – I don't even know if I knew then. All I know is that it was a great learning experience." The project got Morgan's name all over town. He was now a bonafide cameraman with a current credit. Over the next eight years, there were pilots like *Serpico*, an ambitious miniseries called *Harem* which was shot in Spain, and a very daring project starring Dennis Weaver called *Amber Waves*. "Director Joe Sargent saw the *Serpico* pilot I did and told me he wanted me to take a few risks for him. 'Filmmaking,' he said when we met, 'is a series of risks and I've been guilty of not taking enough of them. I'll direct and you do anything you want photographically.'

"So I decided that I wanted to light everything with amber gels – after all, that was the name of the movie. You should have heard the screaming when I walked into the transfer session. How could I possibly make them leave even his teeth amber?"

Donald M. Morgan was making a name for himself. People began to watch. While he was hanging out of a helicopter doing some aerial work on *Dirty Mary, Crazy Larry* and wondering if he would ever shoot a picture again, director Sidney Fury was flying across the country watching Morgan's western called *Santee*. "Next thing I know, I get a call from Fury's office. They wanted me to come in and talk about doing a project called *Sheila Levine is Dead and Living In New York.*

For Morgan, *Sheila Levine* was a ground-breaking picture. As Fury said to him, Morgan was in the big time, now. He was at Paramount, shooting only a few stages from *Godfather II* and *Days of the Locust*. "On a small set, though," he laughs. "I think we lived in one set – her apartment – morning, noon, and night. I didn't want to light it once and shoot the whole movie, I wanted to re-light every time. So we established a morning, afternoon, and late afternoon look.

"We would constantly change the key. I took a cue from one of my early influences, Gordon Willis. We put unbleached muslin over the whole set. We had coop lights shining down through the muslin. Then we blacked all the way around the set, so the walls would stay dark and the ambient light would be in the center. I would then highlight different things, depending on the time of day or the action in the story."

A new wave of directors began doing projects, breaking away from the norm. Morgan's attitude was just what they wanted. Soon he began doing a series of projects with directors Robert Zemeckis (*I Wanna Hold Your Hand, Used Cars*) and John Carpenter.

"John and I rarely went by the book on the television movie *Elvis* or the features *Christine the Car* and *Starman*," he admits. To this day, Morgan is assaulted with questions on *Starman*. "*Elvis* won the Emmy nomination, *Starman* became something of a cult picture, and *Christine* really set a tone for both myself and John Carpenter."

Morgan wanted to create a very specific mood for *Elvis*, the story of music's most enigmatic legend. "A recurring theme throughout the whole film was his memories of a long-dead, twin brother," he says. "As a little boy, he would see his reflection in water and talk to the twin brother that didn't make it. When he was in the depths of depression, he would look at his own shadow on the wall and feel the loneliness.

"In one part of the story, John wanted Elvis's shadow, as he sits in a chair, despondent, to be really hard. My problem was where to put the light. If I put a little lamp on the side, he'd be where the camera angle was but he would be too bright. Then I got this idea – sit Kurt Russell (as Elvis) in the right spot and light him the correct way for the shot. Then, sit someone else off to the side and light that person with a really hard light. That would put the correct shadow in. All we had to do is coordinate Kurt and the other actor to move in unison."

The problem was finding someone who was built like Russell as Elvis. Carpenter scoured the crew. Suddenly all eyes turned in Morgan's direction. "For some strange reason, they thought I looked more like Elvis than anyone else there," he laughs. Make up took grip tape and made Morgan's hair into a pompadour. He lit the scene properly, then took his place in front of the cameras. "We tried, oh how we tried to coordinate our movements," he says, shaking his head. "Now I know why I stay behind the camera!

"It was impossible to know what was in the other person's mind. So, finally, we came up with the idea of a key word. We would both hear it at the same time and make our move. Sometimes, we'd both crack up so much we had to stop. I still laugh every time I see the film. 'That's me. That's my shadow!'"

With the success of *Elvis*, Carpenter and Morgan re-teamed for one of Stephen King's earliest projects, *Christine*. "There was a place in the movie called Darnell's Garage," Morgan recalls. "It is where the kids break in and try to destroy

Christine and she heals herself. We found this half torn down building in an industrial area outside Los Angeles. It looked like it was half a mile long. I wanted that feeling, so I had 10ks mounted on dimmer boards.

"They wanted to shoot day for night, but I didn't. If we did that, we would have had to black out the windows and not see through them. I wanted night for night, that way we could light and see the junk yard outside and pan inside and outside the building. With lights that included 10ks and green hooded practical lights hung outside the windows shooting down, we had the whole interior lit and we didn't have to change anything during a move. Well, maybe the angle of the outside light, but that was it."

Another Morgan/Carpenter teaming still draws audiences today. *Starman* is a fantasy movie with a lot of effects. Morgan and Carpenter chose to do as much as they could in camera. "It was a tough film," he sighs. "Matching was the biggest challenge." By now, major matching sequences and massive aerial shots were second nature to Donald M. Morgan. What fascinated him were the "little" shots that looked so easy on the screen but were a challenge to do. "Jeff Bridges had a ball that glowed," he says. "When he squeezed it, the magic would happen. He could heal things, change things.

"A lot of people ask how we got this to work. All we did was put a ball in his hand and wire it to a dimmer board. When it was supposed to glow, the prop guys would make it happen. Of course, once in a while it would 'over-glow,'" he laughs. "'Oh shit, you burned my hand!' would come out of Jeff's mouth, instead of the line he was supposed to say. We all tried to be as careful as we could," he says dryly. "Jeff included."

For Morgan, one of the most important ingredients in making this dark and tricky film was a man by the name of Dick Barlow. "He was head of the camera department at Warner Bros.," he explains, "and one of the most valuable tools a young cameraman could have. If that cameraman could get his ego out of the way and ask the right questions, that is. He had probably forgotten more about film than we would ever learn." When Morgan faced a challenge that puzzled him, he would go to Barlow and there would be the answer.

Starman's arrival at the deserted cabin where Karen Allen's character is trying to reconcile herself to her husband's untimely death was quite a challenge for Morgan. Using both the real location and a duplicate cabin on stage, he had to make it appear as if *Starman* beams down from the sky, sees Karen through the window, finds a way into the cabin by going under the door, then clones himself into the human form by using a lock of her husband's hair.

Morgan had already shot the sequence where the alien being crashes to earth in Tennessee. An electrician hand held an HMI light as he rode in the helicopter, sweeping the cabin toward the lake. They then turned around to get a reflection on the lake that provided the basic effect of the mother ship's arrival. "All we had to do was add a fog filter to diffuse the lighting effect," he explains.

Then effects had a thousand gallons of gas poured into rubber tires. The tires were then hung in the trees. When they exploded the gas, it looked like a starburst effect, just like a starship crashing. "Explosions are tricky," he says. "If we had shot at a really low light level, the explosion would white out. We exposed for what was there, then dialed the stop as the explosions went off. This made the shot red and rich, rather than white."

Carpenter then wanted a shot of Starman, as a burst of light, looking at Karen Allen through the cabin window as she watches 8mm films of her late husband. To make the film on the projector look real, Carpenter scratched it up and showed it on an old projector.

"After *Starman* sees this, he enters the cabin as a light pouring under the door," Morgan continues. "All we did was raise the door up as the camera on a Louma crane went down, giving the illusion of it going under the door. Once he was inside, we focused on the film and projector. We concentrated on the piece of the man's hair that Starman uses to clone himself. We started with a really dark room, then threw HMI lights in to burn the shot out, making it appear as if the burned out light is Starman cloning himself.

"Stan Winston did the baby. Then we shot a young boy from the back. We then went to a nude Jeff Bridges and, finally, Jeff himself. When he becomes a person, he frightens Karen. Because he saw her husband use a gun in the films, he picks one up, not knowing what it is. He shoots a hole in the window and scares himself as well.

"John wanted us to see the strained look in Starman's face as he realizes what he has done," he recalls. "So, we hung Jeff upside down, with his hair hanging and the blood rushing to his face!"

Morgan had definitely developed a style, although it was not written in cement. "I want light that works for the story. I like to start in the very background and work my way up to the foreground. It's like a puzzle. I very seldom know what I am going to do way ahead of time. I have an image of what I want it to look like.

"Gaffers ask me what key I want and I say whatever we end up with. I don't like to say a 2.8 or a 5.6. I light by eye and what I think will look good and look better through the camera. I go for the contrast, then take a reading. That's when I know the stop."

It is the adventurer in Donald M. Morgan that keeps driving him into new and different situations. For years after *Elvis* and the Carpenter projects he worked consistently. His "non-formula" look influenced major national commercials, television and feature movies, and series projects.

Then there came a series of well thought out, often controversial, and definitely attention getting movies for television, miniseries projects, and cable productions. For the past four (going on five, most likely, with the addition of *Miss Evers' Boys* to his resume) he has won the coveted A.S.C. Award for cinematography, as well as several Emmy nominations and awards. Ask him what makes an award-winning project and he is at a loss for words. He just approaches each one with the idea of making the best visuals possible. And, he chooses the projects because of the visual possibilities.

"What fascinated me about *Geronimo* was the man's courage," he says. "I wanted to show how he withstood the assaults on his world – as a warrior, as a man interred on a reservation, and finally as a legend who was still fighting for the rights of his people."

Try to pin Morgan down to the visual challenges of this historical story and he has to think for a moment. "We did a lot with just the firelight available," he says, "and we did a lot with rain. I learned a great lesson on that picture. I admit, I can be stubborn. When I see a great shot, I will dig in and try to go for it. On this picture, it was a wonderful scene where we had a large shot of the wigwams, the woods behind, trees wonderfully back lit, fires in front of the tents – a monsoon! Production told us we had to wrap. Thunder and lightning were on the way – real lightning. I didn't want to listen. 'Have you ever heard of anyone getting hit by lightning on a location?' They didn't buy it. So I cursed the AD and everyone else as we packed up the equipment and moved down off the location.

"I shut up, fast, when I found out one of the crew members did get hit as he packed the equipment into the truck. I know, it wasn't my fault. I still feel guilty. In retrospect, what we should have done is left the equipment and gone for safety – it was only things."

Morgan sits quietly, for a moment. The memory is real, once again. "Rain was a horrible and wonderful part of this project," he admits. "Not only did it teach me to value life more than a shot, it also showed me the difference between shooting real rain, and shooting movie rain. There was another scene, where Geronimo is turning into a drunk. Confined to a reservation, he has no purpose in life. He tries to talk to a young boy, tries to make sense of their world.

"It's a night shot, in the village. We wanted to see the tents, a little firelight where people are still awake, and nothingness. To give depth to the shot we brought in a Condor. It was supposed to go up 85 feet and provide back light for the night and the rain. Unfortunately, or fortunately, the condor wouldn't go up. I had to focus it almost straight in." In reality, this became a happy accident. By bringing the light in low, he was able to enhance the feeling of being out in nowhere.

He was also able to show the viewer that the scene was shot in real rain. "If you aren't careful, shots done in 'movie rain' can look exactly like what they are," he says. "Even on the biggest budget pictures, there is rarely enough time, money, or equipment to give depth to the rain effect. You throw it in front of the camera and hope the audience buys the visuals. In *Geronimo*, the happy coincidence of a Condor that wouldn't cooperate allowed us to see both dark and light places, instead of an overall high angle skylight. Look at the wigwams in the background and you can see the rain – the real rain. I think it added to the emotional value. Here we have free spirits, caged and uncomfortable in elements that they couldn't control."

Morgan used light, and the absence of light, in many *Geronimo* sequences to enhance the caged feeling in other ways. "I got an awful lot of flack from everyone from studio to director to color timer. They all thought I'd gone over the edge on the opening sequences, where he comes to talk to the Senate," Morgan laughs. "'You can't do it that way. The light is too low.'

"The moment Geronimo surrenders, he gives up everything to save his people. From that day forward, he feels like a caged animal – even in the elegance of what was then a modern hotel and hotel room. By keeping the light levels low, we could show his puzzlement when he discovers running water and electric light. We could also give the rooms the feeling of being caged in. You knew Geronimo would trade these 'modern' things for the freedom of the open sky. I wanted the audience to feel the same way."

Ask anyone who has seen Donald M. Morgan's *Geronimo* what scene stands out in his or her mind and without hesitation it is the final sequence. After Geronimo speaks to the Senate and the President of the United States about the broken promises made to the Indians when the treaty is struck, he walks down a long and elegant hallway and through a door into a blast of hot, white light. "Our version of riding off into the sunset," Morgan says.

"Director Roger Young sprung the idea on me the day of the shoot," he remembers, sobering. "We had no time to design it, no equipment supply houses to call for extra lighting. I took a deep breath, had the crew grab what silks we had and literally caged in the area outside this door. We then nailed foam core to the floor, so the actors could walk on it. We also made a little upward curve outside the door, creating a raised cove. I then blasted two 12ks and dumped every other light we had on the truck into the silks – and prayed. With a little help from post, we had a great 'ride into the sunset' shot to finish this amazing story."

One of the reasons directors and studios keep coming back to Morgan for their visuals is this ability to think on his feet and make something, often out of nothing. He is also known for being fast, but thorough. "If I need time – I take it. If I can get something fast – I don't screw around. And, if I can go for real, as opposed to manufactured, I'll stand my ground and con whoever I have to into doing what is necessary to make the shot more real," he says with a smile. Fortunately, Morgan rarely has to do the conning. He just points something out, and lets the director do the sell.

"Hey, that's what they are there for," he laughs. In *Double-crossed*, another award nominated HBO project for Morgan and director Roger Young, he saw a chance for a better reality in several flying sequences. In the story, Dennis Hopper plays a good guy type drug runner, who has to turn informant. "We were constantly trying to get the audience involved in his predicament and take them along for a ride," he explains. "Although the picture was high budget for cable, it was low budget for effects.

"Which was okay with me. I like to do as much as I can in camera, anyway. Roger and I were still determined to open the story up with a few flying sequences. So, I talked him into doing them for real. Now, it was Roger's job to talk to the actors. Somehow, he got them to agree to do the scenes in the air. That was quite an accomplishment, considering one of the actors hated to fly – even to a location!

"Somehow we packed Roger, the operator, an assistant, myself, the real pilot and our actors into the small plane.

We would do Dennis's lines, with the pilot flying in the co-pilot seat, then we would land, switch sides, and do the other lines. Sure, it was difficult. But you can't tell me the reality doesn't show up there on the screen!"

For Morgan, the last few shots of another project, *Murder in Mississippi*, are also some of his favorites. His unobtrusive support of a very emotional story caught the attention of awards committees and garnered him another honor. "In the end scene, where the boys are killed, we wanted to make the car chases as real as possible.

"When we didn't need to see inside the cars, we positioned the camera car at a certain angle and used the car lights to reflect the wonderful red Georgia clay dust coming from the ground. That allowed us to move freely through the back roads and build the tension.

"When the boys pulled into a barn, looking for safety, that was where I really needed the light. We wanted to let the audience see the boys hiding, and see the cop cars racing by. While we were scouting, I picked two or three important areas along the chase route. We pre-rigged the dense forest with Maxi brutes behind trees, placing everything on the ground because the forest was simply too thick for scaffolding or condors. We flagged everything carefully so we had a nice back light and a gentle rim around the trees for depth. As the cars came in, their headlights picked out the trees, giving us even more of a sense of isolation.

"When the cars surround the two boys, we made it appear as if the car headlights were lighting the scene. We angled a few par lights beyond the headlights to extend the throw. I then had the actors use their flashlights to direct light onto the featured actors. As we were shooting, I stood near the camera and used my flashlight to throw a little extra kick into an eye or a face, anything to enhance the emotionally charged moment where two innocent boys, one white and one black, are killed by these men."

Focusing light on a world out of control is a recurring theme in the pictures Donald M. Morgan chooses to shoot. In 1996, he won his fourth A.S.C. award for *Ruby Ridge*, the tragic story of unnecessary deaths caused by emotions run amuck. "One of the things that attracted me to this project was that there were no good guys," Morgan says. "Randy Weaver and his family were of absolutely no threat to anyone, yet the government spent over a million dollars a day trying to bring them down off Ruby Ridge."

Morgan and director Roger Young worked hard to show this in their visuals. They built the suspense carefully. And when the story got to the crisis point, they used very subtle techniques to enhance the tragedy. One of the most effective shots in the movie is the point where the government soldiers and this family they are stalking really come together.

"I wanted to find a way to show the soldier, as he prepares to fire what he claims was going to be a 'warning shot' at the family, in a dynamic and unusual way," says Morgan. "It wasn't enough to see him get into position. We needed to feel him as he got over his fear and confusion and did what he was trained to do – shoot in what was deemed a hostile situation.

"I thought it would be impressive and dynamic if we saw the gun coming up as the shooter focused on the house. So I went to Denny Clairmont and told him what I wanted to do. Denny and company are famous for creating something for a specific shot, then putting it in their stock for others to use. So, I knew they could help me with this one.

"They tested several different lenses and found that they could attach a gunsight to the iris rods of a camera with a 28mm lens. This way, we could pull up through focus from the background, which happened to be the house on the ridge, bring the scope into frame, and see the cross hairs, as well as the family dog, who was laying somewhere between the woods and the house.

"To give our assistant a little extra help, we brought in a video monitor so he could see what was going on. This way, we could role through the shot, letting some of the edge go out of focus, but giving us a very clear impression of 'business as usual.' We see the man take his place, see him pull up the gun, see his view through the sight, and bring it around to the family, as they ran for the cover of the house. This visual intensified the horror of the moment when the bullet leaves the gun and 'accidentally' kills the mother.

"On *Ruby Ridge*, I was always trying to find ways to show both sides of the story," he explains. "There had to be a reason for some of these mistakes. A reason that basically good men let clouded thinking force them into making these horrible mistakes. One element I thought would work was to add to their physical discomfort. Rain and cold weather are always good tools to cloud thinking, so we decided to shoot the night sequences in the pouring rain.

"We were in an open area, so back lighting the rain was easy. We used the lights from the house where the troops gathered, a flashing red light from the ambulance that was taking one of the dead soldiers away in a body bag, and a few flares set on the ground for depth." Morgan pauses, expecting a strange reaction to the last tool.

"That's the same look I got when Roger Young saw me placing flares on the ground on this remote location!" he laughs. "'Why? What's the motivation?' he asked me. My answer – it looks good. 'But it doesn't make sense.' Maybe they are there to show the way out – that's what I told him." At first, Young didn't buy it, but he'd hired Donald M. Morgan to shoot the picture for a reason. If Morgan believed the audience would buy road flares in a shot, he wasn't one to argue. "Sometimes," Morgan says with a straight face, "you have to use a little unreality to make the reality play.

"You have to find a balance that keeps the audience interested. The flares added color and excitement to the shot," he says.

It is hard for Morgan to explain why he does a lot of things that he does, it is just part of his need to make the shot exciting. His favorites aren't always everyone else's favorites. Often he goes for the simple shots, while people go nuts for the extravagant ones. Sometimes he will be asked about projects where he has to hold himself in, like *Double-crossed* or *Murder in Mississippi*. Other times, people will react to extremely stylized movies like *Dillinger*.

"Don't ask me what they saw in *Dillinger* that got me the awards, I can never figure that out," he says adamantly.

"All I know is the project's director Rupert Wainwright wanted to do something different from every other *Dillinger* project ever shot. Words like flashy, pretty, and stylized kept creeping into the conversation. He loved *Miami Vice* and *Dick Tracy*." That sent Morgan's creative senses into overdrive. As long as the shots were based in the film's reality, he could do what he wanted.

"We tried to make each robbery different. Sometimes we did it with angles, sometimes we did it with light, sometimes with camera placement. In one particular shot, we had this magnificent old vault. We could have done the shot straight – the gang approaching the vault, going in, looting it, and leaving the bank – but Rupert wanted stylized. So I came up with this idea of putting the camera inside among the loot. As the vault opens, we know it is Dillinger and his gang outside, so why did we have to see them? Instead, we blew out the background, smoked the shot, and washed it out so that they were dark silhouettes against a lit background. It added to the mythology of the Dillinger story."

Morgan admits he really enjoyed playing with shots like this on *Dillinger*. Although this was another project based on a true story, the reality of this historical character has been so washed with myth that over-the-top was the only approach. "It's fun to do," he says simply. "It can also be expensive. One of the key scenes is a long, very over-the-top death sequence in which John Dillinger is finally killed by his nemesis, a government agent. It's beautifully shot but totally unreal," Morgan admits. "So many bullets, so much time for him to die. I mean, really, he gets hit, he runs. He gets hit again, he runs in another direction. Sometimes you wonder if this guy is ever going to die! Yet, you buy it, because it is part of the myth.

"It was probably one of the most expensive lighting jobs in the movie," he says. "Fortunately, the city of Milwaukee really wanted us to shoot there, so they went out of their way to give us what we needed. They went as far as taking the modern parking meters out and replacing the street lights with lights they had in storage. They even let us paint the lines out of the road, and let us into their stores to put lights inside.

"Every night, after we finished shooting on another location or on one of our sets, I would walk the street with several members of the rigging crew. We would throw a light in here, extend a light there. We lit for several blocks. And, when we got to the river, we didn't want the depth to end. So, we went across the river and lit the buildings facing back at the camera, just so we could give a sense of place to this all important shoot out.

"Was it necessary? Probably not. However, by lighting this way we were able to shoot any angle without having to relight. That saved time. We used major dutch angles, varied the speed of the camera, and went all over the street in front of the theater, following Mark Harmon as he played the death scene to the hilt. However, I really believe giving the audience that sense of place worked for the story. Sometimes, massive rigging efforts that don't always show in a shot are still worth it because they support the story in so many other ways.

"Did that effort help sell the A.S.C. committee? I don't know. I certainly wasn't thinking about that when we were shooting. I never think about what others might think. It gets in the way. For me, it's about pleasing myself and the director. True, it is a lot easier when we are both tuned into the same visuals. However, that doesn't always happen. That's when you have to pick your fights and stand your ground."

Fortunately, that hasn't happened very often in Morgan's career. He has built a long-standing relationship with several different directors. Directors who hire him because he can push the edge of the envelope when that becomes necessary. Did he do much of that on his latest cable special, *Miss Evers' Boys*? "It's hard to tell when you are working with a director like Joe Sargent," he laughs. "Every shot is different, because he comes at a story from a very different perspective. Joe thinks of light as another actor. His theatrical background and sense of the music in a shot allows me to do things other directors often hesitate to try.

"We were always finding ways to bring the audience into the story and still keep the shots moving," Morgan continues. "One of my favorite sequences is in the hospital where the black doctor is trying to treat a young boy whose lungs are filled with water. Instead of starting on a closeup of the boy, we focused the eye on Miss Evers and the child with a pool of light over them. However, we see them through an old medicine cabinet filled with medical tools. To give the sense of time, place, and condition, we had art director Charlie Bennett paint the glass of the cabinet with shellac. It made the glass look old when the camera moved through the uneven veneer."

Everything Sargent and Morgan did on *Miss Evers' Boys* spoke of a specific approach to filmmaking, that of making the camera a participant in the story. That's a difficult task when a project has to be shot on a very tight schedule. This film, like so many other cable projects, had to be done in something like six weeks, not the six months normally allotted for a feature. "You learn to get the shots quickly and move on," says Morgan casually. "That way, you can save the time for things like *Dillinger's* death scene or whatever else you need.

"That doesn't mean you rush," he adds emphatically. "It does mean you look for ways to make this happen quickly. Sometimes that means shooting at very low light levels and trusting your stock to get what you need. Other times, it is coming up with new approaches to shots."

On *Miss Evers' Boys*, Morgan really challenged everyone on the crew. He was always coming up with moves that required a dancer's agility or stops that made an assistant's hair turn gray. At times, it also required incredible strength and patience. "There was a really important scene between Miss Evers and the doctor who knowingly partici-pated in this experiment of keeping medicine away from blacks with syphilis," Morgan explains. "It was supposed to take place in a hospital, as she wheels a man with an advanced case of syphilis down a long corridor.

"Originally, Joe wanted to lay dolly track inside the schoolhouse we had turned into the hospital. We would then move along side them as they walked and talked. As I looked at the building, I thought of another way of giving the audience a sense of where we were and what was going on. We found a long hallway with a wall of old windows. By shooting the actors from outside, we could play them in semi-silhouette against a great wall of glass inside. All we needed to do was light the faces."

The challenge – getting enough light in so the faces would read against the background. "Suddenly, this became one of those shots where we needed to use up a little of our saved time and the energy and participation of our crew," he says with a smile. "To make it work, I had to tent the outside with silk then expose for the back side of the shot. This made the glass about five stops hotter than the rest of the shot.

"To get a nice rim light on the actors, I had my poor gaffer walk along with them holding a 2500 HMI! As they turned a corner, he panned off, and we used the sunlight pounding through a side window to send them off to their duties. It was a little bit like the last walk of Geronimo – without the blasted out effect."

Will this effort to do something special be noticed by the Emmy and A.S.C. panels again? Who knows? "We didn't do it for any other reason than it looked good," says Morgan. "One of the biggest advantages in doing projects for companies like HBO and TNT is that you can really do something different, even though you can be on a tight schedule. This is a wonderful venue for quality stories about the human condition, a venue for feature work without the intrusion of commercials, network censors, or studio exec-utives saying you 'can't' do that for television or whatever the excuse of the moment is."

******

A.S.C. Award *Geronimo, Dillinger, Murder in Mississippi, Ruby Ridge –* **Emmy Award** *Geronimo, Murder in Mississippi, Miss Evers' Boys–* **Emmy Award Nomination** *Ruby Ridge, Double-crossed, Elvis,–***A.C.E. Award Nomination** *Double-crossed, Geronimo*

"The trick is, it doesn't really matter what the gear is. We have great gear, now, and the work is great. But, in some hands, great gear can look lousy. It's all in what you do with it."

Dennis Muren

Somewhere in a quiet industrial park in Northern California, an innocuous smoked glass door leads to the most amazing mixture of movie magic in the world. Young computer nerds who look as if they still don't shave mix easily with distinguished, slightly balding, and bespeckled mavens of another generation. "Distinguished?" laughs one of the "older generation" of effects gurus. "I don't know about that. George Lucas, maybe. He could be called 'distinguished.' However, if we weren't slightly balding and didn't need glasses, that would mean we haven't been doing our job – tearing our hair out and staring at storyboards trying to figure out how to do what we've already said we could do. Of course, once we've pulled the proverbial rabbit out of the hat, there is still that frame by frame and pixel by pixel image to be conquered."

He calls himself a film technician, others call him a Merlin. However, Dennis Muren A.S.C., Senior Special Visual Effects Supervisor at George Lucas's effects house *Industrial Light and Magic,* is one of the industry's unsung heroes. He is the recipient of eight American Academy Awards for Best Achievement in Visual Effects, not to mention numerous technical awards and British Academy Awards, and has brought everything from dinosaurs to the "Death Star" to life.

"My first 'effect' was to make scratches on slides and project them onto a screen," he recalls, as he settles into an office chair shoved into a corner of one of the many little "houses" on the ILM magic lot. Things are run quite differently at ILM. There are few "big" offices and fancy dressing. Since the place is so spread out and work is done in many locations, Muren prefers the "camping" approach. He sets up his headquarters where it is most convenient, breaking down his portable office when a project is finished. Outside the window on this particular location, jean-clad young geniuses are fighting the Northern California wind and rain as they rush from stage to studio, mysterious thoughts of other worlds flying through their heads. Somewhere in the background you can hear the "ILM House Band," a group of resident special effects wizards "cooling their jets" through a different creative venue. Does Muren join in? "In my mind, maybe. I reserve my music for relaxation in private," he laughs.

At the tender age of six, this La Canada, California-born man became fascinated with "other worlds." "When I saw *King Kong* and the stop-motion movies of Ray Harryhausen, my imagination went wild," he admits. "My parents gave me my first camera and I started shooting my own movies. Stop motion," he explains, "is taking pictures of inanimate objects and making them appear to move by shooting one frame at a time and moving the objects before shooting the next frame.

"I didn't know what I was doing," he admits. "However, a neighbor, Phil Kellison, was working at Project Unlimited, an independent visual effects company. He would take me to the studio and the fairytale would come true. I saw them working on *Jack The Giant Killer* and I even got to meet Harryhausen and visit him in Malibu. To this day, every time I think about the moment I stepped into the studio and saw the six-legged sea serpent, I get a lump in my throat!"

In the 1950s, special effects were not sophisticated. Playing with clay figures and strange configurations didn't carry much punch in the business world. "My parents didn't know if I could ever make a living doing this work," he smiles. "'Major in business,'" they would tell me. So, there I was, taking business courses at Pasadena City College and then Cal State L.A. I was also shooting my own films off the television screen and trying to figure out how these things were done.

"In college, I decided to make my first feature. I had a 16mm camera and shot a low budget science-fiction film called *The Equinox*. It was filled with crude effects including a giant ape-like monster and flying winged being. Nothing like the ones in *Lost World*," he interjects.

"And," he laughs, "just like in one of those old Hollywood movies, I sold my little movie to a producer, Jack Harris, who did *The Blob*. He added about 40 minutes of footage and blew it up to 35mm. It ran at a theater on Hollywood Boulevard and all over the country!"

Then things slowed down, sort of. Fresh out of college, with a produced and released credit on his resume, Dennis Muren thought he could get work somewhere. He would visit people like Bill Abbott at Fox, asking for a job on one of the few effects pictures. He was not, unfortunately, in the Union. "I began freelancing as a camera operator on commercials for Green Giant and Pillsbury. I also supervised effects on educational films. I had joined the 'Hollywood System,' my friends said. I'd 'sold out.' No, I still wanted to do things my way, I just knew I had to join them to beat them."

Then came the fateful day when Muren heard about this new movie rogue named George Lucas who was determined to make a new 'hero's journey' feature called *Star Wars: A New Hope*, "any way he could," Muren adds. "I called John Dykstra and walked into another world of Hollywood effects – the Doug Trumble-trained, hardware-oriented world. I signed on as a cameraman."

This was a whole new world for Muren. "I had learned a lot about lighting the 'most perfect ear of corn or toilet paper roll,'" he laughs. "Now I was learning to program spaceship movements.

"In *Star Wars*, there is a scene with four x-wings above the Death Star. They are flying toward the camera, then they peel off, and sort of flip over," he explains. "We used a stepper motor (motor that moves in repeatable, identical steps) controlled by a computer. By programming this computer to move in exactly the same way over and over again, we could control the Dykstraflex (specially built small camera). Various takes of the same action would then be reproduced in exactly the same way. That meant we could shoot each fighter separately.

"I consciously gave each of these pilots an 'attitude,' a personality, when I was programming these motions. I wanted each of them to move a little differently, as 'human' pilots would," he adds. "Using an optical printer (a camera that re-photographs a piece of film over and over), we could then put each fighter and their attitude into the same shot."

Lucas loved the shot and the meticulous lighting effects Muren created through the computer. A cinematographer as well as a computer programmer, Muren knew how to make light bounce or wrap, within the computer language. Muren had found a home – and a "style." "Actually, I really wasn't satisfied with what I was doing on *Star Wars* or on *Close Encounters of the Third Kind*," he says stubbornly. "I came into *Close Encounters* late in the game. The gear being used was simple motion control. You couldn't vary the speed on anything.

"I remember when we were doing the mother ship, something would go wrong and Doug Trumble would call a halt to everything. He would stand there for 30 seconds and come up with a solution to make the shot look great when he had nothing to work with.

"That is kind of what I was doing when I was younger! I had never seen anyone else work that way," he says warmly. "The trick is, it doesn't really matter what the gear is. We have great gear now, and the work is great. But, in some hands, great gear can look lousy. It's all in what you **do** with it.

"At this point, I knew motion control wasn't as good as it could be," he says. "I had to find a way and a place to perfect it." So, in 1978, Muren left ILM and joined the ranks of "television" people. "George wasn't sure if he would be doing another project, so a group of us began working with John Dykstra at Universal on a television series called *Battlestar Gallactica*.

"Television, of course, was really different back then," he continues. "Movie and television people mixed well. They thought alike. *Gallactica* gave me the opportunity to do what I wanted, show off the power of motion control and the potential of the medium. I did things like move a three-dimensional figure through space," he explains. "A perfect example would be the scenes with the Cylon space ship. We would start with it near the camera and make it dive down toward the Gallactica. This made the ship appear as if it were going farther and farther away as the Gallactica became larger. We would then have it fly away. At the time, this was an elaborate trick of the eye – which we used many, many times."

When Lucas decided on shooting a sequel to *Star Wars*, Muren returned to the ILM team. With *The Empire Strikes Back*, Lucas had promised to take effects into a world never before explored and Muren was ready to help him accomplish that.

"There is a shot of a battle scene on the icy planet Hoth," he says. "At the beginning of the film, a helicopter flies over the planet. You see a Ton-Ton running off into the distance. The camera moves up, flies over him, then looks straight down.

"At the time, that seemed to be an impossible shot to do," he laughs. "But George wanted the shot, so we spent days thinking about it.

"It was a process of dissecting the equipment and defining what it could do," he explains. "We then had to figure out how each element would work together. If what we tried didn't work, we would then try something else. Most everything is solvable," he adds.

"The equipment we were working with, well, we had motion control, animation stands, an optical printer – the same things we had before. What we were attempting was to marry several elements together – elements that were now continuously moving.

"I had read about a man by the name of Bill Cruise," he continues. "He was working on *Damnation Alley*. He took an animation stand, something you hardly ever see, and plotted every frame of film in what we called 'match moves' of previously exposed pieces of film. All we had to do is figure out how the camera worked, then expose the film.

"I got this background that could move all over the place. I didn't want to put light into it, I wanted to put little laser lights into it. I re-developed the film, photographed it, and moved it around on an animation stand.

"It is hard to explain," he admits. "But what this lead to is 'pin blocking,' something we used even more on *Jedi*."

This technique earned Dennis Muren his first Academy Award, establishing him as one of the best effects people photographing miniatures. Suddenly, he was promoted to Visual Effects Supervisor. Budgets, technology, and artistry," he groans. "It becomes a chess game!" He might be groaning, but inside he is smiling. Muren may have become part of the "establishment" but he was now able to tell people how to do things – his way.

"It was time to move on to a more sophisticated technique," he says simply. "We were starting on *Dragonslayer*. Up until this point, there was an amount of strobing in stop-motion. This happened when you tied inanimate objects together frame by frame. In this project, the dragon had to have a life, a breath. The subjects had to move. So, we inserted rods into the characters and programmed their movements through the computer. It was told to break down the puppet dragon's movements to extremely precise segments.

"This allowed us to move the dragon when the camera shutter was open and make the movements appear smooth." This "go-motion" technique earned Muren his second Award for Technical Achievement.

"For a while, we kept repeating ourselves with this technique," he admits. Although films like *E.T. The Extra-Terrestrial* caught the audience's attention, Muren didn't feel this was a step in special effects. "The project simply didn't really call for it," he says. "In doing this picture, I sort of went back and used what I knew from commercials and what I picked up from Allen Daviau. I made the material rich, composed, and classic, lighting with different color keys and fill."

Dennis Muren is constantly asked about the bike chase in *E.T.* and the mine chase in *Indiana Jones and the Temple of Doom*. "Those again," he groans good-naturedly. "They were really repeats of *Dragonslayer*. So was the shot in *Innerspace*.

"However," his smile can't hide just a little of the excitement he feels when talking about the films that won him still more Academy Awards, "We did spend a lot of time on that mine-chase sequence. We didn't have that much money to do it and I wanted to make it real.

"We put registration pins in a Nikon still camera," he says. "This allowed us to put 100 feet of film inside and move it one frame a second. We could then capture a 'chase' through the small replica set. It worked fine for the close-ups, evening shots, and, maybe, not very wide shots.

"So, we had to make the miniatures look as dangerous as the real-sized shots would be. I had to put my mind in the head of a cameraman. I wanted to do it in go-motion, so we wouldn't have problems with depth of field or focus. So we decided to stop animate puppets.

"The smaller the set, the shorter the distance the cars would travel," he interjects. "So, the length of the run was then limited by the size of the camera. We ran the camera through our tinfoil sets on little tiny cars run on a track. These mine cars were carrying claymation figures animated one frame at a time.

"We could get a five-second shot, in whatever direction we were going. If the cars were going about 25 to 30 miles per hour, they could cover a 50 -foot set with one run instead of one double that size."

And, what about the bike chase in *Jedi*? "The background for that shot was done with a Steadicam walking through the woods in Eureka, California. We shot at one frame per second, so it looked like 120 miles per hour. Then we "go-motioned" the rest of the effects into the shot. We did what is now called animatics with dolls for the same sequence. It was 105 shots, pre-visualized on moving storyboards, and done one frame at a time over a grueling three days."

Dennis Muren was getting tired of the same old effects; there had to be another challenge. When he attended a seminar in future technology, he found this strange new technique called Computer Graphics. "I saw a demo of a formation of rocket ships making maneuvers we could never do with models," he recalls.

When *Young Sherlock Holmes* came along, he had his chance to experiment with CGI. "There were three sequences in the movie where I had a very strong point-of-view on each technique," he explains. "At first, I wanted to do rod puppets because we could do them easily. The flying harpies I wanted to do with match moving. However, George Lucas's company had had a CGI department for about six years and I wanted to use them.

"Even though John Lassiter and Bill Reeves, the same guys who did *Toy Story*, weren't part of ILM, we asked them to do seven shots," he continues. "Because of the slowness of the computers, they took six months to complete their effects. Today," he shakes his head, "it would take six weeks!"

In *Young Sherlock Holmes*, a knight steps out of a stained-glass window and tries to murder a priest. "The shot involved the first computer generated character seemingly made of glass. I was determined to design a creature that could be done no other way. Actually, the concept was my wife's idea," he says proudly. "We created a mobile out of separate pieces that were not connected. Bill Reeves and his crews modeled the different pieces and then animated them. Filmed with a film recorder put together on an optical printer, they were then combined with the background."

The film won another Academy Award nomination and Muren was hooked. His ambition was to refine this tool. "A film called *Willow* came along," he explains. "I now had a reason to push the computer department from research and development into full production."

In the story, Willow tries to retrieve his female friend, who has been turned into a possum. The wave of his wand doesn't exactly work. His friend, Fin Raziel becomes a goat, then an ostrich, and finally a tiger. "We did two-dimensional morphing," he explains. "It was originally called 'image blending,' this is where you move one shape into another.

"We created a program which takes images scanned into the computer and digitizes them. Then we merged the scenes together and worked out a way to put them back on to film. Everyone does it now, but back then we were the only ones to accomplish the technique."

Muren's Academy Award nomination for morphing caught James Cameron's eye. "He told me he was going to do a story where he would create a creature that was an amorphous pseudopod, composed entirely out of seawater. For *The Abyss*, he was thinking of stop-motion or computer graphics. For this project, we had to create a computer program that would do reflected and refracted light and animate a figure. We needed to sustain that for 75 seconds!"

In the scene, two of the scientists discover the being. As it rises in the water, it assumes the face of one of the scientists. The second character actually touches the face of the creature with her finger. "To do this, we shot the finger against blue screen touching nothing, then wrote procedural software for a CGI face and matched it to where the finger would be in the frame. At that point, it changes to another face, so we had to morph the two faces together."

Muren was taking computers to much more sophisti-cated heights. "Programming is an interesting art," he admits. "One step after another after another. You learn to transform one image to another, beginning at point A in one scene and moving to point B in a second scene. The idea is to create a program that moves objects from one point to another using a particular percentage of movement. Say you want the second scene to begin to appear at 10 percent into the move, leaving the other 90 percent of the frame intact. The next frame, the move in might go to 20 percent and then 30 percent. This is simple for the computer. It is the programmer who has to adapt to a linear way of thinking and create the codes to tell the hardware what to do.

"What is interesting is that you can give the problem to ten different computer programmers. Each will come back with a different solution. One might be using Photoshop, the other another program entirely. One solution might be great, the other solutions terrible. The computers haven't changed, it is the programmer and the codes, the language, that is the barrier."

The Motion Picture Academy bestowed yet another Technical Achievement Award on the people who created this program and Muren got a nomination for his visual effects work. He tries to pretend receiving the awards is getting old. "It is the work that counts," he repeats. Yet, there is still something about all this appreciation.

"Jim Cameron wasn't sure we could do it," he admits. He had protected himself by making the sequence autonomous. If we didn't get it right, he could always cut it out of the picture. Frankly, we didn't know what we were going to do when we began! The nominations, the awards, they say we did what our director wanted. It's kind of nice to know our peers appreciated the hair pulling and double vision!"

In 1991, convinced that Muren could capture almost anything he wanted to achieve, James Cameron returned to ILM for the effects in his newest science-fiction thriller, *Terminator 2: Judgment Day*. "This time he created a character who could not be cut out of the picture – in fact, he was the star!"

"Unlike the amorphous pseudopod of *The Abyss*, T-1000 is a killing machine," he says. "It could kill with its index finger and even regenerate after taking shotgun blasts. T-1000 had a chrome skin which reflected its surroundings. It could change at will – from a checkerboard to a cop and more. It could even pass through steel bars.

"This was definitely our, 'Oh, shit! How do we do this?!'" Muren laughs. "One of the biggest things here was to get the images into the computer from the dailies. This was the only way we could map them onto the chrome and do digital compositing," he explains. "Doing it this way would eliminate the final telltale flaw which was in the optical process.

"Optical compositing," he explains, "shrinks the film when it is developed. That means the image is different. When you try to overlap different images, they are no longer precise matches. That gives us a halo effect. By scanning the image and using digital software, we could get rid of that halo. We usually got a perfect take on the first try."

In 1993, Muren won over another skeptic when he delivered living, breathing creatures for Steven Spielberg's *Jurassic Park*. "In the beginning, Steven wasn't going to do computer graphics," he says. "It was all going to be stop-motion action. He had already discarded a few scenes that he wanted to do in the original script because they were too expensive. When I saw the script, I asked him if we could test a stampede sequence using computer graphics. We could now, we thought, replicate objects rather easily.

"Thank heaven for Kathy Kennedy! She was the one to give us the go ahead – without her, it wouldn't have happened. Fortunately, this was about nine months before the project really got off the ground.

"First, we did tests. Getting the T-Rex to walk in bright sunlight looked great. When Steven saw this, he brought back several discarded shots. Fortunately, he didn't see the second test! No matter what we did that second time, the animation looked jerky. Fortunately, by the time the show got done, we had solved the problem. It wasn't the program, it was our lack of experience in working it. I think we used Soft Image for this one. Again, the challenge was in the codes we fed into the computer. It took a while to get them right. Editing was vital here," he adds. "You have to watch every element so that you can tweak them until they are absolutely right. If we had done opticals, we might have had two or three passes and that would be it. By working on the computer, you can pay attention to minute details and move things as many times as necessary. And, since light and figures are independently created, you can change one and not the other.

"Lighting, within the computer environment, is also extremely important," he says, changing the subject. *Jurassic Park* was the first film to make massive strides in lighting for the computer. Up until this film, the CGI work revolved around inanimate or contrived images. Although the dinosaurs in *Jurassic Park* were extinct, they had lived. They were real creatures – living creatures. "We had to light them as we would living, breathing beings," Muren explains.

"That's something we had never thought of before! Now we had to create the tools – computer coukaloris, flags and other equipment to make shadows. We had to figure out things like duplicating the inverse square law of fall off. As light goes away from a source, it 'falls off,'" he explains.

"It is no accident that a cameraman broke the program! A computer programmer doesn't know that the tools have to fit the rest of the movie. And, if that programmer has been told, he most assuredly doesn't understand all the subtle filmic concepts."

Muren did, thanks to his determination and understanding of both film and computer mediums. So, Dennis Muren had racked up his eighth Academy Award for a dinosaur stampede, a fight between a prehistoric animal and a van, and a stalking sequence like no other. "What was going to be next? Humans, maybe? Then I realized humans are a variation of what we'd done before. However, we hadn't done natural phenomena. Someone must have a hidden mike in my mind," he laughs, "because I got a call about doing a ghost and a tornado. Well, they are natural phenomena – sort of!"

"For *Casper*, Steven Spielberg wanted the look of the Harveytoon," he explains. "We started with concept art. The idea was to create a 3-D sculpture that had the facial expressions and characteristics we thought would work. We concentrated on eyes, mouth, facial movement. Anything that would sell the idea of this figure interacting with the real world and in a real way.

"Unfortunately, by the time we got to the shooting, we realized what we had didn't work. We fed the stage notes, taken by Amblin Animation's animation director Phil Nibbelink on an Amiga computer (2-D models) into our computers. We found that live action lenses and computer lenses read things differently. We had to bend and stretch the material to make it work."

Their idea was to fool the audience the way they did on *Jurassic Park*. "It was the jeep shot all over again," Muren says. "What was the jeep and what was the CGI image? Here, we had to meld human elements into CGI elements as seamlessly as possible."

Animating the body was tricky, "but the bigger challenge was Casper's bald head," Muren says, unconsciously running his hand over his hair. "It didn't seem to be a problem on the set, but get it into the computer as a 3-D character and we had a major problem. Cinematographer Dean Cundey could use a cutter to take light off an object on the set, but there was no such thing as a cutter in the computer world. How could we take the light off that shiny object!?"

Since the ghosts were supposed to be opaque, lighting was a problem. Whatever was used would bleed through the figure. "We had to light in the computer by keeping everything away from the body. We also had to come at it from all sides at the same time. In essence, we rimmed the figure with computer light, and made the rest transparent – the eyes, however we made opaque, because the eyes are the window to the soul.

"No one believes me, but the hardest job we've ever done is the compositing on *Casper. Lost World* doesn't even come close! Just let the next person who tries to do it, prove me wrong!!

"For *Twister*, we created many techniques including what we call 'particle animation,'" Muren says. "We had no idea what that was or how to do it when Steven came to us with the idea of doing a tornado movie," he adds. "I knew nothing about tornadoes. So, I went in with the 'we can do it' attitude. Steven Spielberg thought we could so we weren't about to disappoint him.

"I had this great idea, a documentary-type point-of-view of the effect of a tornado. I wanted to see a handheld-type shot through the windshield of a car. We would look past the driver, go around a turn, and see a tornado off in the distance. It rips a barn up in the air, flies a tractor that crashes, and throws a tire through the car windshield. All in one shot!

"No, this was not a real barn or real props," he says, smiling. "This was a totally computer generated barn, which sent computer generated debris everywhere. We were even able to darken skies that had been shot for us to fit the appropriate mood for the shot.

"See, waiting around for the 'right' background could be a thing of the past now that we can duplicate and manipulate Mother Nature in the computer," he adds. "That was the test – if we could do that we could do the rest. The test greenlighted the movie. Then director Jan De Bont signed on, and the project got made with another crew. For me, the tests had been enough!"

For his next project, Dennis Muren seemed to return home, "to correct what I did years ago, when George Lucas and the rest of us were young, foolish, and up for anything new," he laughs. "For the *Star Wars* restoration project, we finally got to do things we wanted to do in the original, but didn't know how.

"We never really liked Jabba," he admits. "He looked like the manufactured figure he was. Now, because the computer software can replicate about anything we want, we were able to replace the awkward figure with what George had always wanted Jabba to be.

"Remember, when we did the first projects, there was no such thing as 'digital animation.' We still used stop-motion and unsophisticated techniques to blend the effects together. As the computer became more sophisticated and the resolution sharper, we could start doing finer and finer movements."

Press Dennis Muren to pick shots from *Jurassic Park: The Lost World*, the Spielberg/ILM sequel to their biggest CGI movie and he is very reserved in his judgment. He insists that there were more technological 'leaps' in the first picture. "We made more leaps to make the dragon mover work in the first picture," he says. "The leaps were just different in *Lost World* because we knew more about composite technology. When we did the first picture, we didn't know how to manipulate the programs to meld things like Spacecam shots following motorcycles through a round up of dinosaurs or pull downs by hunters. We couldn't do broad daylight shots that would last this long or show 30 CGI animals kicking up dust. It's the interaction that has changed. We can make muscles and skin look better. We can speed up the process. Now we have interactive software to make these things happen."

And, where did that software come from? Muren's determination to grow ILM's technology, that's where. Pre-*T2*, Dennis Muren realized there was something missing in ILM's technological battery of tools. He took a year off to study the use of MAC equipment. He believed ILM's stumbling block was digital compositing. It wasn't the people, but how the people talked to the computers.

"There was an input scanner we had co-built with Kodak," he says. "The people working with it couldn't decide on the resolution and depth. Kodak's specs were high and took an enormous file size. At least, that's what they said."

Muren was determined to find a way to get around this stumbling block. He found an earlier version of PhotoShop and, along with John Nowell, experimented. What he came up with was the absolutely necessary specs needed to make the moves required.

"CGI compositing happens in three stages," he explains. "The first stage, getting the image into the computer, second, manipulating that image, and third, getting it out on film.

"We could work with the first stage. However, the computer equipment we had was a piece of junk. I wanted to throw it in San Francisco Bay," he laughs. "So, during my sabbatical from ILM, I found time to research. What really worked was the film recorders used for business slides and presentations. A company called Management Graphics had a machine called Solitaire. Using that, I was able to ask it to scan real movie photo images with a full color range and output them again. We didn't need laser equipment like everyone said. We needed equipment that could take our images, take our instructions, and turn them back with a new refinement."

Because Dennis Muren took the time to investigate, even sinking several thousand dollars of his own money into a flatbed scanner, "which I immediately took apart to find out how it worked," he laughs, there are now extremely successful composited images on the movie screen – with no flaws. The morphing in *Terminator 2* began the process. As of 1997, the round up in *The Lost World* is the most sophisticated. "Is it?" Muren asks, with a straight face. He looks off at a little office, housing several of ILM's computers. It is one of the company's rare closed door sessions. From the look on Dennis Muren's face, there is a feeling that 40 tiny dinosaurs attacking a man, hunters rounding up a dinosaur herd, and dust blowing around the interactive elements of man and beast is going to look "elementary" in a very few short years – if he has anything to say about it.

******

American and British Academy Awards for Visual Effects *Jurassic Park, Terminator 2: Judgment Day, Indiana Jones and the Temple of Doom, Return of the Jedi* – **American Academy Awards** *The Abyss, Innerspace, E.T.: The Extra-Terrestrial, The Empire Strikes Back* – **Academy Technical Achievement Award** *Creator of Go-Motion Figure Mover* – **Academy Award Nominations for Visual Effects** *Willow, Young Sherlock Holmes, Dragonslayer* – **Emmy Award Visual Effects** *Caravan of Courage*

"Remember, you would be feeling things that were different from what was real because your only visual reference was through the eyepiece of the camera. This way my brain could see where everything was going to be through my left eye and I could pre-roll the horizon level with the camera as I tilted up to complete the shot."

David B. Nowell

The atmosphere in Canyon Country, a suburb 35 miles outside bustling Los Angeles, is quiet. The occasional neighing of a horse or the whizzing sound of an off-road vehicle is far different from the constant chatter and non-stop traffic jams of "the city." It doesn't matter to David Nowell that it takes him half an hour more than most people to get to "the studios." Although his job is in the Hollywood system, his "office" is high in the air above the bustle of Los Angeles, Rome, Sydney, or wherever the aerial shots of the moment are being done.

"No, I was not in the military," he laughs. It is a question often asked, a seemingly natural progression from flying for the service to flying for Hollywood. "I wasn't even interested in aviation, stunts, or Hollywood as a kid," he continues. Born and raised in Los Angeles, Nowell graduated with a B.A. degree in Communication Arts and Film from Loyola Marymount University. "It was now time to take Hollywood by storm," he says with that calm sense of humor that has gotten him through more than a few hair raising experiences.

Unfortunately Hollywood wasn't ready for this particular storm. "After graduating from college, I spent two years trying to find work of any kind, let alone get into camera," he adds. "It was the early 1970s and virtually all productions were done by the Union, which was fine until you tried to get into the Union. The motto then was: 'To qualify to become a member of the Union you have to work 30 days on a Union show, but to work on a Union show you have to already be a member of the Union.' You can imagine it was a little difficult to get in back then."

Finally a friend, who was an established assistant cameraman, was going to do an undercover, non-union show. He brought Nowell in and trained him as a second assistant/loader on *The Mad Bomber.* "I finally started meeting people who could help me in my career as a cameraman," Nowell says. "John Cassavettes gave me a chance to work on *A Woman Under the Influence* as an assistant cameraman. He eventually made me one of the operators. That was when I knew, looking through the eyepiece of the camera, that this was what I wanted to do."

During this period, Nowell worked on a few features as an assistant, meeting the right people. One of these was Rex Metz, who at the time was one of the top aerial camera operators in the business. Through this connection with Metz, Nowell was introduced to the fledgling aerial camera company, Continental Camera Systems.

C.C.S. was just starting out with a brand new design for a helicopter camera platform that would compete with the established Tyler Camera Systems. The old method of putting a camera on a Mitchell hi-hat and then onto a mattress spring to take out the helicopter's vibration – like the strafing beach shot in *The Longest Day* – was now part of ancient film history. The industry now had sophisticated gimbaled and isolated camera platforms from Tyler and was soon to receive one from Continental Camera Systems.

"Of course, they had no money to pay me either as a machinist or as an assistant cameraman," Nowell says ruefully. "But the opportunity was there for me to go out on jobs and meet new people while I was teaching them the use of this new camera platform." It didn't take long for Nowell to connect with those who needed aerial work.

"In 1974, I finally got into the Union as an A/C through the efforts of John Carroll, the head of C.C.S. John was also instrumental in providing me with opportunities to work as an aerial cameraman.

"Most of the well-known aerial cameramen, David Butler, Frank Holgate, and Rex Metz, would only shoot the 35mm jobs. This left me with wonderful opportunities to learn the art of aerial photography doing the 16mm jobs myself. You still weren't allowed to make any mistakes because a producer of a 16mm job wanted it perfect, too."

Soon David Nowell got his first 35mm job on a feature called *Hustle*. "When David Butler was unable to complete the day's work, I was asked to take over. It's like they say about anything I guess, it's being in the right place at the right time."

What were some of the skills that Nowell picked up during this time? "From the input of different cameramen I would hear: 'Grip the mount lightly, let the mount do the work, be easy on the zoom and focus controls,'" he says. "Things like that. It really came down to me finding out what worked best for me.

"One thing I was always a stickler for was having the horizon level in the frame as I tilted from the ground up to reveal the horizon," he explains. "I always hated it when I saw other cameramen correct for their horizon after it was already in the shot. What I did was open my left eye and see where it was as the helicopter was rolling out of a turn.

"Remember, you would be feeling things that were different from what was real because your only visual reference was through the eyepiece. This way my brain could see where everything was going to be through my left eye and I could pre-roll the horizon level with the camera as I tilted up to complete the shot.

"I learned other techniques literally through the seat of my pants from the camera platform. Both the Tyler and the Continental mounts required that a door be removed from the helicopter and the camera platform placed in the back seat area. Both had a counter-weighted arm that had a gimbal in the middle. This gimbal allowed the arm to pan, tilt, and roll. Each platform had pistol grips under the camera that gave the camera operator control over zoom, focus and camera on-off."

As the equipment changed, Nowell's vehicles changed as well. "We started using a helicopter called a Bell 47, the type you saw on *M.A.S.H.*," he explains. "It had limited space and very little power. Next we used a Bell J2-B which had a lot more room, but not much more power. We finally came into the jet age with the Bell Jet Ranger helicopter. This still is one of the best helicopters to use when it comes to the Tyler or Continental 'side mounts,'" he explains.

"One of the techniques critical to an aerial camera operator's reputation is the 'zoom out or pull back' shot with a helicopter. If you ever see a 'pull back' shot where the zoom suddenly hits a stop during the movement of the helicopter, it's probably been done by a newcomer," Nowell explains. "You have to start the shot by carefully zooming back on the lens. Then you tell the pilot to start pulling back in the helicopter as you slowly stop zooming the lens at the wide end to blend its movement into the pull back of the helicopter.

"A lot of this will depend on your relationship with your pilot," he admits. "The closer the relationship, the less that is said because you know what the other guy is thinking. When flying with my longtime friend Rick Holley shooting opening shots for China Syndrome, he yelled at me to keep rolling. He had an idea for something he could see coming up ahead.

"We had been filming Jane Fonda and Michael Douglas as they drove their Bronco on Interstate 5 just north of L.A.," Nowell explains. "Rick radioed Michael to change lanes and get in close to the right shoulder. Rick dropped us right next to the vehicle, calling out focus distances as we approached. I was able to get a tight shot of Jane as she talked with Michael.

"We then 'pulled back' to show the Bronco about to exit the freeway. The whole shot lasted a little over a minute. None of this had been planned and we didn't have another chance to do anything different. The director loved the shot so much when he saw it the next day that it was used, uncut, for part of the opening title sequence."

In 1974, C.C.S. introduced the Astrovision system. It was a periscope similar to what is in submarines except there were two of them and they were installed in a Lear jet, one out the top and one out the bottom. Cameras were mounted onto these periscopes inside the Lear. The Astrovision now allowed for 360 degree pans and 45 degree tilts – the tilt coming from a small moving prism located behind a small window in the end of each periscope.

With video taps on each of the Astrovision periscopes, all functions were done by remote control while looking at a video monitor in the control console. Most aerial shots of jets had been done from a B-25 bomber because of its excellent use of camera positions. The problem with the B-25 was it was becoming too slow as commercial aviation was developing faster jet aircraft. The Lear with the Astrovision installed had no problem keeping up.

"Because the Astrovision was one of the few systems, at this time, that was operated solely by remote control, I was getting some serious 'stick time' that no one else in the industry was able to get," Nowell recalls. "It was during this time, say late 1975, that Francis Ford Coppola and Vittorio Storaro approached C.C.S. about supplying aerial camera platforms for a little film they were going to do called *Apocalypse Now*. Little did we know what we were getting into.

"We sent over two Continental mounts. One was for David Butler to use in a Jet Ranger that Francis bought just for our use on the movie. The other was for me to use in the Army Huey helicopters. The plan was for Butler to be able to photograph the armada of helicopters during any part of the attack sequence without seeing me, while I shot other pieces of the sequence hidden inside the larger helicopter. This setup worked very well. We were able to get two for one coverage anytime we went up to fly.

"We also had a Continental belly-mount that would bolt to the underside of our Jet Ranger. The special effects department strapped Roman Candle launchers to the skids facing forward and we were able to get great P.O.V. shots of rockets being fired toward the Viet Cong village.

"Months before we left for the Philippines, we had Francis' private airplane, a Mitsubishi MU-2L, outfitted to take the Astrovision system. We were going to use this setup specifically for filming the jets that were going to do the big napalm drop on the jungle. While Butler waited to shoot from the Jet Ranger and Vittorio's crew waited on the ground, I waited in the MU-2 circling over the coast line, counting sharks in the water below, until the Philippine Air Force Blue Diamonds finally arrived to drop their napalm tanks into the jungle set.

"And all this so we could make the shore line safe for Robert Duvall to go surfing. Remember, . . . 'The smell of napalm in the morning does smell like . . . victory.'"

Since the collaboration of Aerial Coordinator J. David Jones, Aerial D.P. David Butler, and Nowell worked so well, they were asked to do the aerial work on Peter Hyams' new film, *Capricorn One*. The film called for a huge air chase sequence at the end between an escaping astronaut clinging to the wing of a bi-plane and two military helicopters trying to shoot it down. The whole chase would be taking place through a canyon area just north of L.A. "Peter wanted very specific things: The camera would only shoot either straight forward or straight back; he didn't want side angles. Whenever the bi-plane banked, the camera had to bank, too. That way, the bi-plane's wings were always level in frame.

"We all racked our brains over this one," Nowell admits. "You see, at the time, the only mount that could shoot straight forward was a belly or nose mount. The problem, you couldn't pan, tilt, or roll the camera You couldn't use a zoom lens either. The gyro stabilized ball mounts were still years away from working properly, so that left us with either the Tyler or Continental side mounts.

"I finally figured out what to do. If everybody didn't laugh, I knew I could make it work. Well, they didn't laugh, but they thought I was nuts. I built a platform specifically for a Hughes 500 helicopter. This allowed me to bolt a Continental mount, seat and all, on the outside of the helicopter. This way, I could face the camera mount forward or rear. The camera operator had complete control over pan, tilt, roll and zoom.

"We had written on the side pod of this rig, 'E ticket ride,' remembering the most exciting rides from Disneyland's old ticket method. Believe me, this ride was definitely worth the 'E ticket.'"

By this time Nowell had put in the necessary time as an assistant camera operator as required by the Union. Even though he had been operating and shooting aerials for years, it was time to make the move officially. In 1977 he became an official camera operator.

"As an operator, you had to be behind the camera, but as an Aerial Operator I would often become the D.P. of these sequences as there was no room for the D.P. to be with you. This was terrific training. Directors and producers were trusting my decisions knowing my background of aerial and ground work. More and more, they were letting me do everything, even though I was considered just the 'operator.'

"I think the problem with the young guys becoming Aerial Operators today is that most of them have been technicians for a specific piece of equipment and eventually are capable of operating them, but most have had no real film background. Most have never gone through the production chain of assistant cameraman to operator to D.P., and I think this lack of training affects their careers. I don't see the producers and directors putting that much trust in them.

"The time I spent as a ground camera operator was very special. I started doing a lot of work with cameraman Charlie Correll, at first doing B-camera, but eventually becoming his A operator. We did some TV and one small feature until we did *Star Trek: The Search for Spock*. It was great. A major feature, anomorphic, what could be better? Right after that, we did a TV series called *Our Family Honor*. It was during a hiatus on this show, that I was asked to do the aerials on *Top Gun*.

"This was another situation like *Apocalypse* where we had no idea what a huge hit this picture would be. I could tell something very special was going to happen every time I talked with director Tony Scott. Nobody before had taken the time to get specific shots with such exacting lighting conditions. Since an aircraft such as an F-14 Tomcat is very expensive to pay for, producers usually want shots to be done fast no matter what the look. But Tony would take the time to get the shot he wanted even if it meant getting out his own checkbook.

"I had done plenty of other films involving military aircraft, like *The Great Santini*, but nobody had wanted to do aerial shots from the ground like Tony wanted to do. After Tony saw the aerial work I did for him, he asked me to be involved in the ground shots as well. We took cameras with long lenses, some up to 1600mm, on top of a mountain overlooking a dry lake near Fallon, Nevada. From this vantage point, we could be at the same altitude as the F-14s while they did all their maneuvers: flying toward us, flying away from us or flying left and right.

"You just can't get the high dynamic feel of speed or maneuverability of an aircraft when you're flying with it at the same speed and direction," Nowell explains. "But fix that camera position and you can really see and feel all this, especially through the look of a long lens. While sitting on this mountain top waiting for the F-14s to arrive, Tony would describe how he wanted to cut this sequence together. Using rock music, he wanted the aerial dog fights to feel like a *Rocky* heavyweight fight sequence.

"I've worked with Tony on just about all his features and commercials since then and learned new things each time, but the best for me was this shooting technique. I've used it myself ever since, from *Iron Eagle 2* to directing the aerial sequences on *Outbreak*. You can't beat doing some great aerial shots from the ground."

Around this time is when the gyro stabilized "ball" mounts were coming into their own. Although they had existed since the mid-1960s, their reliability and track record had not been good. With the advanced electronics design of Howard Preston, the Gyrosphere began the era of reliable and sophisticated stabilized aerial photography. Because Nowell was at the top of the aerial field, and was one of the few people with a background using remote control cameras, he was a natural to begin using this new tool.

"I think it was only the second time I had ever used the Gyrosphere when Stephen Goldblatt asked me to shoot the opening sequence for *Lethal Weapon*. The shot required flying a long distance over Long Beach before coming to and circling an apartment building, then zooming into a window to see a young woman lying on a sofa. To cover the distance in the beginning of the shot required shooting at six frames per second, then as we approached the building ramp the film speed went up to 18 frames per second for the effect that Stephen wanted.

"I had never operated this system at six frames, nor had I any experience with changing the frame rate during a shot. I had to calculate as best I could my input on the controls. In effect, this had to be one fourth their normal input, since we were shooting at 6 f.p.s. and projecting back at 24 f.p.s. My usual habit of seeing dailies as often as I could was essential because the projected effect of this whole shot would be completely different than the real-time feel of the shot.

"Thankfully the director, Dick Donner, had scheduled two nights for this shot. I wanted to fine tune my operating after I saw the first night's work. It wasn't that the first night's shots were bad, but with the difficulty of looking at a very slow shutter plus the video being dark, I was virtually blind on part of the beginning of the shot. With the chance of a second night, I knew what to do even though I couldn't see it very well."

Aerial Units were becoming larger for Nowell. Instead of just the aerial shots, he was being asked to include ground shots, actors, stunts, and lighting. They were becoming full-blown 2nd Units. It was in 1989 that Nowell moved up to Director of Photography for a 2nd Unit on a film called *Ghost Dad*.

Soon after that Paramount wanted Nowell on the 2nd Unit of a new project. *Flight of the Intruder* was going to involve the normal shooting, but one requirement added a new dimension. "We outfitted an A-6 Intruder with four camera positions using special camera mounts that had been developed by Grumman Aircraft Co. for test purposes on the F-14 program. These mounts had previously been used on the films *The Final Count Down* and *Top Gun*.

"We mounted one in the cockpit looking forward over the shoulders of the pilot and the bomber/navigator (they sit side by side in this aircraft). The second was under the belly of the plane. It could look either forward or aft for take offs and landings on the aircraft carrier. The third could be mounted under either wing looking forward or aft. Another was high on the tail looking down on the fuselage.

"Essentially, I had to be in the cockpit to run these cameras. So, after two days of poking and probing for a flight physical, being thrown into the pool with all my flight gear on to see if I could keep myself from drowning, hurled upwards at 15 g's in an ejection seat trainer, and hung from the ceiling by parachute lines to see if I could escape from my harness, I was now officially cleared to fly in Naval aircraft. The first two flights were from a runway at Barber's Point NAS in Hawaii, but the next one came from our work on the deck of the U.S.S. Independence aircraft carrier.

"Nothing in the world short of being fired from a cannon will prepare you for the experience of being catapulted from the deck of an aircraft carrier in a Navy attack aircraft," he laughs. "It's a nine-g kick in the back that leads to a six-g acceleration of zero to 150 mph in about 2.3 seconds."

After the completion of *Intruder*, Nowell realized there needed to be a change in the direction of his film career. "I had done so many shows and worked with so many directors that were good and talented people, but had no idea how to do aerials," he explains. "I was getting a little frustrated, showing them how to do everything while they took all the credit for what was being done.

"The producers from *Iron Eagle 2*, which I had shot the aerial work, approached me with the idea of shooting the aerials for *Iron Eagle 3*. I told them I thought it would be a better idea for me to take on the job of director as well as cameraman. It made more sense for me to do it rather than teach someone else what to do. The producers agreed and I embarked on a new segment in my life in features as a director/cameraman. This background led fairly soon to my being taken on in a commercial production company as one of their director/cameramen for commercial work."

Career opportunities were changing and so were pieces of equipment. New and innovative tools were popping up all the time. "The hand held GPS or Global Positioning Systems were just getting cost effective when Stephen Goldblatt and I were heading to New Orleans to work together on the opening shots for *The Pelican Brief*," he adds. "I had just purchased one of these GPS units, figuring it would be worthwhile at some point, on some show.

"Stephen knew he would be directing most of this shoot, but knew at some point he would have to leave to do a 1st Unit shot and would be sending me off to direct the remainder of the sequence. The one thing he wanted to do ahead of time was pick all the locations for both his section of the shoot and mine.

"We spent a day in a helicopter flying around the featureless landscape of swamps and lakes outside the New Orleans area. With the GPS, I was able to store in memory all the locations Stephen liked. Later, I was able to calculate where and when the sunrises and sunsets would take place. I then mapped out the entire shoot based on this information, even though it wouldn't take place for another three days. When the day came to start the shoot, the GPS guided us to all of our spots at the precise time and compass heading of each sunrise and sunset.

"Somebody once asked what my favorite shoot was. I think of everything I've had a chance to do in my lifetime as a cameraman, there are two shoots that stand out the most. The first was being one of 25 operators to film the 1984 Olympics in Los Angeles. More than anything, it was the spirit of being involved with this event. The Olympic spirit is something very real when you are right there in the middle of these games," Nowell says, sincerely.

"The second shoot would have to be filming the weightless sequences for *Apollo 13*. Ron Howard's producer, Todd Hallowell, had asked me to shoot some of the aerial sequences for the film. During our conversation, he mentioned this zero-gravity work they had planned. As I pressed him for more information, I realized this was something I would dearly love to be involved with. I convinced him that I had a good lighting background from commercials and 2nd Units and would be the ideal person to head up this particular unit. He agreed.

"As we started putting this unit together, we realized we had to have the crew's complete commitment to this project because of NASA's requirements. We started with lighting tests inside our set pieces which were placed inside a mock-up of the interior of a military KC-135 aircraft. This aircraft is affectionately known as the 'vomit comet.' Andy Ryan, the gaffer on this unit, came up with some great lighting tricks. Because we would be shooting with extremely wide angle lenses, usually between 10mm and 17mm, all lighting within the capsule sets had to be practical or coming through windows. Since our shots were so wide, in order to see the entire interior to get the full effect of zero gravity on the actors, there were few places to hide any lights.

"Unlike what would be happening later on with the 1st Unit capsule set, we would only have about eight inches of room outside the set to be able to light from. Andy came up with an ingenious mirror and motor setup so we could reflect moving light into the set to simulate the rotation of the capsule through sunlight. He also came up with some fiber optics that could be poked through the instrument panel to simulate light from computer faces or other gauges. Once Ron had approved the lighting and filming techniques we thought would work, everything was packed up and shipped to Houston to be put into the KC-135 that is based at Ellington AFB.

"The idea behind creating zero gravity is this: The KC-135 climbs at a steep angle to 34,000 feet, at this altitude, it dives over toward the ground at a descending rate equal to an object falling through space. Since there is no wind inside the aircraft, all objects become weightless and start to float. This lasts for approximately 23 seconds before the aircraft reaches 24,000 feet and has to level out. It then climbs again to repeat the process.

"All totaled, we did 564 of these maneuvers over a period of several weeks to achieve the necessary footage for these sequences. Since everything becomes weightless, we had to bolt the sets to the floor of the aircraft. All lights and cables were then clamped or bolted to the set. This left the actors and ourselves as the only objects able to float during the 23 second weightless period.

"We rigged the set pieces with batteries and video cables at our pre-determined camera positions. This way, whenever we changed shots, all we had to do was unplug the camera body and move to the next station and plug in ready to go. This whole shoot was an extreme exercise in 'time is money.'

"Because of this, we carried a third backup camera fully rigged and ready to go should there be a problem with either of the two main cameras. Sure enough, on the very first flight, the electronics died on the B-camera. Within minutes, we were back shooting. It may have seemed excessive at first to have all these extra backups, but at $9,000.00 per hour for the use of the aircraft, the cost of the backups were minimal when they saved the shoot.

"Aside from the extreme mental and physical strain to complete this part of the production, we all had a great time. Not many people got motion sickness as you might think. Our greatest bit of fun was anytime you didn't have to shoot during a weightless maneuver or 'parabola.' All it took was a slight shove and you could send one of your crew members floating past the set and into the interior of the plane. You couldn't do anything about it until you could catch a rope or a bit of the set to stop yourself. Then you would spin yourself around in mid air and float back to another position. This was even better than the *Capricorn One* E-ticket ride. As we all know, *Apollo 13* was a huge hit and it was great having been part of it."

Nowell moved on to another kind of E-ticket ride, working with the new technology of computer generated images or CGI. "It has begun to invade the world of aerials," he says. "Some CGI use has real advantages, like adding low level power wires into a shot in *Outbreak* where it would have been far to dangerous to do it for real," Nowell explains. "But some use of CGI is taking away actual aerial shots. Although these shots may look very spectacular, the very fact that they couldn't have been done for real seems to take away a certain dimension or feel that is there when you work with the real thing. The computer still can't generate realistic backgrounds for certain work."

"In *Mission Impossible*, we went to Scotland to film the countryside and its railway lines for the high speed train and helicopter sequence. The plan was for ILM to create the entire exterior of the train in CGI and then composite the actors onto the roof of that train. That left us with filming all our shots pretending as if the train was there. This was interesting, trying to picture in my mind what the pans and tilts should look like during the shot as if there were a real train hurtling down the track at 150 mph while we descended and moved closer to the imaginary roof where the imaginary actors were fighting.

"We had to do something similar for Steven Spielberg's *Lost World*," he adds. "I was already slated to direct the aerial sequences, but they asked if I could help with some of the dinosaur round up scenes since I would have to work with imaginary things in the frame similar to the work on *Mission*. We took the Gyrosphere equipped with a VistaVision 8 perf camera and put it on an off-road racing truck. Off we raced across the fields with jeeps and motorcycles, panning and tilting as if we were following the capture of a herd of dinosaurs."

David Nowell's latest project has been *Air Force One*. "This has been another collaboration with my friends from *Outbreak*, director Wolfgang Petersen and D.P. Michael Ballhaus A.S.C. The sequence we just finished was the 'aerial rescue' that takes place at the end of the movie. The 747 of the President, (Harrison Ford) is running out of fuel. All the pilots are dead and the only people left on board are the President, his family, a secret service agent and one aid.

"A military C-130 flies in close to attempt a rescue of these people before the 747 crashes into the ocean below," Nowell explains. "Special Forces Rangers get themselves from the C-130 to the 747 by way of a cable they have stretched between the two aircraft.

"This entire sequence was done with real airplanes, no miniatures or CGI planes on this one. But we took a step backwards, as far as equipment goes, to be able to shoot these scenes. The whole sequence takes place just before sunrise. This meant, for me to shoot with the proper light, I only had the 15 minutes before the sun comes up and 15 minutes after the sun went down in which to shoot. It took me seven to complete everything from the production shots to all the plate shots too.

"The reason for stepping backwards on equipment was I had to shoot everything with T1.4 speed prime lenses. None of the new sophisticated equipment is capable of shooting at that f-stop or if they could use the speed lenses, they didn't have the capability of changing lenses in a matter of seconds like I needed. So we did everything from the good old B-25 bomber. This way I could change lenses in seconds or change camera positions by crawling from the tail section of the plane to the bomber position or back again.

"This sequence took major planning and briefings before each flight. The crew of each aircraft had to know almost to the minute which shot we were doing, which included compass heading, altitude, action of the aircraft, etc. This was the tightest I have ever had to plan a shoot. Luckily all three aircraft crew were perfect, the weather co-operated, and I didn't have but one or two glitches in the sequence scheduling."

Recently, cinematographer Jeffrey Kimball asked Nowell to come to Florida to do a shot for *The Wild Things*. Kimball felt that David Nowell was the only person to capture the shot – so the production scheduled their time around Nowell's. "So, why am I off to Florida for the third time? I still haven't done the shot!" That is part of the breaks when Mother Nature, a movie schedule, and a hot cinematographer/director are thrown into the mix.

"It is often the 'hurry up and wait' syndrome," Nowell says, lightly. "At the moment, I'm working on a movie called *I Know What You Did Last Summer*. We left Van Nuys on Tuesday and flew for three hours to Santa Rosa to scout the shot with the director. Unfortunately, it was raining by the time we got here. The scout was canceled and rescheduled for the next evening if the weather was good.

"With the camera system now mounted on the helicopter we picked up the director and flew in perfect weather conditions to rehearse the shot on Wednesday evening. After the rehearsal, we were told we wouldn't be used until Thursday evening because 1st Unit was behind due to the rain the night before! On Thursday, we were told we wouldn't be used now until Friday evening because 1st Unit still hadn't finished. Finally, we shot on Friday evening and traveled home Saturday. A one day shoot turned into three days of sitting around the hotel! Good thing I took a few things with me to occupy my attention in that oh-so-fancy hotel!

"That isn't the worst of the syndrome," he laughs. "I remember spending nine days waiting to even start a commercial. A Japanese company had picked a lake location high in the mountains just outside Portland, Oregon. Every day we would push the helicopter out of the hanger and look to the skies. Sometimes, we could get airborne but could never get to the lake location because the clouds were still too low or it would start raining and we would return only to push the helicopter back into the hanger.

"This went on for four days. We knew the weather report was calling for this weather pattern to continue for at least another five days. Finally, the production company sent us home to wait to be called back when the weather looked good.

"I had no sooner walked in the front door than the phone rang. It was the production company saying come back up immediately. They had looked outside and had seen blue skies, so the weather must be getting better. I called the pilot, who had gotten the same phone call, and asked him what he knew about the weather change. All of his sources still indicated rain for the next five days. So we all trooped back up to Portland because the company thought it best and we waited in the hotel for the next five days while it continued to pour. The company finally scrubbed the Portland shoot and we finished the commercial three days later at Lake Powell in Utah."

******

1982, 1984 Emmy Award for Outstanding Aerial Cinematography
David Copperfield Specials

"You can stretch the palette a lot more when you are doing projects that allow more freedom. Of course, I am always afraid each time I push it a little farther than the last. But, I will always remember something Michael Chapman once said. 'When the fear goes, it's time to move on.' I live with this fear everyday."

Salvatore Totino

Outside the windows of Salvatore Totino's home the rain is coming down in sheets. The sound of a ferocious Southern California storm pounding the large glass windows is all but drowned out by upbeat music. It is the background to some of the unusual visuals playing across the large television screen in the sun room. The floor to ceiling audio/video unit is relatively new and Totino is proud of the changes that are being made in this comfortable "old California" home. "We're getting the house ready for a new addition," he says, eyes flashing away from his newly cut reel. "Our first child will be here in a few months."

The sound surges as he turns his attention back to the screen. "That's a Marlboro commercial," he says, "although you would never know it. And that's the latest Soundgarden video," he adds, as a desert scene covered with orange and yellow colors fills the screen.

The song is "Burning In The Hand." The screen is filled with barren desert. The members of the band are wandering aimlessly across the landscape. At first, everything is dead – a deserted mobile home, the shell of a 1950s truck buried in the sand. As the band enters an old building, the wind blows, sealing them in.

"The challenge was how to make a desert interesting," says Totino. "We tried to do it with props – like a half-buried airplane wing, with sound and visuals – f4s flying over and with effects – a lightning storm and a tree catching on fire. Most of all, we used camera tricks – grad filters and a pinhole lens. The lens," he explains, "is courtesy of Clairmont Cameras. By using a piece of metal with a small hole in the center, in front of the lens, you can focus on very interesting points in your shot. Add changes from using both normal and reversal stock and the visuals are really striking."

Totino reverses the tape and replays the Marlboro spot. It begins in the snow. Two cowboys, one young, the other old, are driving horses back to their ranch. "The storm begins to spook the horses," Totino explains. "Instead of leading them into a corral, the older cowboy pushes on to a hidden cave. Shelter for the night. In the morning, they finish their journey through new snow.

"When we were scouting for Marlboro, we looked at some beautiful sacred Indian lands," he adds. "We flew in a ten-seater plane. As we were leaving, I saw our production designer carrying a little bag of dirt. He was bringing it back home to match the color of the landscape for some scenic set designs. I just about freaked," he laughs. "Would disturbing the land be the reason we had a little bit of a 'rough' flight back?" he shrugs. "Any way you look at it, every job is an adventure!" he adds. "Shooting with real horses and actors, in a cave at night – that was a challenge! So was trucking in all the fake snow we needed for the 'morning drive' to the ranch."

Totino turns his attention back to the video. "When a cinematographer specializes in music videos and commercials, keeping a reel fresh with startling images and unusual techniques is extremely important. I always like to keep mine visually interesting and offbeat," he explains. "I'm adding a recent Nestee spot directed by Alex Pryas and designed by Nigel Phelps (*Aliens*) in a few days. This is an extremely stylized concept, with no hint of the 'product,' except the logo at the end."

"The 'story' follows students in a business school class. The room is 40 feet by 22 feet high and about 12 feet wide. We lit everything from the top and used monochromatic colors with a hint of yellow in the sets. The perspective is through a 6mm lens. In post, we used Power Windows to get the effect of a 10mm without distortion.

"Backed by very strange music, the camera dollies in very slowly, following a dominatrix-type teacher wearing glasses as she walks to a box of chalk, takes a piece, then scratches on the board. We use close-ups on a thermometer, the chalk, then cut to students wincing with pain, screeching. We see eyeglasses shatter. '*Time for Nestee.*' We cut back to the teacher who is tied to a chair – suddenly the logo appears over the shot."

Totino is one of the top commercial and music video cinematographers in the business. His work is more than ground breaking, it is often on the edge – or over the edge. However, what he does is often grounded in a very classic style of cinematography. Somewhat in the minority, he prefers to first try to do effects in camera as opposed to in post production.

"When we go to post, it is to enhance what we have done with very specific elements in mind. In the Soundgarden piece, we used Power Windows to do things like draw a line across the screen and color correct what is above the line or below it. Doing this, you can change the color of the original image by changing the color of the sky and not the sand or vice versa."

He picks up the remote and punches it. Another eye-catching video fills the screen. An intense looking black and white H.I.S. Jeans commercial called "Cropduster" is a bit sexist and simple. A young flyer has his eye on a beautiful farm girl as she hangs laundry on a line. He tries to get her attention. Desperate, he starts throwing his clothes out the window of the plane as he flies over. When she sees the H.I.S. Jeans, she drops everything and runs to meet his landing plane. The two take off together.

Did Totino shoot color film and drain out the color in post to black-and-white? "No, we shot black-and-white film," he smiles. "The agency wanted to shoot color so they would have the option later. The director and I fought hard to convince them that black-and-white film was the best way to go. The combination of heavy red filters and old fashion arc lights helped us to intensify the black-and-white imagery." Striking and simple, as Totino says. The image caught the Clio committee's eye and won him the 1995 Gold Clio Award for best cinematography.

With a reputation for using the strange and unusual, you would think Totino ignores the rules of filmmaking.

"Filmmaking is different than making music videos or commercials," he smiles. "There are no rules in this world," he says as he punches the button on the clicker, freezing the frame. "I take it back, there is one rule – don't follow the rules. Personally, I have one other rule – do as many of the effects in camera that you can." Over the past few months, Totino has really stretched his creativity with some of the strangest rule breaking techniques.

He smiles at the new U2 video "Staring at the Sun." "Going into this video I knew most of the effects were going to be done in the Flame program, but I still wanted to do as much as possible in camera," he says. "Performance videos are difficult and you often want to do something a bit out-of-the-ordinary to give the performance a different look.

"Director Jake Scott had a few specific ideas in mind. To accomplish his concept, we did a few tests prior to the shoot. I decided to use another of Clairmont's devices. This time, it was the over and under rig (see artwork) for the shutterless camera – doing a kind of poor man's process. Since you can't look through the camera to focus, I put a shutter camera on top of the shooting camera. This helped us dissolve from shutter shots to shutterless shots in post."

Totino will use whatever he can to push the limits of the equipment available, depending on what the job calls for. "Sometimes, you get a great idea and you can push it just a little too far," he adds. "The shutterless camera worked great for Jake Scott's job. However, there was one time when I pushed things just a little too far. It was on another Nestee commercial. I was underexposing a scene and Alex Prayas asked me if I was on the edge. I said I'd never been quite this on the edge. He trusted me and gave me permission to go for it. Next day, after dailies he looked at me and said, 'I guess you fell off, didn't you?' The two of us had a great laugh and went back and did it the right way!"

You can tell that Totino loves what he does. The jobs are always intense and can take anywhere from one day to two or three weeks to shoot. "Everything changes from job to job and I like that," he says. "Sometimes, I will get a six-page treatment and have no idea what the spot or video is about,

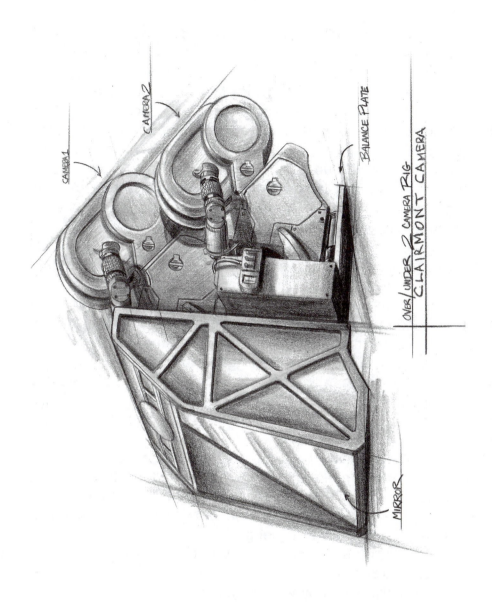

even after I've read it. At other times, I can get boards that tell the story shot by shot. Of course, we don't always follow what is in the sketch.

"There are always a lot of different pressures, especially in commercials," he says, getting serious. "On some commercial shoots, we usually complete shooting most of the story board and then do the product last. The whole job can go really smoothly up to that point, and the minute the product arrives on the set everyone gets tense. That's because the agency becomes so focused, the product shots are all important to their client.

"I remember one series of international spots we were doing for a beer client," he recalls. "We had to have a different bottle for each country. That meant we had to shoot each cut – master, insert, everything – four times. The positioning, even of the hand in wide shots, became so very important to the client. Sometimes," he laughs, "products and their entourage can be more difficult than the biggest Hollywood stars!

"It is ironic, we can spend more money on a three-day shoot than feature people spend on four or even eight weeks of a picture considered 'low budget.' That's why the pressure is sometimes so high.

"Then again," he says, as he clicks the television off, "we have done projects with no money and still finished with incredible visuals. For me, what I can do with my camera and lighting is a lot more important than how much I have to spend on the toys. That's the challenge."

Totino thrives on the challenge of this ever-changing world of short shoots. "You never know what is going to come up," he says. "One day you might have a huge budget and all the toys. The next day, next job, there is nothing to work with and you have to readjust your approach and call on spur-of-the-moment possibilities.

"Not too long ago, I had a commercial for Bud beer. We were supposed to shoot in a bar: The lighting was limited. The area was small. We used a partial front surface mirror in the foreground of the camera. This reflected the bar lights, making it appear bigger and grander than it really was.

"For a *Live* video, we wanted one light source to cast shadows on a wall. The shadows had to be intense and contrasty, but we didn't want them to affect the talent. We couldn't underexpose or push the contrast in post, so we brought in a scenic artist to enhance the light, the contrast with a 12 dollar gallon of paint!"

That is part of the fun of doing these mini-productions. Totino never knows what is going to happen when he gets to the set. He spends a great deal of time in preparation, only to change everything once he begins the shoot. "At times, there is a great gap between prep and the production," he admits. "Sometimes we get there and everything is in place but you get a sudden idea of how to make it better.

"Of course, there are times when you wish you were any place but on that particular set. I remember doing a commercial with Bryan Brown as the talent. Part of the gimmick was a tarantula walking on his leg. Well, obviously, they weren't going to let this valuable actor have the thing walk on his leg! To get the actor's point-of-view, the director had me do a handheld shot – with the tarantula walking on my calf! At one point, the thing disappeared up my pants! You should have seen how fast I threw the camera at my assistant and ran!

"It was an intense, but funny, moment. For me, the more fun we can have, the more creative everyone can be. That goes for product shots, music videos, and features."

Yes, Totino has been offered feature film work. There is a script or two sitting on his desk in the other room. "Sometimes people see something on my commercial reel and they want me to duplicate that look for their project," he says. "It isn't always possible to do, because the look and feel of one spot doesn't always fit for another. The end result of each job comes out of a whole lot of different elements and those elements are what helps to give each job its own individual character.

"At the moment, I'm waiting to hear about a project budgeted at eight million. Low, for a feature. The director said he wanted to go with a cinematographer who knew no rules and had no boundaries. That's me," he says enthusiastically.

"Yes, I would like to do features and I feel that my experience in commercials and music videos would lend a lot to a motion picture."

How did this son of Italian immigrants, living in a New York suburb, get into this fast paced world of no-holds-barred creativity? "I wasn't exactly the greatest student," he laughs. "Frankly, I had trouble in school. My 'counselors' tried to steer me toward trade school. I went to a private college for two and a half years and ended up working for an electrical contractor."

Totino got his first break into the business at a family gathering. "Italian families are big on 'reunions,'" he adds. "At one of those major get-togethers, I found out a distant relative was in the film business. He worked at Fairbanks Films, a commercial production company where the Scotts were, before they started their own house. I got a job as a production assistant. I had no idea what that meant, so I went to the movies and read the credits. When I saw that the 'PA' got a credit, I thought it must be something important."

After the first day on the job, Totino was "booked" by the producer for the next week. "I didn't even know what 'booked' meant," he laughs. "Suddenly, I found myself 'free-lancing' at the same company for a year and a half."

Totino moved from production assistant to director's assistant to studio manager and soon bought a still camera and taught himself black-and-white photography. "I asked a lot of questions, but in 1985, in New York, not many cinema-tographers were willing to give away their secrets." he says. "It was a closed Union. I became very aware of that when Union projects came into the studio. I would go near something and there would be a shout – 'Don't touch that!' If you see someone who needs help, the natural inclination is to offer it," he says. "I learned not to. They didn't want 'us' (non-union) to help 'them' (union)."

Fortunately, Totino eventually found a camera assistant who was willing to teach him. "'You want to be a camera assistant? Pick up those cases!' he said. For three days, all I did was lug equipment from one place to another. When he saw I really wanted to learn, he invited me to the camera rental house. Whenever I had a day off, I would do camera preps with him. That's how I learned," he adds.

Totino began going along on jobs, doing slates and other "second assistant" duties. "I had the opportunity to work on some of these jobs because in New York, in the 1980s, a lot of Union people were not doing music videos, most weren't Union jobs then. They were afraid they would get caught and fined so non-union people had a chance to work on these non-union jobs and learn the ropes."

After getting into the union as an assistant, Totino worked on "tabletop" commercials for over a year. "The new thing in tabletop commercials was to 'move the camera and the product a lot.' The lighting on tabletop commercials is very specific and rigid. For me it was difficult to stay within those boundaries."

Totino started to become influenced and more en-lightened by seeing more creative commercials. "There was a W. R. Grace spot that was directed by Ridley Scott," he re-members. "Ridley created a postapocalyptic world and he made this 18th-century bank building look really cool and futuristic. He didn't go by any 'rules' but only did what he thought would work for the spot." Watching this made Totino start to see things in a different light.

He was one of the lucky ones. With his electrical background, Salvatore Totino could understand the intricacies of lighting. He began to learn, and learn fast. "I saw a great deal of creativity and a great deal of experimenting," he recalls.

Totino first got his break as a cinematographer in 1993, shooting second unit on a New Order music video directed by Peter Care. "A few weeks later Peter hired me for an MTV promo, I got paid about five hundred dollars. The spot was filled with flash frames that turned out to be in-camera cuts. We would turn the camera on and off quickly, re-adjusting the compression of the frame every time. When the shots were edited together, we got the feeling he wanted."

"I was moving up but was so naive and inexperienced as a cameraman," Totino laughs. "I used to make these massive lighting diagrams and take them home to study. I thought that was the way to learn to become a good cinematographer but finally realized that experience is the real teacher.

"I relate shooting commercials and music videos to cooking," he gets philosophical. "It is how you feel that day and what you feel you can bring to the party. You can be inspired by the environment around you, photography, what you read, and what you see day to day, then you put the ingredients together. That's how my mother taught me to cook. That's how I cook today, I concentrate on the ingredients. You may be selling 'soap suds' but it is how you do it, how you create the visuals that stand out in the audience's minds.

"Often," he adds, "it is more than creating a mood or an emotional reaction − it is also creating a hunger. Make the audience want the product, and it will sell. Take a recent *Jaguar* commercial. We put a beautiful girl, an exquisite car on an almost unreachable, but magnificent cliff above San Francisco. Of course, we wanted to shoot it at night.

"I hate when night shoots are over lit," he adds. "To make sure that the night felt like a real night, I wanted to use a single light source that made the environment look like it was lit by a real moon. With the single source, I was able to move the camera without restriction. The wind and rough terrain made it difficult to hang a large light source over the car.

"To get that shot, I decided to point a Musco light into the fog using it to wrap the light around the car," he explains. "Traditionally, cars are lit with much more light, however, my gut instinct told me it was the right way to go in this situation. Even shooting the car at a 1.42 split stop, on an 18mm lens, the shot looked gorgeous. It was well worth the risk.

"In the Live music video 'Lightening Crashes,' we are telling the story of the life and death of the lead singer. An angel appears in each of the scenes. We did everything in camera through double exposures. We did two shots, one with the angel and one with the lead singer. To add to the surreal atmosphere, we created a flickering light around the head of the angel by taking chaser lights, like what you see in store windows and reflecting them off a stainless steel salad bowl.

"Don't laugh," he says, trying not the laugh himself. "You use what works! You use what your creativity suggests.

"Yes, the process was time-consuming. You had to shoot one pass of the scene then rewind the film to shoot the second layer without disturbing the set. But it was worth the effort. The shot was really different and lent itself to the performance video."

Totino recently finished a Powerade commercial shot in downtown Los Angeles. "The boards called for a young man in training, pushing himself past the point of exertion. In his mind, he can't go any farther. That's where Powerade comes in. After he drinks it, he pushes on – racing through a tunnel (downtown Los Angeles) and into the light. We added uncorrected fluorescent lights to the existing lights in the tunnel for the run.

"Of course, I had to make things a little more difficult," he laughs. "I varied the camera speed from normal 24 frames per second to a higher 96 frames per second, as the runner ran the tunnel. This allowed the flicker to become more pronounced, separating the runner from the background. As the runner bursts into 'the light,' he goes into a blast of white light from a hot Musco."

This freedom of creativity puts pressure on the cinematographer. "It's fun, because you don't have to keep continuity for two hours as you would in a feature film and you have the option of playing with things in post if you want.

"Look at the Nestee spots, or the U2 video," he continues. "Those are only a few samples of what a cinematographer can achieve in the world of music videos and commercials. On a recent commercial with director Dominec Sena for Fleet Bank, we wanted to use wide lenses and throw the background out of focus. Due to the nature of wide lenses, this is extremely difficult to do. To add to the difficulty, we also wanted the talent surrounding the main talent, who were moving at a normal speed, to move in slow motion. To achieve this, we had to shoot on live locations with motion control cameras and green screen. Then we composited three or four passes of the same scene together. One pass was with talent walking normally. The second pass was background talent with the camera at higher speeds. Sometimes, we had to do that two times to make several different speeds for background talent. The last pass was an empty plate without anything in the background. In post, as the shots were being composited together, you could change the focus on any layer. This made it appear as if the technique was done in camera. That's a great example of using in-camera and post techniques together.

"Today, to be a good cinematographer, you have to know a lot more about photography than just where to put the lights. You need to know what those lights do, what the camera does, and how to use them to paint. You also have to know about exposure, film stocks, and what happens after you open the lens."

Commercials don't have to make sense, as they did in the days of the "hard sell," when all that counted was the product. "We've done spots where you don't even know what is being sold," Totino laughs. "Look at the Nestee commercial. I've done several Nike spots where the only reference to the product is in the voice over.

"Music videos go even farther," he adds. "This is where you can be outrageously creative. I've done soft and beautiful for Springsteen and out-of-this-world visuals for Soundgarden.

"You can stretch the palette a lot more when you are doing projects that allow more freedom. Of course, I am always afraid each time I push it a little farther than the last. But, I will always remember something Michael Chapman once said. 'When the fear goes, it's time to move on.' I live with this fear everyday."

******

1995 Clio Award *H.I.S. Jeans*

References

Box, Harry C. *Set Lighting Technician's Handbook - Film Lighting Equipment, Practice, and Electrical Distribution.* Second Edition. Boston: Focal Press, 1997.

Brown, Blain. *Motion Picture and Video Lighting.* Revised edition. Boston: Focal Press, 1996.

Carlson, Verne and Sylvia Carlson. *Professional Lighting Handbook.* Second edition. Boston: Focal Press, 1991.

Carlson, Verne and Sylvia Carlson. *Professional Cameraman's Handbook.* Fourth Edition. Boston: Focal Press, 1994.

Elkins, David. *Camera Terms and Concepts.* Boston: Focal Press, 1993

Ferncase, Richard K. *Film and Video Lighting Terms and Concepts.* Boston: Focal Press, 1995.

Fitt, Brian and Joe Thornley. *Lighting Technology - A Guide for the Entertainment Industry.* Boston: Focal Press, 1997.

Millerson, Gerald. *The Technique of Lighting for Television and Film.* Third Edition. Boston: Focal Press, 1991.

Reid, Francis. *Lighting the Stage.* Boston: Focal Press, 1995.

Samuelson, David W. *The 'Hands On' Manual for Cinematographers.* Boston: Focal Press, 1994.

Sandstrom, Ulf. *Computerised Lightboards.* Boston: Focal Press, 1997.

Focal Press

Related Titles

Filmmakers and Financing
Business Plans for Independents
Second Edition
by Louise Levison

The Second Edition of this book contains completely revised and updated financial and industry data. The book will teach the reader how to create a business plan to present to a potential investor. With its easy-to-follow format and its step-by-step approach, this unique guide will bridge the gap between the filmmaker and business.

January 1998 • pa • 192pp • 0-240-80300-0

The On Production Budget Book
by Robert Koster

Offers both the novice and the experienced producer the best possible guidebook to creating and fine-tuning their budgets. Based on the leading film budgeting software, *Movie Magic,* this book takes the reader through each line item in the budgeting software and describes the background for that item, how it fits into the overall production, and, any issues or pitfalls that may arise.

June 1997 • pa w/ CD-ROM • 224pp • 0-240-80298-5

The Complete Film Production Handbook
by Eve Light Honthaner

A comprehensive and practical, step-by-step guide to organizing and running a film from pre-production through post production and delivery. Covers the essentials of business, from sample pre-production and post production schedules to contracts and company policies relating to insurance, talent management, and even customs and immigration details.

1996 • pa • 400pp • 0-240-80236-5